QUALITATIVE METHODS
IN PSYCHOLOGY
A Research Guide

Peter Banister, Erica Burman,
Ian Parker, Maye Taylor and
Carol Tindall

Open University Press
Buckingham · Philadelphia

Open University Press
Celtic Court
22 Ballmoor
Buckingham
MK18 1XW

email: enquiries@openup.co.uk
world wide web: http://www.openup.co.uk

and

325 Chestnut Street
Philadelphia, PA 19106, USA

First published 1994
Reprinted 1995 (twice), 1996, 1998, 1999

Copyright © The Authors 1994

A catalogue record of this book is available from the British Library

ISBN 0 335 19181 9 (pbk)   0 335 19182 7 (hbk)

Library of Congress Cataloging-in-Publication Data
Banister, Peter, 1947–
    Qualitative methods in psychology : a research guide / Peter
Banister . . . [et al.].
       p.   cm.
    Includes bibliographical references and index.
    ISBN 0–335–19182–7 — ISBN 0–335–19181–9 (pbk.)
    1. Psychology—Research—Methodology.   I. title.
BF76.5.B35   1994
150´.72—dc20   94–25724
                                                  CIP

Typeset by Graphicraft Ltd, Hong Kong
Printed and bound in Great Britain by
Biddles Ltd, Guildford and King's Lynn

CONTENTS

PREFACE

This book is an introductory text to the area of qualitative research, intended for advanced undergraduate and postgraduate students. Its emphasis is very much on *methods* within psychology, and it assumes some basic knowledge of the discipline; we thus expect the reader to have a preliminary acquaintance with the approach of psychology and more conventional methods, including some familiarity with the philosophy of psychological research, the research process, research methods and quantitative approaches. Thus the book is not aimed at introductory psychology students, but is a resource for academics and professionals who use psychological methods in their work.

The book is intended to be a main text for those interested in utilizing qualitative research methods. There has been an increasing demand in recent years for this contrasting approach to conventional psychological research, especially from people who are concerned with the application of psychology to real-world problems. This book is a resource text for advanced undergraduate/postgraduate research methods courses, as well as a response to demands from research funding councils for increased taught postgraduate input in this area. Not only do we provide an understanding of the assumptions underlying such research methods, presenting them as both a *critique* and a *complement* to quantitative approaches, we also present here a practical guide to how to carry out such research, along with the basis for a critical evaluation of it.

The reader will find here chapters that cover a selection of the major techniques within qualitative methods, with sections on 'how to carry it out', illustrations from appropriate research, ideas for possible research projects, worked examples and a critical analysis of the advantages and disadvantages of each method. It is hoped that you will be able better to appreciate a range of approaches, their relative drawbacks, advantages, contrasts, limitations and appropriateness for a number of research questions. As well as providing a general overview, the text acts as a bridge to other literature in the area, and each chapter concludes with suggestions for further reading.

You will find here that we draw on perspectives that are often outside the conventional Anglo-American tradition which has dominated psychology during the twentieth century, but in a pragmatic handbook style, emphasizing the practical use of such perspectives. We attempt to pull together a variety of techniques and perspectives not only from British and American perspectives, but also from more Continental European traditions, in one convenient source.

All the co-authors have carried out research using qualitative methods and are committed to this general approach; this book arises from our experiences in running a course on these methods as part of an MSc in applied psychology over a number of years. We found that no one text was suitable, so we decided that the best solution to this problem was to write a book ourselves, based on our course. Thus what you read here has been used extensively in teaching, and has been refined and developed as a result of feedback from our students. Through our teaching, we have been exposed to the many problems experienced by students who are interested in utilizing qualitative research methods, but who have encountered only quantitative approaches as part of their undergraduate curriculum; it is hoped that what we present here will support you in your inquiries.

Particular emphasis in the book is laid on the advantages and disadvantages of departing from the conventional psychological world of reliance on what is taken to be empirical objectivity. We want to encourage you, the researcher, to go beyond positivism, and to do psychology in a way that is useful and relevant. A common thread throughout the book is an emphasis on reflexivity, not only concerning the research process and its outcomes, but also in terms of acknowledging and using your own position as a researcher.

This is not an edited collection of articles. The five co-authors, all of whom teach on the postgraduate qualitative methods course, were responsible for the initial drafts of particular chapters: Peter Banister took particular responsibility for Chapters 2 and 10, Erica Burman for Chapters 4 and 8, Ian Parker for Chapters 1 and 6, Maye Taylor for Chapters 3 and

7, and Carol Tindall for Chapters 5 and 9. Each chapter was subsequently collectively discussed, reworked and rewritten as appropriate to develop a lucid argument for qualitative research throughout the course of the book, thereby ensuring that the finished text stands as a comprehensive review and guide to the area. This does not mean that this is a coherent seamless text; just as there are contrasts and conflicts (as well as continuities) between the assumptions underlying quantitative and qualitative research, so there are tensions and differences in approach between the various qualitative methods and researchers. Such divisions are inevitable, given the nature of research. Indeed, some of these researchers would not accept the designation 'method' at all, seeing this as partaking in the scientist division between experience, theory and action. Please note that we have attempted systematically to use 'we' throughout the book, to signify that this is a joint endeavour; however, when 'I' is used, this refers to the actual initial writer of the chapter, who, it is recognized, may have a specific stance or particular experiences and values in relation to the topic under consideration. The move from general to specific author marks this shift.

We recognize that readers may want to use this book as an aid to carrying out research using a particular methodological technique from within qualitative methods, and may thus just look at the appropriate chapter. However, we think that a few words here about the book in general may well encourage you to read a little more than just one particular chapter.

The book starts off with a general introduction, which sets the scene in terms of the background, history, advantages and disadvantages and philosophy of qualitative methods. The next six chapters then concentrate on what we consider to be currently the major different research approaches within psychology practised under the general heading of 'qualitative methods': observation, ethnography, interviewing, personal construct theory, discourse analysis and action research. These chapters follow a common format and include a brief résumé of the specific area, its historical development, a description of the method as applied to a particular research example, a review of the advantages of the approach and a discussion of problems with the method. Each chapter concludes with suggestions for further reading. Your attention is particularly drawn to Chapter 2 on 'observation', as this chapter introduces the reader to a number of issues that permeate the subsequent chapters; these include vital considerations such as ethics and reflexivity.

The questions raised by the final three chapters of the book are common to each of the specific methodologies discussed in Chapters 2 to 7. Chapter 8 covers the general approach of feminist methodology, which is of growing importance in qualitative methods, and needs to be considered by all researchers. Chapter 9 is on the important topic of research evaluation, and the issues raised here are of use to all who are carrying out qualitative research. Finally, Chapter 10 not only provides useful advice on the writing up of qualitative research, but also attempts to tie a number of threads that permeate the book together; the reader's attention is drawn to the specific sections on reflexivity, ethics, the role of values and the relationship between psychology and social change.

Our collective thanks are due to our students, who have helped us to refine our thoughts, and to appreciate the problems faced by those who are intending to start research using the exciting and challenging approaches of qualitative methods.

1 | QUALITATIVE RESEARCH

IAN PARKER

Qualitative methods have emerged in psychology only fairly recently as an array of alternative approaches to those in the mainstream, and it is difficult to define, explain or illustrate qualitative research without counterposing it to those methods in psychology which rest upon quantification, methods that have determined the shape of the discipline so far. However, it is not necessary to set quantitative and qualitative traditions in diametric opposition to one another, and we would lose sight of the value of much qualitative research if we were to do so. It would be wrong to assume, for example, that a qualitative researcher will refuse to summarize data numerically or that she should always disregard material that has been gathered through rigorous sampling techniques or is represented in statistical form. However, the process of reducing material to manageable proportions and abstracting certain types of information from it is fraught with difficulties; the logic of such a process of reduction and abstraction is that it will eventually reach a point where the context completely disappears. The over-enthusiastic quantitative researcher, who in psychology is often an experimenter of some kind, may be content and confident with his results when that has happened. A *qualitative* researcher, on the other hand, will be focusing on the context and integrity of the material and will never build her account directly, or only from quantitative data.

In this chapter I will explore definitions of qualitative research before moving on to illustrate how the role of interpretation functions to create both irremediable problems for a psychologist who wishes to confine himself to quantification, and valuable opportunities for a researcher using the qualitative methods described in later chapters in this book. In the course of the book we will be describing and assessing a variety of approaches, some of which are usually treated as if they were quantitative methods, and we will be dealing in detail (in Chapter 9) with evaluation and (in Chapter 10) with report writing. First, then, we should identify what is distinctive about qualitative research.

Definitions

Qualitative research can be defined first in a simple, but quite loose, way. It is the interpretative study of a specified issue or problem in which the researcher is central to the sense that is made. A researcher's selected domain of interest here will be a particular aspect of action and experience, but it could just as well be a reflexive study of part of the discipline of psychology itself. With regard to the first of these types of domain, it is important to differentiate the language of qualitative research, how we talk about our object of study, from that of many quantitative researchers who want to study what they term 'behaviour' directly. One of the features of measurement in quantitative methodologies is that it attempts to screen out interpretation, and to imagine that it is possible to produce a clear and unmediated representation of the object of study. This sits uneasily with the belief that nothing definite can be concluded from data, or that it is only possible to confirm the 'null hypothesis' (the hypothesis that the results will not be significant), but a belief in direct and unmediated perception of behaviour is a starting point of much orthodox psychological research. Many qualitative researchers would argue that this is impossible because our representations of the world are *always* mediated, and that since research always includes an interpretative component it is better to use the phrase 'action and experience' as one which more easily includes and respects the role of interpretation.

Study of an aspect of psychology is included here as a possible focus for a piece of work because the researcher is central to qualitative work, and so it is sometimes useful to turn around and look at the nature of the discipline that defines what human psychology is supposed to be like. Psychology is about people, and, despite the attempts of many psychologists to deny the fact, it is conducted by people who have much in common with those they study: psychology is one of the disciplines in which subject (the investigator) and object (the investigated) coincide. Moreover, everyday accounts of action and experience are the source of theories in psychology and these theories then trickle back out from the discipline into the explanations that people give of themselves and their lives. Qualitative research as interpretative study often involves a questioning of the boundaries between the inside and the outside of psychology. We will meet this issue again when we come to consider the position of the researcher.

We can be a little more rigorous now about definitions, but here we must also be open about the way they are used in psychology in a number of contrasting and overlapping ways. Qualitative research is part of a debate, not fixed truth. Qualitative research is: (a) an attempt to capture the sense that lies within, and that structures what we say about what we do; (b) an exploration, elaboration and systematization of the significance of an identified phenomenon; (c) the illuminative representation of the meaning of a delimited issue or problem. There is no single qualitative method, and quite different aims will be accomplished by different interpretative approaches. Discourse analysis, participant observation or personal construct work, for example, may only produce redescriptions of language, social interaction or the self, while interviewing and ethnography will touch upon and change a person or a community, and feminist methodology and action research will always involve reflection and transformation of experience and action.

The second reason why we cannot appeal to a single definition is that it is in the nature of interpretation to be contradictory and for there always to be a surplus of meaning, additional things that could be said, that we cannot limit or control. Quantification all too often fuels the fantasy of prediction and control, but qualitative research in psychology takes as its starting point an awareness of the gap between an object of study and the way we represent it, and the way interpretation necessarily comes to fill that gap. The process of interpretation provides a bridge between the world and us, between our objects and our representations of them, but it is important to remember that interpretation is a *process*, a process that continues as our relation to the world keeps changing. We have to follow that process and acknowledge that there will always be a gap between the things we want to understand and our accounts of what they are like if we are to do qualitative research properly.

The role of interpretation

The history of quantitative methods in psychology is a catalogue of attempts to wish the gap away. The gap between objects and our representations of them is not peculiar to this discipline, but common to all sciences. The gap appears in three forms. They have been termed the 'methodological horrors' (Woolgar 1988) and described as follows: (a) *indexicality*, in which an explanation is always tied to a particular occasion or use and will change as the occasion changes; (b) *inconcludability*, in which an account can always be supplemented further and will continually mutate as more is added to it; and (c) *reflexivity*, in which the way we characterize a phenomenon will change the way it operates for us, and that will then change our perception of it, etc. As a set of problems endemic to scientific inquiry, a number of strategies are routinely employed to control the methodological horrors, such as appealing to a hierarchy of existing scientific knowledge that should not be questioned, treating the problem as a technical one or as a trivial difficulty, or deferring the task of dealing with it, leaving it to others to solve as a philosophical problem. Qualitative research does not pretend that we can fill the gap between objects and representations once and for all. Rather, because it is an essentially interpretative enterprise, it works *with* the problem – the gap – rather than against it. One only has to consider the attempts to work against it in much quantitative research to see why this alternative way of doing psychology is preferable to the old.

The repression and return of meaning in positivist research

The 'crisis' in psychology at the end of the 1960s and beginning of the 1970s was an expression of an awareness of the impossibility of dealing with interpretation by attempting to suppress it (Parker 1989). The old way of doing things was characterized, using terminology from the philosophy of science, as an 'old paradigm'. The logic of the crisis was that the old set of assumptions and practices which held the scientific community together and set it certain types of puzzles to solve would give way to a 'new paradigm' (Harré and Secord 1972; Reason and Rowan 1981). The old paradigm and all too much contemporary quantitative research in psychology is underpinned by a positivist conception of science. A positivist attempts to discover the laws that he thinks govern the relationships between 'causes' and 'effects', and the preoccupation with independent and dependent 'variables' in psychology is one expression of the hold of positivism. Before I turn to look at different views of science which eschew positivism I should underline the strength of positivist ideas in psychology until the 'crisis'. Not all quantitative research is positivist, but it had become apparent by the 1960s that each attempt to deal with methodological problems thrown up by the old paradigm, a paradigm marked by a fetish for quantification, made the problem worse. Let us take six of these interlocking problems.

Ecological validity

Some degree of ecological validity (that is, trying to make the research fitting to the real world) is necessary if the findings of a study are to be extrapolated to a wider population than the sample used in the study and if the findings are to be generalized beyond the particular situation constructed by the researcher (Brunswik 1947). If one conceptualizes the research setting (whether it be a laboratory experiment, field study or interview) as the intersection of different variables, ecological validity should then be increased either by ensuring that as many variables as are present in the 'real world' are present in the research setting or by restricting the number of variables to the barest minimum so one knows that one is targeting only those that are relevant to the study. The problem with this is that either solution, of course, actually serves to undermine rather than guarantee ecological validity; for to make the research setting like the real world we would have to refrain from measuring the 'behaviour' of our 'subjects', and to exclude all 'confounding variables' we would have to make the setting as unlike the world as possible (Mixon 1974). The latter option obviously will not work, and if we tried to implement the former, and we were still operating as positivists, we could only do it by *deceiving* our 'subjects', measuring their behaviour surreptitiously, and embroiling ourselves both in another set of 'confounding variables' and in another problem.

Ethics

Deception of subjects is both a methodological and a moral issue (Kelman 1967), and is part of a second deeper issue to do with the treatment of subjects as objects or as people like ourselves. The peculiarly reflexive quality of psychology means that it must express a moral/political stance; it must in some respects be a moral science (Shotter 1975). It has to negotiate the boundaries between ethical and unethical research. The confusion between the terms 'subject' and 'object' in quantitative psychology (in which we call people 'subjects' but treat them as 'objects', and we pretend to be objective but are still always deeply subjective) is a symptom of how deep a moral problem there is. The psychology of the research setting, and the struggle to make sense of what is going on, is set up in positivist research as a battle that must be won by the researcher if he is to extract good data. There is a continual tension between 'personal reactivity' (the attempt by the 'subject' to understand and control the research) and 'procedural reactivity' (the ways in which the demands of the situation limit their room for manoeuvre). When psychologists agonize about deception or the depersonalization of those they treat like objects, however, they then find themselves faced with the (to them) unbearable prospect of being open about the hypotheses and giving the game away. The discussions of informed consent, debriefing and minimizing harm in the literature are all ways of trying to solve the problem without letting the subject win the battle. Research need not be set up in this way, but when it is the solutions will always fail.

Demand characteristics

A third problem is that subjects attempt to make sense of the research, and will always formulate their own version of what the hypotheses or aims of the study are. The 'subjects' are not always right, but doing this extra unwanted work constitutes over-engagement in the study, over-engagement from the researcher's point of view (and this extra work does not compensate for the researcher's subterfuge and deception). In some cases subjects are anxious to confirm what they think are the desired outcomes of the study, and much work has been done on the power of these 'demand characteristics' in experiments (Orne 1962). In this way the confusion that is deliberately engineered by the researcher is compounded by the confused way the subjects work their own agendas into the study. In some cases the confusion is also increased by the subjects as they engage in the wilful disruption of what they think are the hypotheses. Neverthe-less, most of the time the spiral of misunderstanding is quite unintentional, and there are good reasons to suspect that our 'subjects' are usually too compliant (Rosenthal 1966). Again, the only options left open within the positivist tradition to deal with demand characteristics produce, at the very least, the first two problems I have already identified: to tighten up the procedures so that the subject cannot possibly guess or interfere with the hypotheses destroys ecological validity, and to reveal the purpose of an experiment unravels the rationale that ostensibly scientific psychologists live for.

Volunteer characteristics

When subjects are compliant, and seem to behave well, this may be be-cause of a further problem that plagues experimental and much other research, and that is usually treated under the heading of 'volunteer characteristics'. This phenomenon only appears when people are allowed to volunteer to participate in research in the first place. If a strict sampling of the population were to be carried out and only certain identified indi-viduals were selected to take part and they *did* take part, then the char-acteristics of the subjects would thereby be controlled for. The practice, for example, of requiring psychology students to participate in studies as part of their credited work for an undergraduate course enforces participation. However, this practice immediately produces ethical problems, and the nature of the sample, the types of people investigated, is not representative (Sears 1986). Similarly, a degree of coercion would be necessary to ensure that any other collection of people identified by the most thorough strati-fied random sampling procedure took part in the final study. The types of people who choose to take part in psychology studies tend to be younger, brighter, friendlier, less conventional or authoritarian, but with a strong need for approval (Rosenthal 1965). To relax control and to allow people to come forward to be studied also, particularly owing to that last char-acteristic, throws us back to the problem of demand characteristics. The types of people who volunteer may be odd, then, and the people who carry out the studies certainly affect the research.

'Experimenter' effects

Despite the rhetoric of falsifiability in scientific psychology, and the injunc-tion that a piece of research should aim to test a hypothesis rather than simply show it to be true, experimenters, and not only experimenters, are always anxious to get a good result. This is just one source of the general anxiety that a researcher exhibits, which she communicates to the sub-ject and which then affects the way the subject feels (Rosenthal 1966). This is usually treated as a problem of 'bias', and once anxiety and desire for the study to succeed are characterized in this way a series of unworkable correctives can be quite logically, but mistakenly, called for. The only way to ensure that the 'experimenter' is unable to 'bias' the result is to prevent him from meeting the subject or to know anything of the context from which the data was collected (for then he would know which condition was which, and this would 'bias' interpretation). Experimenter effects can be controlled by the use of double-blind procedures, but even here anxiety and desire seep through the patterns of relationships between researchers and between surrogate researchers and subjects. At its most efficient end point, the procedure should guarantee that the subject never meets anyone remotely connected with the research, that is anyone, and we would then be caught once again in the traps of ecological validity. This process in-creases the artificiality of the research situation and the *sense*, even if not a deliberate intention on the researcher's part, that deception is taking place (Shotter 1975). These correctives are only needed, and they are then always self-defeating, if the issue is seen as one of 'bias' to start with.

Language

Positivist approaches are faced with an insuperable problem when subjects start to make their own sense of the research setting, and the most hard-line experimental psychologists will be making sense of the situation they have constructed for their subjects, which is surplus to that which they want to measure and report (Gauld and Shotter 1977). All quantitative approaches become mired in this problem as soon as the subjects and the researchers start to talk; and the fact that human beings use language is the most important and disruptive problem that these approaches face. It is understandable, though not surprising, that language, the medium through which social life is maintained, is absent from most studies in psychology. Sometimes the instructions are written in a brief standard form to screen out the chatter that governs the rest of our lives outside the laboratory, but whichever technique is employed to stop people talking brings into play the guesswork that underlies demand characteristics and researcher effects, and sets severe limits on ecological validity. The pretence that people do not speak is also the core of the repression of meaning in positivist research (Harré and Secord 1972). The recognition of these problems combined with the recognition that language is crucial to self-reflection and the development of psychology as a moral, as opposed to an amoral, science fired the paradigm 'crisis'. An outcome of the crisis was a 'turn to language' in psychology which enabled a connection to be reforged between research in the discipline and work in anthropology, sociology and other human sciences.

Alternative foundations: philosophies of qualitative research

Qualitative research did not emerge newly born from the 'crisis' in psychology, and it would be a mistake to subsume it only under the 'new paradigm' heading. Many qualitative methods, such as ethnographic and action research, have a longstanding history in sociology and anthropology; some, such as personal construct theory, arose years before the 'crisis' as part of a humanist protest against the mainstream; and some, such as feminist research, were developed in the 1960s as a reaction to the grip of masculine assumptions about rigour and hard science. There is no one correct qualitative method, but there is a strong underlying sense in all the approaches described in this book that much, perhaps too much, is lost when material is quantified and that we need to base research on different conceptual foundations from those occupied by orthodox psychology. There are actually *two* contrasting foundations that can be constructed to ground qualitative research in distinctive models of the person and the social world. The first is that of realism, and the second is that of social constructionism. It is often felt, quite understandably, that qualitative methods do not meet the standards that science demands of researchers (Silverman 1993). There is a significant difference, however, between the image of science that most psychologists adore and the nature of science. It does not have one fixed nature: the procedures that a science should follow have been disputed, as have the claims made for it as the only purveyor of truth.

Realism

For a realist, any science must operate with adequate models of the objects of study, and the methods used to investigate and explain the way those objects operate must be appropriate to the object (Manicas and Secord 1983). The favoured method in the natural sciences is often an intensive study of a particular case rather than the accumulation of data across a sample of instances. The natural and the social worlds are layered with structures which define the tendencies or powers to act of objects. Chemicals, for example, have certain structures by virtue of which they function in particular ways; they are endowed with particular 'powers' in different situations and in the presence of other chemicals. It is in the nature of human beings, and a 'power' they have, to reflect upon their actions and to give account of those actions, and this means that a properly scientific approach to the study of action and experience should employ methods which engage with rather than try to screen out these powers. Positivist research in psychology that tries to ignore the powers of human beings is unscientific. A realist will not be opposed to quantitative research that aims to describe qualities common to a group (nomothetic research), but will insist that we can only develop an adequate account by intensive study of particular cases (idiographic research). A realist view, then, aims to put psychology on a more secure scientific basis (Harré 1974).

Social constructionism

While realists are committed to the view that there are underlying structures to be described, social constructionists will insist that all forms of knowledge, including scientific knowledge, produce images of the world that then operate as if they were true (Gergen 1985). This does not mean that social constructionists are necessarily opposed to 'science', but it does mean that they have a more sceptical view of how science operates, and they will insist that there is always a moral aspect to research. Research questions are structured by personal and political interests that need to be explored rather than hidden away, for it is when they are concealed that they do the most damage. For a social constructionist these strictures apply to even the most ostensibly 'neutral' natural sciences. In the case of psychology, in which the object (investigated) is endowed with the same qualities of reflection as the subject (investigator), the exploration should not only be one which respects the specificities of each case (idiographic research), but should also be one which explores the particular meanings that are produced on this occasion (hermeneutic research). A social constructionist view, then, sees science as a form of knowledge which creates as well as describes the world.

When we adopt either a realist or a social constructionist view of science and of ourselves as qualitative researchers in the best traditions of science we are likely to disappoint our colleagues in psychology. However, we have to point out that they cannot themselves, in their own quantitative work, live up to the expectations they set qualitative researchers, and that the model of science that underpins much psychology can be successfully challenged.

Working through the horrors

It is now possible to characterize qualitative methods in more detail by considering how a researcher can work interpretatively *within* the methodological horrors and transform them into methodological virtues.

Indexicality

The work that goes on in a research setting is something that is quite particular to that situation, and we can take the 'problem' of ecological validity and turn it into an aspect of the research itself. All meaning is indexical, which means that it will change as the occasion changes and as it is used in different ways. An explanation changes as the occasion changes, and so the best alternative to suppressing this change is to *theorize* it. In this context theorizing does not mean that esoteric and obscure metaphysical systems of thought should be brought to bear on the research, but rather that patterns of influence on the research setting be identified and an account be developed as to how these patterns have played their part in the outcome of the study (Henwood and Pidgeon 1992). There is a general issue here concerning the relationship between empirical and theoretical research, a relationship which changes when we move into the area of qualitative methods. While quantitative research sees theory as a domain of work that is conceptually distinct from empirical work, and sees empirical work as the 'test' of a theory, qualitative research brings the two domains together. A qualitative researcher must, in some respects, be a theorist, for each occasion sets particular puzzles that must be addressed as the research proceeds. (Similarly, a 'theoretical psychologist' who takes the turn to language seriously must, in some respects, be a qualitative researcher, for theory never floats in a realm free from context.)

An attention to indexicality in the research setting means that we must reformulate what we understand by validity and reliability. In quantitative research *validity* refers to the degree to which what has been measured corresponds with other independent measures obtained by different research tools. The correlation between a test and other tests of the same thing, for example, will be a measure of how far that test is picking up what it claims to be picking up. *Reliability* in quantitative research is the extent to which the same results will be obtained if the research is repeated. In the case of psychometric tests, for example, the reliability of the test is measured by the correlation between different applications of the test. Validity and reliability are discussed in quantitative research as properties of the research tool, whether it be the test protocol or interview schedule. There is an assumption built into this way of treating the materials that are brought to the research setting, which will often be quite inappropriate to qualitative research. There is an assumed separation between theoretical and empirical work and between the research tool and its application here which is mistaken, and there is a failure to theorize change.

The search for both validity and reliability rests on the assumption that it is possible to *replicate* good research. A qualitative researcher, however, will never make the mistake of claiming that their work is perfectly replicable. It is certainly possible to repeat the work that has been described, but that repetition will necessarily also be a different piece of work: different at the very least by virtue of the change in the researcher, informants and meanings of the research tool over time. The meaning that is produced in the course of research is something that has to be followed and recorded carefully and sensitively, and an account of the process of tracing and presenting the analysis as the 'results' of the study is an account of *change*, and this entails change in the research tool itself. The aim in qualitative research is not so much replicability as *specificity*. Ecological validity is sustained when the particular meanings of the research setting are explored. When that exploration is thorough and when it is done with the informant rather than against them, demand characteristics, volunteer characteristics and experimenter effects are rendered visible and accountable. The process respects the importance of language and the rights of the informant to speak. In this way the research setting does become more like 'real' life. However, for this new guarantee for a stronger form of ecological validity than that found in experiments to hold good we have to underline the clause which says that the findings of the study are as fragile and mutable as real life is.

Inconcludability

The notion of ecological validity can only be reworked when the impossible task of constructing a research setting which is so throughly controlled as to prevent the outside world seeping in has been given up, and when the search for 'facts' which are separable and distinct from the world has been abandoned. Qualitative research draws its strength from the ways in which accounts of action and experience reinterpret and understand facts anew, such that their shape, function and very nature seem to change. While a positivist who believes that it is possible to capture facts and arrange them in mathematical form will see inconcludability as a fatal problem, qualitative researchers who follow the changes in meaning in the course of research will both understand and welcome the opportunity for others to supplement their account. There will always be a gap between the meanings that appear in a research setting and the account written in the report, and that gap is the space for a reader to bring their own understanding of the issue to bear on the text. It is in the nature of much 'scientific' psychology to resort to a variety of rhetorical devices to persuade the reader that certain facts or laws have been 'discovered'. One of the ways in which the fact-like status of the results are supported is through an appeal to 'sampling'.

Sample size is often used to guarantee the strength of claims made for results of quantitative research. The greater the number of subjects the better able the researcher is to generalize to the rest of the population. Equally, though, the greater the sample size, the less the researcher is able to respect the specificities of each subject's response and the meanings of the response to the subject. There is always the 'problem' that another account can be added, and as the number of subjects rises more of the material goes missing as responses are gathered together into manageable categories for statistical analysis. The better solution to each problem with positivist research is to turn to the meanings employed in each setting and to explore the sense which underlies and structures a particular case, whether it be the life story of an individual recorded in a diary or the set of discourses that hold a text together. The turn to a single case study is also more in keeping with the most sophisticated practice of the natural sciences.

In practice, quantitative research will sometimes abandon claims to be able to generalize from a study, and may even sanction the use of single case studies if the measurement is rigorous enough. A single case study may be necessary if only a small number of potential subjects are available, and there may only be the one who has the particular characteristics that the researcher wishes to focus upon. This departure from normal sampling procedures is, however, normally undertaken reluctantly, and the results will be discussed in relation to the probable wider population that this case may be a member of. Much qualitative research, however, will treat every study as if it were a single case study, and the aim is to provide an in-depth examination of the meanings at work rather than a skim over as wide a surface as possible. It should be noted, however, that some researchers will want to use a qualitative approach as a pilot study or as supplementary work to support more traditional methods. There is some impatience now, in addition, with the argument that qualitative research can only justify its analysis by saying that it is telling a 'plausible story' (Silverman 1993).

But either way, rather than apologize for the failure to study a sample, the qualitative researcher should clearly state the reason why a particular selection of informants was chosen. The results of qualitative research are always provisional, and changes in the demands of the research setting, as well as of the volunteers and researchers, place a moral responsibility on the researcher to allow readers of the report to offer different interpretations. This also opens up the research to a reflexive survey of the assumptions that have guided it.

Reflexivity

The ways in which we theorize a problem will affect the ways we examine it, and the ways we explore a problem will affect the explanation we give. The reflexive spiral bedevils quantitative research and means that claims to have really refuted a hypothesis or to have ever discovered facts about something dissolve the moment the problem is reformulated. In personal construct terms (and personal construct research is too often treated as if it were a quantitative method), once we acknowledge the way the perceptions of the researcher define the problem we must abandon the 'accumulative fragmentalism' that underpins positivism. Qualitative research does not make claims to be 'objective', but it does offer a different way of working through the relationship between objectivity and subjectivity. Objectivity and subjectivity are always defined in relation to one another, and the mistake that positivists make is to assume that the relationship is like a conceptual zero-sum game in which a diminution of one, the erasure of subjectivity, will lead to an increase in the other, the production of a fully objective account.

For qualitative research, on the other hand, we arrive at the closest we can get to an objective account of the phenomenon in question through an exploration of the ways in which the subjectivity of the researcher has structured the way it is defined in the first place. Subjectivity is a resource, not a problem, for a theoretically and pragmatically sufficient explanation. When researchers, whether quantitative or qualitative, believe that they are being most objective by keeping a distance between themselves and their objects of study, they are actually themselves producing a *subjective* account, for a position of distance is still a position and it is all the more powerful if it refuses to acknowledge itself to be such. Research is always carried out from a particular standpoint, and the pretence to neutrality in many quantitative studies in psychology is disingenuous. It is always worth considering, then, the 'position of the researcher', both with reference to the definition of the problem to be studied and with regard to the way the researcher interacts with the material to produce a particular type of sense. In many cases it will be helpful to explore this position in a reflexive analysis. A reflexive analysis which respects the different meanings brought to the research by researcher and volunteer is an ethical enterprise, and characteristics, whether of the situation or the person, are treated as valued resources rather than factors that must be screened out.

It will also be right on some occasions to acknowledge the role of subjectivity in the process of change that occurs in the course of research. The informant may be using the researcher as a 'witness' for her story, and the telling of the story may change her understanding of it. It may be that the informant will wish to ensure that some material does not appear in the report, and there will certainly be some aspects of the research that the researcher will want to censor deliberately. Such issues both exacerbate the problems with objectivity that quantitative research is mired in and intensify the ethical dimensions of the research process. Qualitative methods cannot, for example, comply with the demand that research should not have any 'effects'. The activity of studying something will always change it, will affect it. The production of knowledge in science starts at the moment a scientist starts to speak about the phenomenon, and that speaking will restructure the way it will be understood by others.

Language and truth

Psychologists immersed in quantitative methods often find it difficult to understand how qualitative work connects with their concerns. We should not underestimate the challenge qualitative methodology throws to mainstream psychology. Nevertheless, quantitative research preoccupations do need to be taken seriously, and if qualitative research needs to refuse questions that are habitually posed in the mainstream it must at least explain why it will not address those questions. Such questions come to the fore when the research is presented in a public, usually written, form.

We are able to recognize a good experimental report or journal paper in large part owing to its adherence to a particular genre of writing. Psychologists are trained to conform to the conventions of quantitative research, and these conventions stipulate rules that must be followed at all levels of the report, from the use of introduction, method, results and discussion sections to the use of the third person throughout. Similarly (as we point out in Chapter 10), with qualitative research, the use or misuse of terminology will commend or mar the study. It would be quite wrong, for example, for a qualitative researcher to refer to herself as the 'experimenter' or her interviewees or co-researchers as 'subjects'. In some cases the use of the term 'data' to refer to the material that has been selected for analysis will be acceptable, or writers may even feel that they are right to say that they have 'discovered' something; but these are borderline concepts that evoke the quantitative world of 'facts' and 'laws' and many qualitative researchers will want to eschew them.

The language we use reproduces particular images of research, and of psychology, and it has not been surprising, perhaps, that qualitative research has been of interest to feminists in psychology for some years (Wilkinson 1986; Burman 1990). (The reader may have noticed that I have departed from British Psychological Society conventions for gender-free writing in this chapter by referring, for rhetorical effect, to quantitative researchers with the male pronoun and to qualitative researchers as if they were always women.) Qualitative research speaks a different language from that spoken by many psychologists tied to the quantification of action and experience, but it needs to speak more clearly. We do need to specify the criteria by which a piece of qualitative research should be judged. If not, it will by default be judged against a mistaken model of science, the person and the world (Chapter 10 explores this issue). In some cases the task is to reframe, to reformulate the parameters that would be set by a quantitative study. In other cases the task is to defend a completely different way of doing psychology.

Qualitative research may not be the panacea for all the ills of psychology, and its role in a study or report may sometimes be marginal. It may be the voice that carries through the sense of the phenomena under investigation, while the quantitative research component circumscribes the scope and extent of the topic. However, even when a qualitative method is employed in this modest way, we should be careful to assess its role fairly and to accord it due value. We have explored the rules by which we should judge qualitative research in this chapter, and in the following chapters you will find a range of methods that have made a more than modest contribution to a scientific understanding of action and experience.

Useful reading

Henwood, K. and Pidgeon, N. (1992). 'Qualitative research and psychological theorizing'. *British Journal of Psychology*, 83, 97–111. Reprinted in Hammersley, M. (ed.) (1993). *Social Research: Philosophy, Politics and Practice*. London: Sage.

Reason, P. and Rowan, J. (eds) (1981). *Human Inquiry: a Sourcebook of New Paradigm Research*. Chichester: Wiley.

Sears, D.O. (1986). 'College sophomores in the laboratory: influences of a narrow data base on social psychology's view of human nature'. *Journal of Personality and Social Psychology*, 51(3), 515–30.

References

Brunswik, E. (1947). *Systematic and Unrepresentative Design of Psychological Experiments with Results in Physical and Social Perception*. Berkeley: University of California Press.

Burman, E. (ed.) (1990). *Feminists and Psychological Practice*. London: Sage.

Gauld, A.O. and Shotter, J. (1977). *Human Action and Its Psychological Investigation*. London: Routledge and Kegan Paul.

Gergen, K.J. (1985). 'The social constructionist movement in modern psychology'. *American Psychologist*, 40, 266–75.

Harré, R. (1974). Blueprint for a new science, in N. Armistead (ed.) *Reconstructing Social Psychology*. Harmondsworth: Penguin, pp. 240–59.

Harré, R. and Secord, P.F. (1972). *The Explanation of Social Behaviour*. Oxford: Basil Blackwell.

Henwood, K. and Pidgeon, N. (1992). 'Qualitative research and psychological theorizing'. *British Journal of Psychology*, 83, 97–111.

Kelman, H.C. (1967). 'Human uses of human subjects: the problem of deception in social psychological experiments'. *Psychological Bulletin*, 67, 1–11.

Manicas, P.T. and Secord, P.F. (1983). 'Implications for psychology of the new philosophy of science'. *American Psychologist*, 38, 399–413.

Mixon, D. (1974). 'If you won't deceive, what can you do?', in N. Armistead (ed.) *Reconstructing Social Psychology*. Harmondsworth: Penguin, pp. 72–85.

Orne, M.T. (1962). 'On the social psychology of the psychology experiment: with particular reference to demand characteristics and their implications'. *American Psychologist*, 17, 776–83.

Parker, I. (1989). *The Crisis in Modern Social Psychology, and How to End It*. London: Routledge.

Reason, P. and Rowan, J. (eds) (1981). *Human Inquiry: a Sourcebook of New Paradigm Research*. Chichester: Wiley.

Rosenthal, R. (1965). 'The volunteer subject'. *Human Relations*, 18, 389–406.

Rosenthal, R. (1966). *Experimenter Effects in Behavioral Research*. New York: Appleton-Century-Crofts.

Sears, D.O. (1986). 'College sophomores in the laboratory: influences of a narrow data base on social psychology's view of human nature'. *Journal of Personality and Social Psychology*, 51(3), 515–30.

Shotter, J. (1975). *Images of Man in Psychological Research*. London: Methuen.

Silverman, D. (1993). *Interpreting Qualitative Data: Methods for Analysing Talk, Text and Interaction*. London: Sage.

Wilkinson, S. (1986). *Feminist Social Psychology*. Milton Keynes: Open University Press.

Woolgar, S. (1988). *Science: the Very Idea*. Chichester: Ellis Horwood; London: Tavistock.

Acknowledgements

Thanks are due to Deborah Marks for her helpful comments on an earlier draft of this chapter.

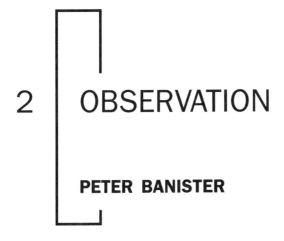

2 | OBSERVATION

PETER BANISTER

In this chapter, we turn to what is probably the most basic and oldest method in the whole of psychology, one which in some way or other is involved in every other method used by the discipline. Observation is a process we all are continuously engaged in, and in the eyes of the public, psychologists are notorious for spending their time watching (not to mention analysing) other people. Even when we are not working as psychologists, we are always forming hypotheses, making inferences and trying to impose meaning on our social world, based on our observations. Issues are raised in this chapter which are pertinent to most other qualitative methods in psychology, and this is why it is located near the beginning of this book. The reader is advised to look at what is covered here, as it is of relevance for any research utilizing qualitative methods.

All psychological research, including both quantitative and qualitative methods, involves at least some element of observation; this may be something as simple as reading (or perhaps misreading) a dial on a machine, or as complex as observing group interactions. Many of the major developments within psychology have come from the initial observation of a serendipidous event; this is defined by Reber (1985) as the finding of one thing while engaged in a search for something else. He uses Pavlov as an example, but other instances abound, including Skinner and superstitious behaviour, Piaget's observations of the systematic failure of children on intelligence tests (which led to his theories on cognitive development) and

Freud's insights, which developed from his initial observations of systematic links between earlier experiences and current problems in his patients. Sometimes, observations of a single event have sparked off a whole series of related studies, and have opened up huge new areas of psychological research; an example that readily springs to mind here is the Latané and Darley (1970) research on 'bystander apathy', which was initially inspired by the tragic death of Kitty Genovese in New York.

In any psychological study, quantitative or qualitative, the researcher should always be alert to unexpected as well as expected reactions of participants to the situation; often such reactions may provide vital pointers to future research, as well as providing useful feedback on the current study. Qualitative methods have the advantage of focusing in on real-life problems, of reflecting the world as it actually is, and are more likely to come up with unexpected results. This chapter will include a small-scale observational study based on an everyday occurrence which none the less produces interesting findings. Although it is closely linked to observation, participant observation (where the observer becomes part of the group which is being observed, often without the knowledge of the group) is covered in this book in Chapter 3, on ethnographic study, as it shares many features with such approaches.

Background

The term 'observation' derives from Latin, meaning to watch, to attend to. Dictionary definitions (e.g. *Oxford English Dictionary* 1989) tend to stress that it is concerned with the accurate watching and noting of phenomena as they occur in nature, with regard to cause and effect or mutual relations (note 'in nature', as opposed to an experiment, which concentrates on the manipulation of conditions, often in artificial conditions). This definition is extended by Reber (1985), who points out that all psychological methods involve observation, but stresses that a distinction should be made between research that is controlled by the manipulation of independent variables and research that is carried out by the use of naturalistic observation. It must be stressed, however, that the observational method can be successfully used in laboratory settings; the crucial distinction that needs to be made here is in terms of whether or not deliberate manipulation of variables is involved. The essence of observation in the context of this book is that it is concerned with naturally occurring behaviour, which can take place in any setting. Variables can nonetheless be examined, for instance by looking at behaviour in different settings or by selecting people to observe who have different demographic characteristics. A more specific definition to use in this context (although not without problems of its own) is that of Marshall and Rossman (1989: 79), who define observation as 'a systematic description of events, behaviors and artifacts in the social setting under study'.

Given this long historical background, it is difficult to separate out observation as a qualitative method from much traditional research, as it is intertwined with and permeates through all psychological methods. A distinction can be made in the context of this book, though: in common with other qualitative methods, with observation there is a commitment to try to understand the world better, usually from the standpoint of individual participants. Thus we are concerned with such aims as getting to understand 'real' people in their everyday situations, to learn about the world from different perspectives, to experience what others experience, to unravel what is taken for granted, to find out about implicit social rules, etc. It must be noted, however, that our 'findings' (in common with some other qualitative approaches) can be divorced from the experiential knowledge of those being observed; indeed, at times one may be looking at aspects of behaviour (e.g. non-verbal cues) of which the person being observed is not consciously aware. In this context, it must also be stressed that observation, unlike many other qualitative methods, does tend to be from an outsider rather than an insider perspective. In addition, the method can be used as a very useful precursor to later studies, opening up possibilities and making suggestions for future research.

In the context of this book, it must be pointed out that observational methods are not necessarily within the Reason and Rowan (1981) conceptualization of 'new paradigm' research, their ethos of (in particular) collaboration and participation being not always applicable to this approach. The method can be very much 'objectivist' in its standpoint, with the researcher sometimes using the material gained very much for her or his own ends. There are obvious ethical problems here, which can be compounded by the (not necessarily invariable) tendency of psychologists not to feed back and share findings with those who have been observed. Some have called the method a potential 'act of betrayal', where what is private is made public, and those observed may have to take the consequences of what has been written about them. An example of this is the participant observation study of Ditton (1977) of the practices of bread roundsmen, where he revealed working practices such as the recycling of stale bread and deliberate cheating by underdelivery of large orders. Ethical problems are not inevitable, but always need to be carefully attended to. There are ethical guidelines that must be adhered to, and this area is so important that it is considered in detail in Chapter 10. It could be claimed that there are fewer problems in naturalistic observation, which is a necessary everyday activity we all engage in continuously (even if not consciously!) when interacting with others. Pavement walking, for example, would be impossible unless we observed fellow walkers, and literally took steps to avoid colliding with them.

As has been suggested above, the typical observation is (though not invariably) a field one, where one attempts to record in a relatively systematic fashion some aspect of the behaviour of people in their ordinary environment, usually in as unobtrusive a fashion as is possible. It is thus basically a 'watching' operation, but does embrace a whole variety of different approaches and techniques. There are very different methods in approaching observation, and it is beyond the scope of this chapter to consider all the possible permutations in detail. Nonetheless, it is important for the reader to be aware of the range that observational methods encompass. Among different approaches that can be included here are variations in:

1 Structuring of the observation, which can range from highly structured detailed observation to very diffuse unstructured description.
2 Focus in observation, ranging from a very narrow concentration on specific aspects (such as a single non-verbal cue) to a broad focus.
3 Knowledge of those being observed about the process, which can vary from being known to all (for instance, in the observation of a teacher's classroom technique) to being known by none (where one is, for instance, secretly observing people interacting in a public social setting such as a library).
4 Explanations given to those being observed for the observation. These can vary from full explanations to no explanations, and may even include highly ethically dubious false explanations, where participants are told that the observer is watching something different from that which is really of interest.
5 The time scale of what is being observed, varying from one-off observations to extended observations over time.
6 The methods used, which can vary from simple note-taking to the use of devices such as audio and video tape-recorders, from checklists to stopwatches.
7 Feedback given to those observed, which can range from a full sharing of observations and interpretations to no further contact at all with the participants.

These approaches can obviously be permutated in a variety of ways, and it must be noted that there are even set techniques that can be used. These tend to be on the more quantitative side of the discipline, but mention of them may be useful here. There are a number of examples.

Bales (1950) developed techniques for analysing group interactions, where specific instances of verbal behaviour are recorded in terms of whether the contribution is positive or negative, whether it is asking for or giving suggestions, etc., with the aim of attempting to look at group participants in terms of labelling them as 'task' or 'socio-emotional' specialists.

Minuchin (1974) divided family dynamics in terms of up/down, near/far and in/out relationships, as a first step towards family therapy. Here, the interaction and interdependence of participants are concentrated on, looking at characteristic patterns and strategies adopted by participants to cope with others in the family.

Third, there is analysis of non-verbal cues, using content-analysis. As Argyle (1987) indicates, there are a wide variety of cues that can be looked at here, including style of speaking, voice tone, loudness, interruptions, speed, hesitations, address codes, paralinguistics, silences, clothing, hair style, make-up, facial expressions, use of eyes, body contact, touch, body movement, gesture and proximity. There are even further variables which are currently under-researched, such as smells. Vrugt (1990) provides the example of analysing the non-verbal behaviour of the Dutch Queen during her annual televised presentation of government policies for the year, attempting to find if it was possible to detect when the Queen's opinions were discrepant to those of her government, and finding that speech disturbances, object manipulation and looking up were clear indicators of such discrepancies.

Webb *et al.* (1981) advocated the development of 'unobtrusive measures', where one attempts to establish findings on the basis of observing evidence left behind by people. Their research includes the examination of carpet wear and 'nose-prints' on glass protecting screens as indicators of the relative popularity of art at exhibitions. They also cite discarded rubbish studies, where the contents of people's rubbish bins are looked at in terms of such variables as their consumption of alcohol.

Examples abound in the literature of interesting and important studies which have been based on observational methodology. Three are given here.

First, Albert and Kessler (1978) examined greeting rituals on telephones, including the methods used to end personal telephone conversations. They found that in general there was a four-part ritual, including a summary of the call, a justification for terminating the call, some positive comment and some indication that the relationship would continue.

Second, Argyle (e.g. 1987) has published a myriad of studies on non-verbal behaviour, including such important areas as postural moulding and eye-gaze in the regulation of social encounters. He suggests that postural moulding (i.e. the copying of body posture) often indicated that the dyad concerned were getting on well with each other, while eye-gaze (and the breaking of eye contact) was important in synchronizing conversations, signalling to the other when you wished him or her to take over, for example.

Third, Cary (1978) looked at procedures used by pedestrians in the public use of pavements, finding (in this study using students on an university campus) little support for Goffman's (1963) notion of 'civil inattention', where two pedestrians are meant to look at each other until they are about 2.5 metres apart, and then to look away when actually passing. Such social rules might well change with different populations.

Example

The method has a lot of potential, and could be used in many settings. Examples that readily spring to mind include looking at patients' interactions with hospital personnel in terms of their perceptions of differences in status, gender differences in pupil–teacher interactions in schools, speech accommodation in professional and other settings, and the play of children with special learning difficulties.

As has been highlighted above, there are many different ways of carrying out observational qualitative research. This section will start by talking about general considerations, before going on to take the reader through a particular example. The assumption underlying this chapter is that the reader is interested in carrying out conventional, non-intrusive, non-participating, qualitative observation.

Obviously, specifics will vary, but in general there are three crucial questions that need to be considered initially. First, 'why' is the research being carried out; what is the research question that is being considered? This can be formally stated in terms of a hypothesis (e.g. that more active play will be observed in male children than in female children), or may more usually be formulated in terms of a statement of intent (e.g. 'the activity play of children will be observed'). Often, this may initially arise from personal interest or concern, informal observation, the interests of others, other research, experience, etc., which leads to a literature search. Ideally, it should be rooted in the relevant literature; otherwise, the absence of relevant literature (and possible reasons for such an absence) should be discussed.

Second, 'who' is the research to be carried out on, or (better) who is the research about? This includes not only the actual sample of people to be used (e.g. what age children to use, how many to observe), but also *where* the study will take place (e.g. in a nursery, in their homes), over what period of time, etc. Decisions will be needed as to ethical and other concerns, such as how much ought to be revealed to those being observed or how to disengage oneself from the field.

Third, 'what' is to be recorded? How, for instance, is 'active play' to be defined? Are time-samples to be taken (e.g. just the first ten minutes will be observed), is only play alone to be recorded, what environmental and other constraints will be needed to be taken into account? What recording methods are going to be utilized? Will a single child be concentrated on or will single instances be taken from different children?

Other general points to keep in mind include the following.

Pilot studies are strongly advisable, to discover and smooth out problems, and to refine techniques. Here, you might start by informally observing the area of interest, and then go on to carry out a preliminary observation using the methods which you are intending to use subsequently, checking to see if the chosen method is feasible, that it is producing useful material, etc. It may not be possible to videotape in a particular nursery, for instance, because the cameras cannot cover all the potential play area and behaviour may arise that is difficult to record, or it may be found that too much is lost by only using pencil and paper recording methods.

Observational research is often best done with at least one other observer, and the comparison of independent observations may help to indicate if there are any reliability problems in terms of recording. It is also useful to discuss findings with another person, which may help to avoid idiosyncratic recordings and interpretations.

Notes need to be taken at the time, and subsequently systematically and quickly written up. They are usually useful in addition to any more formal recording (such as a videotape, which may miss out crucial material). Such notes should include reflections, personal feelings, hunches, guesses and speculations as well as the observations themselves and anything else observed (and these different aspects should be clearly differentiated). Descriptions should be reasonably full, allowing the writer to remember the observation from the account several months later, and the reader should be able to visualize it reasonably accurately. It is often useful to take two copies of such notes, to allow one to be cut up, to simplify any subsequent analysis. Writing up is likely to take several drafts.

Ethical considerations are always crucial in research, and must be carefully considered. Observations in natural settings are often made without participants being aware of the process, and they are usually unable to say that they do not wish to take part in the research. Individuals should not be identifiable from the research report and should not be harmed by the publishing of the data. Research generally should not be carried out if the researcher has reason to believe that participants would refuse if given the opportunity to do so.

When it comes to writing up observational research reports, there are no standard ways in which this should be done. Chapter 10, on research report writing, makes general comments that are useful here. The example that follows is based on an attempt to provide a systematic narrative account of a particular observation carried out in a chosen social setting to answer a specific research question. Obviously, if a structured observation was being utilized, then the following suggested procedure would only be partly appropriate. An important point to bear in mind is the criterion of replicability: ideally, sufficient detail should be provided to allow the reader to follow precisely what has been done, which should be in sufficient detail to allow the study to be repeated from what is provided. Often, we take many things for granted, and we are not aware that we are doing so. One way to aid thinking here is to make notes under the following headings:

1 *Describe the context*, including the physical setting. Do remember that aspects such as the date, the time, the weather or the lighting may be of crucial importance, and noticing these things will certainly aid replicability.
2 *Describe the participants.* Who they are needs to be noted, including such potentially important variables as age, gender, ethnicity, clothing and physical description. Note that the boundary between description and interpretation is often a fuzzy one: how do we 'know' the ages of others just by looking at them, and how accurate can we be?
3 *Describe who the observer is*, as this is likely to affect what is seen, what is recorded and subsequent interpretations. If the observer has any prior links with those observed (and thus insider knowledge), this should also be made clear.
4 *Describe the actions* of the participants, including both verbal and non-verbal behaviours (where this is possible). Some coding may be needed for some of the variables (e.g. body posture), to aid recording. The sequence of actions over time is likely to be important, and needs to be carefully noted.
5 *Interpret the situation*, attempting to give an indication of its meaning to the participants and to the observer, what their experiences are likely to be, what their background might be, etc. In this, the evidential basis for the interpretations must be made as clear as possible; these could be from direct observations, from the observer's own experience or from the observer's projection of their own expectations or habits. Often, this is very difficult to do, as we may not be consciously aware of how social reality is constructed until our social expectations are violated in some way or other. Metaphors are sometimes useful here, to aid the explanation that is being put forward; for example, 'waves of people' may convey a lot more than a simple record of the number of people and how they were moving.
6 *Consider alternative interpretations of the situation*, again giving reasons for the conclusions arrived at. If one looked at the situation from another perspective, might this affect the conclusions reached? Would a child view the situation in the same way, or somebody from the Amazon

jungle, or a Freudian, or a behaviourist? It does not matter how far-fetched these examples may seem. It is most important to recognize that many alternative interpretations may be possible in any given observation.

7 *Explore your feelings in being an observer* (reflexive analysis is always important in qualitative research), including your experience of the observation. Again, ethical considerations are useful here, especially in highlighting the ways in which we may affect what we study, with consequences that are often beyond our control.

A particular example will now be given, and worked through. Let us say that we are interested in observing peoples' queuing behaviour.

Why

We are interested in following up work done by Mann (1977) on queuing behaviour. He found in field experiment based studies in Jerusalem that queues only formed when there were six or more people waiting for the same bus. We are particularly concerned to see not only whether this finding holds good for the United Kingdom, but also what other variables may affect queuing, in a 'real-life' setting. Mann's use of a field experiment can be criticized, for instance, for producing the results that he claimed to have found: what he might have discovered is solely what people in Jerusalem do when presented with a queue of strangers, and may bear no resemblance to their normal queuing behaviour, which could possibly be a lot more anarchic. A real-life study may help to uncover all sorts of other behaviours and variables which need to be taken into consideration when we look at queuing in the real world. Work of this nature might provide interesting cross-national findings, indicating differences in social rules that might be of interest to people travelling to other countries. In addition, work of this nature might help in the design of street furniture, and might perhaps have implications for the design of social skills courses for, *inter alia*, people re-entering the community after having been institutionalized for some length of time (especially people who may have problems with aggressive behaviour; somebody was knifed to death at Waterloo Station in London recently in an argument about queuing for train tickets).

Who

In order to compare our findings with those of Mann, we decided to concentrate on queuing at bus stops. After some pilot work, we decided to concentrate on a particular bus stop in Manchester, where there is no shelter (as the restricted space affects how people stand to wait), and where there is plenty of pavement space (so people are free to queue or not). Our earlier work found that rain affects queuing (people often shelter nearby, and then rush for the bus when it arrives), so we decided to carry out the study at a dry time, in an evening rush hour, when the buses are well used. This example merely reports the results for the observation of one particular queue over the five minutes immediately before a bus is scheduled to come (the stop is near the start of the route, so we know that it is reasonably likely to be on time). All the people who turn up to catch the particular targeted bus will be recorded. We decided that ethical concerns are minimal, as we are merely watching naturally occurring behaviour from a window overlooking the bus stop, where our presence will not affect what is being watched. We felt that it was not necessary to tell our participants about our study; indeed, in this case, it may well be virtually impossible to find them again.

What
We decided to attempt to take detailed paper and pencil based notes, as it was felt that a videocamera might be observed. Moreover, because of the distance involved, it would have to be selective or produce images that would be too small to provide useful material. Pilot studies indicated that it is impossible to hear conversations, so we concentrated on the non-verbal behaviour of all the participants. This was a relatively unstructured observation, where we attempted to record all that occurred during the five minutes period. Observation was undertaken alone, as no other observer was currently available. What follows is the detailed written account produced immediately after the observation period, following the format outlined above.

The observation

Description of the context
The observation was carried out from 17.35 to 17.40 on Friday 8 October 1993 in Lever Street, Manchester; the weather was dry but overcast, and there was little wind. Lever Street is a one-way street, the traffic coming in 'waves', being governed by traffic lights at the beginning of the street. The 183 bus stop for Uppermill was observed from the first floor window of Australia House immediately above the bus stop (but about seven metres away) by the observer.

Description of the participants
In all, 14 people were observed during the observation; to avoid needless replication, their details are provided in the next section.

Description of the observer
The observer was a man in his forties from the Manchester Metropolitan University psychology staff (i.e. one of the authors of this chapter).

Description of the actions of the participants

At the start of the observation period, nobody was standing at the bus stop. After one minute, a young man wearing a shellsuit came up, and stood right by the stop, on the south side of it; he stood looking around, particularly towards Piccadilly, where the bus comes from. He was followed after another minute by two conventionally dressed women in their fifties carrying shopping bags, which they put down on the pavement two metres from the first person, also to the south side; they turned to face each other, and one started to speak, while the other nodded her head. The man glanced at them, and started to tap his feet on the side of the litter bin by the bus stop. At three minutes, two more smartly attired women in their early twenties arrived, each carrying a black briefcase. They stood one metre away from the last two, well back from the pavement, and started talking to each other, both facing towards Piccadilly. They were followed in rapid succession by a single man in his forties wearing a black overcoat and carrying a briefcase, three women in their teens in casual clothes, and two more men in their twenties wearing city suits. Each stood in a vague line from each other, at variable distances from each other, those furthest from the bus stop standing closer to the next person. The bus, which was driven by a male bus driver, turned the corner, bags were picked up and the queue filled up the gaps, becoming more orderly. The bus stopped marginally short of the head of the queue, and the bus doors folded inwards. The two older women got on it first, followed by the two younger women. The young man who was first to arrive then boarded, followed by the remainder of the queue; order was not entirely maintained, as three further younger women in casual clothes rushed up from elsewhere, and pushed in before the two men who were at the end of the queue.

Interpretation of the situation

This was an everyday situation for the participants, who were a varying batch of people. It might be assumed, bearing in mind variables such as the time, the age and gender of those observed, their clothing and the location of the observation, that some were shoppers, some city office workers, some shop assistants, some unemployed. All seemed familiar with catching buses, and appeared to be holding some implicit rules about queuing, which broke down slightly in this context. It must be noted, though, that none of the participants seemed to be particularly upset at what might have been construed as queue jumping in this study. In terms of the original interests, this research indicates that queuing behaviour in the United Kingdom seems to occur (in marked contrast to Mann's research) even with one person, but it also suggests that there is a need to investigate other variables, especially as the queue order was not the same as the bus boarding order. It could be that there are social rules as to who is given preference in such settings (what is the impact of age and gender, for instance?), or differing expectations by the participants as to the social expectations and rule-following of others (should those carrying heavy bags or using season tickets be given precedence, for instance?). Further investigation is obviously needed as to whether these results are replicated in other similar observations.

Alternative interpretation of the situation

It could be suggested that the bus driver deliberately stopped the bus before the stop, as he wanted to give preference to the two older women who were laden down with shopping bags, or he thought that the young male at the head of the queue was just hanging around, and was not a potential passenger. It may be that he resents picking up young males in shellsuits, as they have caused problems on his bus in the past. It could be that some of the potential passengers were smoking when the bus came up, and lost their place in the queue while they extinguished their cigarettes. The younger females who rushed up at the last moment could have been psychology students who were carrying out a field experiment on the effects of queue jumping. There may also be relationships between other variables, such as gender, age and preferred interpersonal distance, which could account for the results found. Moreover, there could be possible different types of personality or cultural codes (Manchester is a multicultural city) that are related to queuing behaviour.

Feelings as an observer

The presence of the observer seemed to have had no effect on the behaviour of the participants, and the observation felt ethically comfortable, as it was watching people in their everyday situations. This method produces a rich wealth of data, and sometimes unexpected results. What is clear is that the observation above is only a selection of non-verbal behaviours, it being impossible physically to record all the observable actions of some 14 people over even a five-minute period; for instance, the first male's foot-tapping is noted as started, but no record is made as to when it stopped. No record was kept of smoking behaviour, which (as has been suggested in the 'alternative interpretations' section) could have been crucial. Over even a brief period of time, the relative positions and body postures of participants will change with respect to each other: participants will need to monitor whether the bus is coming on a fairly continuous basis, as well as converse with and/or watch others. As the number of people increases, the detailed amount recorded decreases; a video recording might be of assistance here, but is likely to pose further problems. Interestingly, the sample of people seem in this study was somewhat atypical in terms of demographic characteristics of Manchester bus users, with more males and less older people than would normally be expected; this could be related to the particular time of day and/or route chosen for observation. As well as the questions raised above, it might be interesting to speculate as to whether these findings would be replicated elsewhere in the country (or even in other parts of Manchester). The fact that there was obviously sufficient room on the bus for everyone queuing may have meant less resentment at queue jumping. What is also worthy of note is that the observation provides detailed estimates of gender, age and clothing, but says nothing about ethnicity. This could be a reflection of biases of the observer, which could be conscious or unconscious. There is often a taken-for-granted element that is difficult to avoid. Often, we are so rooted in our own culture, time and background that we do not realize how myopic we are. What led, for instance, to the interpretation of 'unemployed' made above? Whether somebody from another culture would notice, record and emphasize the same features is an interesting point; even another viewer from the same culture may well have recorded the scene differently. Age estimates are particularly problematic, but in certain circumstances gender assumptions may also be incorrect. At best, this is an interesting observation, but one that needs to be looked at in the context of considerable further research.

Assessment

Advantages of observation as a method

Although this very short observation only provides the briefest description of five minutes of queuing behaviour, it has produced much material that can be related to previously published literature in the area, it has provided some unexpected results, it is open-ended and it has suggested many avenues for further research. A picture is provided of a 'real-life' naturalistic setting (with no problems of ecological validity), and many interesting questions are raised. The research results are generally accessible. Though there may be problems with the recording of the observation and its interpretation, the researcher intrudes very little into the situation, and his presence is not obviously reactive. It is hoped that sufficient details are provided to allow readers to make their own judgements about the findings, and how they can be interpreted. The method can tell us not only what is going on, but also who is involved, when and where things happen. It can illuminate processes and it can examine causality, suggesting why things happen as they do in particular settings. It can give access to phenomena that are often obscured (e.g. non-verbal cues) or not amenable to experimentation (it would be difficult to replicate the findings of the observation above in a laboratory based study). Situations can be examined that cannot be replicated in a laboratory, such as weddings, political meetings, prisons, behaviour in bars, football crowds and religious behaviour. The chronology of events can be taken into account, and continuities over time can be looked at. The use of modern technological equipment such as video recorders (though not without their problems, an issue we will take up below) allows permanent records to be made, which can be independently analysed and reanalysed in detail, ensuring some reliability of interpretation. Observation can, of course, be part of a more mixed method approach, where a variety of different techniques are used, focusing in on a common research question.

Disadvantages of observation as a method

There may be external validity problems. At times, the results can end up being very subjective, depending more on who the researcher is (and their biases) than the situation being observed. Researchers may well notice different aspects of the situation. In the example above, a strong anti-smoker may have noticed smoking behaviour to a greater extent, while somebody who was more fashion-conscious might form different opinions about the likely background of the participants based on a keen observation of the clothes worn. A researcher can produce results that are over-impressionistic, carelessly produced or just idiosyncratic. The fact that somebody is known to be interested in a particular phenomenon may well affect peoples' behaviour, and this is likely to be different when the observer is present and when he or she is absent. There have been cases in educational research where a school has carried on utilizing a method that was being observed, when in the ordinary course of events (when it was not being observed) it would have been abandoned. As well as selectivity in terms of the observation, inferences within interpretations are obviously subject to research bias. Although the example in this chapter avoided reactivity of the observer on the situation, there is always the possibility that the observer may have been influenced in some way by the situation. Given that the social world is socially created (as Berger and Luckmann 1967 suggest), it is often very difficult to be able to stand back from a process that one is already part of; moreover, perceived reality may be structured through the very framework being utilized.

The 'why' may be poorly formulated, leading to a concentration on the wrong (or unimportant) aspects of a situation. As has been mentioned, one should be aware of the likely interdependence of observations and interpretations.

The 'who' may be a poor sample, the time chosen may be inappropriate.

As suggested above, the rush hour may sample from a different population of bus users. This is likely to be a particular problem if the observation is carried out in a setting with which the researcher is unfamiliar. Special care needs to be taken in cross-cultural settings, where the implicit social rules are likely to be unfamiliar to the observer. The observation may be for too short a time, thus missing out crucial material; it may be for too long a time, ending up simply skimming the material, or being overwhelmed by too much information.

The 'what' may also be problematic, as there may well be internal validity problems. The observer may be blind to what is being looked at, may not understand it, may think that they have seen something or may influence the ongoing process both consciously and unconsciously. Although videocameras and recorders have been heralded as the way of ensuring that accurate records are available, it must be realized that they also have disadvantages. They are inevitably selective, giving at best only a partial view, they only represent one particular viewpoint and the angles taken may influence interpretations (for instance, a standing figure may be evaluated differently if a camera goes from head to toe, rather than from toe to head), and they are likely to be reacted to. Even using paper and pencil recording has problems: as the above example indicates, it is inevitably selective, and the very act of note-taking will lead to material being missed. Our sense organs and attentional mechanisms are inadequate for the task.

Observation as a method can be very time-consuming and labour-intensive, especially as it creates an enormous amount of data which then becomes very hard to winnow. It is therefore very important to decide how much is likely to be needed, and to consider carefully what precisely it is that will be analysed.

In common with many other methods and theories in psychology, the approach is imbued with assumptions that people *do* make sense of their social world, do carry around with them (albeit probably at an unconscious level) a set of implicit social rules, do behave purposively, etc. But people may be inconsistent or behave in an unthinking manner in social situations, sometimes even following inappropriate scripts. Langer (1978) suggests that for a lot of the time in social interactions we do not behave in a thoughtful fashion, but rather act 'mindlessly'. Thus the findings may be so completely idiosyncratic as to be not worth discussing. As has been mentioned above, it could be that observation may actually produce a structured and crystallized 'reality', rather than a reflection of the messy nature of things as they really are.

Control by the observer over the phenomena being observed is usually minimal, and it may not be possible to predict when certain events are going to occur. In the example discussed above, what if the bus had been cancelled, for instance? This might have produced further interesting results, illuminating a different set of social rules.

All research should involve the careful consideration of ethical problems. This has been touched upon above, and will be discussed further in Chapter 10. It is often assumed that there are fewer ethical problems with observational studies than with many other approaches in psychological research, but ethics do need to be carefully thought through and discussed with others before starting a study. The British Psychological Society guidelines see natural observation as being unproblematic, but we need to consider the extent to which we have a right to record the behaviour of others in public social settings, and issues such as anonymity and confidentiality also need to be carefully considered. We are still accountable for what we produce in observational reports.

Awareness of the potential pitfalls we have outlined should lead to attempts to try to avoid them, or at least minimize their effects. For instance, if one is trying to reduce the impact of the observer on the observed situation, then checking to see if results replicate themselves over time or with different observers would be useful. With experience, too, note-taking becomes an easier activity.

In conclusion, despite the potential drawbacks, observation will produce rich and exciting results, which may well help to challenge existing assumptions about social life, experience and rules, and to point the way to new developments. Admittedly (and this is true of all methods in psychology, quantitative and qualitative), a lot still depends on who the researcher is, but following the guidelines above should help to minimize the problems of this effect. Of all psychological methods, naturalistic observation is probably potentially the least reactive and the one that is most likely to produce valid results and insights that are very much rooted in 'real life'. In conclusion, I would concur with Lofland (1971: 93) that observation 'is the most penetrating of strategies, the most close and telling mode of gathering information.'

Useful reading

Cohen, L. and Manion, L. (1989). *Research Methods in Education*, 3rd edn. London: Routledge.

Judd, C.M., Smith, E.R. and Kidder, L.H. (1991). *Research Methods in Social Relations*, 6th edn. Fort Worth, TX: Holt, Rinehart and Winston.

Miles, M.B. and Huberman, A.M. (1984). *Qualitative Data Analysis*. London: Sage.

Robson, C. (1993). *Real World Research*. Oxford: Blackwell.

Weick, K.E. (1968). 'Systematic observational methods', in G. Lindzey and E. Aronson (eds) *Handbook of Social Psychology Volume II*, 2nd edn. Reading, MA: Addison-Wesley.

Weick, K.E. (1985) 'Systematic observational methods', in G. Lindzey and E. Aronson (eds) *Handbook of Social Psychology Volume I*, 3rd edn. New York: Random House.

References

Albert, S. and Kessler, S. (1978). 'Ending social encounters'. *Journal of Experimental Social Psychology*, **14**, 541–53.

Argyle, M. (1987). *The Psychology of Interpersonal Behaviour*. Harmondsworth: Penguin.

Bales, R.F. (1950). *Interaction Process Analysis: a Method for the Study of Small Groups*. Chicago: University of Chicago Press.

Berger, P.L. and Luckmann, T. (1967). *The Social Construction of Reality*. London: Allen Lane.

Cary, M.S. (1978). 'Does civil inattention exist in pedestrian passing?' *Journal of Personality and Social Psychology*, **36**, 1185–93.

Ditton, J. (1977). *Part-time Crime: an Ethnography of Fiddling and Pilferage*. London: Macmillan.

Goffman, E. (1963). *Behavior in Public Places*. New York: Free Press.

Langer, E.J. (1978). 'Rethinking the role of thought in social interaction', in J.H. Harvey, W. Ickes and R.F. Kidd (eds) *New Directions in Attribution Research*. New York: Halsted Press.

Latané, B. and Darley, J.M. (1970). *The Unresponsive Bystander: Why Does He Not Help?* New York: Appleton-Century-Crofts.

Lofland, J. (1971). *Analysing Social Settings*. London: Wadsworth.

Mann, L. (1977). 'The effect of stimulus queues on queue-joining behavior'. *Journal of Personality and Social Psychology*, **35**, 437–42.

Marshall, C. and Rossman, G.B. (1989). *Designing Qualitative Research*. London: Sage.

Minuchin, S. (1974). *Families and Family Therapy*. Cambridge, MA: Harvard University Press.

Oxford English Dictionary (1989). 2nd edn. Oxford: Oxford University Press.

Reason, P. and Rowan, J. (eds) (1981). *Human Inquiry: a Sourcebook of New Paradigm Research*. Chichester: Wiley.

Reber, A.S. (1985). *Penguin Dictionary of Psychology*. Harmondsworth: Penguin.

Vrugt, A.J. (1990). 'When a Queen speaks to her nation: a non-verbal analysis'. *British Journal of Social Psychology*, **29**, 367–73.

Webb, E.J., Campbell, D.T., Schwartz, R.D., Sechrest, L. and Grove, J.B. (1981). *Nonreactive Measures in the Social Sciences*, 2nd edn. Boston: Houghton Mifflin.

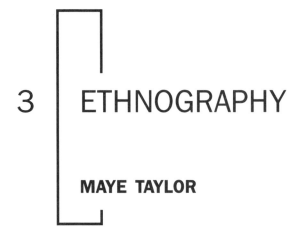

3 | ETHNOGRAPHY

MAYE TAYLOR

Ethnography is, perhaps, the original and quintessential qualitative research method; hence its inclusion here in a book on applied qualitative research methods. It has its roots in anthropology and sociology and in recent years has become a model for research in social psychology and a key source of new paradigm research. Many of the principles embodied in ethnography have become key to the broader movement of qualitative research. In short, ethnography is a basic form of social research involving making observations, gaining data from informants, constructing hypotheses and acting upon them. The ethnographer participates actively in the research environment but does not structure it; the approach is discovery based, the aim being to depict the activities and perspectives of actors.

Background

Ethnography is concerned with experience as it is lived, felt or undergone, and thus involves a concern with phenomenological consciousness. To research this, the ethnographer participates in people's daily lives for a period of time, watching what happens, listening to what is said, asking questions, studying documents, in other words collecting whatever data are available to throw light on the issue(s) with which the research is concerned. As ethnography is crucially a multimethod form of research, this chapter differs slightly from the other chapters in the book, in that much of the emphasis will be on the principles of ethnography, and methods as outlined in other chapters can then be linked to these. Participant observation, in particular, which many researchers see as synonymous with ethnography, forms the base method, while interviewing and action research inform later stages.

As a mode of qualitative research, ethnography only succeeds to the degree it enables the reader to understand what goes on in a society or a social circumstance as well as the participants. As Reason and Rowan (1981) explain, ethnography has to be involved, committed, relevant, intuitive, but above all it has to be alive. Ethnography goes beyond mere story telling, to encompass elicitation and documentation of cultural knowledge, as exemplified in Griffin's (1985) work on young working class women making the transition from school to work, the detailed investigation of patterns of interaction of 'football hooligans' by Marsh *et al.* (1978) and the holistic analysis of the Moonies carried out by Barker (1984). In addition all these investigations demonstrate the important principle argued by Glaser and Strauss (1967) that it is vital in ethnographic research that theories are developed and tested during the process of the research itself.

Contrary to some views, ethnography is not new: it has a long history, rooted in anthropology and cross-cultural research. Witness Fanny Wright's 1821 study, 'View of society and manners in America', and Harriet Martineau's 1837 'Society in America' study, quoted in Reinharz (1992), both of which provide prime examples of ethnography giving powerful insights into 'everyday life'. Specifically, in these two examples, the lived reality of women's lives. Psychologically ethnography is very interesting in itself, in that it bears a close resemblance to the routine ways in which people make sense of their world in everyday life. It could be seen as the most basic form of social research, for when we are a 'novice' in a new world and trying to make sense of our new situation we will probably:

1 Make observations and draw inferences.
2 Ask people questions.
3 Construct a working hypothesis.
4 Act on it.

Observation of 'freshers' in their first few days at university would constitute a research project that would aptly demonstrate people doing this, and student counselling services are well aware of those students who 'get it wrong' at this time. There is a significant drop-out rate at this stage, for example, and ethnographic studies that give detailed pictures of the experience of being a fresher could provide valuable information on critical incidents, which could help to shape appropriate institutional responses.

However, it is the formalized multimethod form of ethnographic research that takes it beyond 'everyday' sense-making activity into the domain of formal psychological research. This multimethod approach reduces the risks that can stem from reliance on a single kind of data, which might mean that one's own findings are method dependent. It also means that triangulation is possible, allowing the researcher to compare data collected by different methods. This is discussed in more detail in Chaper 9, on evaluation.

Essentially, then, ethnography is characterized by:

- gathering data from a range of sources, e.g. interviews, conversations, observations, documents;
- studying behaviour in everyday contexts rather than experimental conditions;
- using an unstructured approach to data gathering in the early stages, so that key issues can emerge gradually through analysis;
- comprising an in-depth study of one or two situations.

It is clear that this type of research is concerned with the interaction of factors and events; one does not exist in any meaningful sense without the others, and the research itself is embedded in the very social world it is seeking to study. Ethnographic researchers thus recognize that they are part of the social world they are studying, and that they cannot avoid having an effect on the social phenomena being studied. The issue is: 'rather than engaging in futile attempts to eliminate the effects of the researcher, we should set about understanding them' (Hammersley and Atkinson 1983: 17); so that this approach is not a matter of methodological commitment but an existential fact. Reason and Rowan (1981) further 'defend' the subjectivity so involved, and claim that it was precisely because psychologists wished to get away from subjectivity and what they see as naive inquiry that they set up the whole apparatus of experimental method, quasi-experimental method tests of statistical significance, dependent and independent variables and so on. They further argue that while this apparatus does counter some of the problem of naive inquiry, it also kills off everything it comes into contact with, so what we are left with is 'dead knowledge'. I certainly agree with their stated view that 'in human inquiry it is much better to be deeply interesting than accurately boring'.

Following on from the principle that ethnography involves abandoning attempts to eliminate the effects of the researcher in favour of understanding them, one could argue that this would be an important feature in the practice of any social research that inclines towards laying claim to the notion of relevance to the real world, a central concern of this book. Another link we can make here is with research that puts emphasis on the research having a closeness to how people actually conduct their lives. So, according to Adelman (1977), ethnographic case study, for example, recognizes the complexity and embeddedness of social truths and represents something of the discrepancies or conflicts between the various participants.

The relevance to research in educational contexts, for example, is clear. Many research questions are based on the identification of a problematic area of practice where there are disagreements about what is to be done (and about what is the cause of the 'problem' in the first place). Intrinsic to such a study should be a consideration of whether it will contribute in some way to improvement in the practice of what is being studied; there is a fuller account of this in Chapter 7, on action research. Much of the research on equal opportunities work in schools, for example, has relied heavily on the ethnographic approach to highlight the diverging experience between certain particular groups, and the dysjunction between theory and practice: a good example of this is the Girls into Science and Technology (GIST) project (Kelly 1984).

If there is, as Adelman argues, complexity of 'social truths' then the multimethod approach of ethnography gives the advantage of being able to develop converging lines of enquiry. Yin (1988) develops this point in case study research, claiming that the findings are likely to be more convincing and accurate if they are based on several different sources of information in corroborative mode. The intending ethnographic researcher is advised to look at examples of ethnographic research and ask questions like: what is there in this study that I can learn from and apply to my own situation and research question? In addition to those already quoted in this chapter, readers might find Wilson-Barnett (1983), Burgess (1990) and Lee (1993) helpful. It will be evident from these studies that methods have to be chosen that fit the purpose of the inquiry. This is no different from any other approach. As mentioned before, the ethnographic researcher can use interviews, observation and documents, particularly diaries; the example in this chapter, for example, relies heavily on participant observation and a detailed research diary. Whatever the method(s) of data collection used, the principle of reflexivity, that is, how the researchers position themselves within the context, process and production of the research, is of central importance in understanding the perspectives of the people being looked at: the researcher and researched are part of the same social world. Further, it is important that those observations are in context, following the ethnographic principle that humans behave differently under different circumstances.

The 'doing of it' raises two key issues, of access and of field relations. Obviously before you can study anything you have to get access to the setting and to the 'actors and actions'. The way in which this access is negotiated, and thus the field relationships are established, can have a significant impact on the quality and quantity of data that the researcher can obtain (the example later in this chapter will highlight this). Sometimes parts of any setting will not necessarily be equally open to observation: some people may not be willing to talk and even those who do agree to talk to you may not be prepared to divulge all the information they have available.

When observation is central there are many situations that might be excluded, psychotherapy and counselling sessions, for example. However, participant observation in co-counselling groups is possible, where the researcher is a fuller participant, and this is mirrored by feminist counsellors, in that the participation *per se* lessens the objectifying of the other participants, and directly addresses the problem of inequality of power in field relations. Much counselling and psychotherapy research is evaluation based and tends to rely on what the clients say about their experience (Toukmanian and Rennie 1992).

Even when access is granted there is still 'actual' entry into the 'real' and everyday of the setting, which sometimes involves the researcher in having to get behind fronts put on for their benefit, such as 'extra macho' behaviour displayed by young men for the benefit of a woman researcher that was not typical of the everyday interaction in the youth club under observation. Sometimes the researchers might find themselves working around the function of gatekeeper, and this can involve the researcher in intricate and delicate negotiations within the setting when access has been obtained. For example, much research about the therapeutic (or otherwise!) factors in residential institutions for difficult adolescents floundered not at the door of the director of social services who had given permission for the research, but at the door of the recreation room, when the 'informal leader' of the residents controls events and thus what the researcher is allowed 'to see'.

People in the field will seek to 'place' or locate the ethnographer within their own experience, so negotiating field relations can be fraught with difficulty. Many researchers have puzzled at the hostility they have met, not suspecting that they were seen as government spies or tools of management. Concern with what kind of person the researcher *is*, rather than the purpose of the research, can often render the research impossible, with questions such as can they be trusted, can they be exploited, can they be manipulated, could they be a source of support? These issues may well still be present when people have agreed to participate, since, as highlighted in Chapter 4, informants set their own, as well as concur with the 'official', research agendas.

Morgan's (1972) ethnographic study of a northern factory illustrates how these fieldwork issues work in practice. He quotes a story of how one of the women in the labour force offered to wash his shirts! Morgan interpreted this as perhaps an unconscious attempt to neutralize some of the ambiguities of his participant observer research role. Morgan reflects on his own ambiguous position in the department, where his gender placed him in the work context in the same position as the foreman and managers, who were all men, but the occupational role he had taken up as participant observer placed him in the same position as the female employees. He discusses how much he learned about gender, and how it is shaped through interactional contexts. Morgan's work underlines how important it is to give attention to impression management and basic interaction skills, to how you participate, as well as to how inventive or interesting your theoretical questions and analysis are. There have been lots of humorous stories told at the expense of action research social workers dressing themselves in old jeans and suchlike in order to 'blend in', only to find themselves confronted by street smart young people in designer label clothes.

It is evident that there are some fieldwork roles that are clearly fixed, i.e. characteristics that the researcher can't stage manage, such as gender, age, races or colour. It is important to accept that no position of gender or ethnic neutrality can be claimed in ethnographic research. This has only recently been accepted, but it is a principle that is important in evaluating findings as well as accepting how the actual research process will be influenced. Many ethnographers argue that sexist and cultural stereotypes influence the research process in certain situations, with women seen as non-threatening, for instance, but this often means that they are treated with more suspicion than male researchers when anything serious is being researched (Hunt 1989). In terms of ethnicity we are now very aware of culture, power and personal style, and of how many anthropologists (the original ethnographers) objectified their research subjects despite the stated aims of their research.

Here field role relationships are influential. People are not 'social facts', inhabiting the place, institution etc. and just waiting to be studied and to reveal their all. There is thus a question of more than just observing, which raises the spectre of immersion that could result from the participation. The time for the research activity *per se* would be eroded, so the aim throughout is to maintain one's role definition. If a researcher starts feeling 'at home' and *all* sense of being a stranger is lost the critical analytical perspective can be diluted. It is wise to bear in mind, in this context, Gold's (1958) classic paper on participant observation, where he suggested four 'ideal' type researcher roles, ranged along a continuum from 'complete participant' through 'participant as observer' and 'observer as participant' to 'complete observer'. This captures the delicate balance needed between the relatively objective observer and the relatively subjective participant.

Ethnographic researchers have specific problems with recording evidence in situations where they are being 'bombarded with material', and memory can play tricks. A particular one is the way in which subconsciously data can be transformed in line with an emerging theory as to 'what is going on'. If you commit the data to audio, video or detailed field notes you have records. It is often impossible, and inappropriate, to audio or video record, so field notes are most common, and consist of relatively concrete descriptions of social processes and their contexts, which sometimes have to be written up out of the immediate situations if it is clear that note-taking would be an intrusive activity. These field notes will be the record and it is vital that they encompass the features on which your analysis will be based. Analytical notes as your research proceeds are also useful. While you are reading your own field notes or documents, or transcribing a tape, it is helpful to construct a commentary, especially if theoretical ideas arise. Again these should be chronologically sorted so that it is clear when they were noted or the ideas occurred. The formulation of precise problems, hypotheses and an appropriate research strategy is, as Glaser and Strauss (1967) claim, an emergent feature of ethnographic research. So these analytical notes constitute the 'thinking out loud' process that is a central part of the reflexive enterprise. Some noting of the feelings of the researcher is also encouraged, to add information to the analytical process so that it can be both a resource for, and a record of, developing interpretations.

Ethnography can provide relatively concrete descriptions or rather more developed typologies; that is, when a set of phenomena is identified that represents sub-types of some more general typology. Much work, for example, has been done on a typology of psychotherapists' difficulties and a typology of the strategies they use to deal with such difficulties. Work with a co-therapist in group psychotherapy provides an excellent opportunity for such research, often using critical incident analysis by recall, immediately after the group, whereby each therapist in turn raises incidents from the group where they saw the other therapist intervene. What the therapist was feeling at the time of the intervention is noted, as well as what was actually said. To take another example, Glaser and Strauss (1968) developed a typology of 'awareness' contexts in hospitals in respect of terminally ill patients, which, when linked with the medical control of information, can present a picture of the difficulties patients have in getting information and shed light on the strategies they employ to deal with this.

Example

Ethnography, as previously indicated in this chapter, is a multimethod form of research, it often combines a variety of techniques, so it is possible to check construct validity by examining data relating to the same construct from participant observation, from observation, from interviewing and from document analysis. For the purpose of illustration here participant observation will be highlighted as the method to demonstrate ethnographic principles in practice. However, given the limitations of a chapter and the extended and complex nature of ethnography, the example will be in outline only.

You should read this in conjunction with Chapter 2, where we looked at the place of observation as a method in psychology. In *participant* observation, the observation is varied in that the observer 'becomes part of the group' which is being observed. All the points raised, particularly the three crucial questions of 'why', 'who' and 'what', need to be borne in mind, given that the researcher is occupying the complementary roles of observer and participant. It is important to remember that the researcher will be actively participating in a social world in which people are already busy interpreting and understanding their environments for themselves. The participant observer is engaged not only in making his or her own observations, but also in 'tapping into' this subjective world. Thus participant observation is about engaging in a social scene, experiencing it and seeking to understand and explain it, and it is this understanding which requires systematic and sustained study.

In a casual conversation with a group of police officers in a different context, it emerged that West Ham United football supporters were the new folk devils, viewed as being the most difficult of all supporters, so much so that extra police were always on duty when West Ham were the visiting team. They were viewed and portrayed as amongst the most violent, racist and sexist of all football supporters; the notorious ICF (Inter-City Firm) of the 1980s was quoted as evidence in support. For my purposes it offered a good ethnographic social psychological project, which could concern itself with making sense of a social phenomenon and the opportunity to carry out some cultural analysis.

I chose this study quite deliberately once the topic had presented itself to me via the conversation with the police officers. I would be a 'stranger' in a very distinctive culture and was offered an opportunity to study male behaviour, albeit in one context, from very close quarters. I was anxious to put to the test the 'making sense' aspect of ethnography and therefore did not choose an area of familiarity or one connected with action, in view of my later chapter on action research. I would most certainly be 'the novice in the new world'. I wanted to know what those supporters were like, how they behaved to get that reputation and something about why West Ham, a London East End football club with a reputation for good football, as exemplified, as I already knew, by Bobby Moore and Trevor Brooking, should attract such supporters. Participant observation, I assumed, would clearly provide the material needed to address the questions and perhaps give me insight into the process of 'becoming' a West Ham supporter!

For the purpose of the study I chose to do the following things.

1 To attend ten away matches and four home matches, during the 1992–3 season, when West Ham were in the First Division (the season when they won automatic promotion to the Premier League of English football).

2 To travel to the respective grounds with the fans by coach or train as appropriate, which included walking in ranks, with mounted police escorts, from the station to the ground at away games.

3 To use the cafe before the game and at half time.

4 To stand on the terraces to watch the away games in the visiting supporters' enclosure, and for home games to stand behind the goal.

5 To buy match programmes and the fanzine to use as documentary evidence.

6 To talk to as many fans as possible, men and women, in informal 'interviews'.

This allowed me to observe the West Ham supporters in several different contexts and provided me with enough material to draw conclusions. In total I spent about 100 hours with the fans. These were the regular group of travelling fans, in the order of about 1,000; the ratio of men to women was usually about 10 to 1 and there were a number of young children, with a wide adult age range.

I did not announce my 'academic status' but it became known during an incident at the second game, when I was routinely body searched by the police as I came through the turnstiles. When I was asked what I had in my bag, my response of 'a book and an orange juice' was met with derision: it was said that 'West Ham fans can't read'. The interaction was observed by several fans and one of them jokingly asked what my book was. I answered truthfully that it was a psychology book, and from then on I was known as 'the clever bird who reads books', and ascribed my status accordingly. I thus gained access and acceptance, my 'field role relationships' established from that point.

Analysis

This section can provide only a small glimpse of the sort of episodes, incidents and talk that I observed, but in line with the nature of ethnography I will try to communicate the quality of the experience. From the outset it was obvious that it was not just a question of watching the football, but that social ritual figured strongly in being a West Ham fan and that there was a well rehearsed sequence of behaviours which played a large part in this. I was expected to take my part in the regular renditions of 'We're forever blowing bubbles' and 'Billy Bond's magic army' at appropriate times when pointed at. The various song leaders have evidently become an accepted feature, and they point at different people in turn, which is the signal for them to lead the next bit of the song. From my observations it would appear that these rituals are very well established. As each West Ham player comes out on to the pitch for the pre-match practice, he comes towards the fans, and each player is acknowledged and greeted by having his name chanted and then applauded. Nicknames are used for some of the players, Martin Allen being 'affectionately' known as 'Mad Dog'. The cry of 'givus a ball' follows these greetings and a player always obliges by kicking a practice ball into the crowd, which is the key for the supporters' version of terrace handball, which continues until kick-off. On several occasions when West Ham were playing very, very badly, this game was taken up again during play, with the supporters very pointedly not watching the football match itself. On one occasion, when West Ham were playing even more badly, there was a call from one of the 'leaders' of 'sit down for West Ham', a large section of the crowd immediately sat down on the terraces with their backs to the pitch and an impromptu 'cabaret' ensued.

The language of some of the fans was crude and offensive. Other fans apologized to me at times, and there were a number of occasions when the swearing supporters were told to 'watch their language' by other fans in the vicinity, because of the presence of women and children. In my immediate hearing the language was not racist. West Ham had, at this time, a number of black players and the kind of comments they got when missing a goal or making a poor pass were substantially no different from the abuse that the white players got. Much of the unsolicited comment was in the form of humour. At the game at Barnsley, the day was dark and gloomy and grit and dust was being blown off slag heaps across the pitch. A fan in front of me suddenly screamed, pointing at the sky, 'What's that?' His friend hit him on the head and said, 'You daft s––, that's the sun.' Cries of 'Oh come on West Ham, we're in pain up here' rang round the ground. The humour was always well to the fore, winning or losing, home or away.

At all the away games there was considerable barracking from the home supporters, which was greeted with evidently rehearsed songs. I learned a new version of 'The Blaydon Races' at Newcastle that was not complimentary. In fact the rewording of the home team's 'song' was a regular part of the fans' repertoire of behaviours. The 'song' would not only be reworded but sung in an exaggerated local accent calculated to incense the home supporters. That same Newcastle game held a sequence which was to underline the difference between what was clearly expected of West Ham fans and what I myself had experienced. The fans were held behind, as always, by the police to let the home supporters leave first. There was a long delay in opening the gates, it was wet and cold and after the usual renditions of 'why are we waiting' they suddenly started waving at the now empty home supporter's terraces, laughing and chanting 'you're not singing now' and 'you're supposed to be at home', to the evident puzzlement of the very large numbers of police present. West Ham had lost the match, incidentally.

I filled several notebooks with my observations, dividing the recordings up into short time sequences and using what was happening in the game as an organizing device to locate the incidents. These notebooks constitute a diary, using the Bruyn (1966) indices of time, place, social circumstances, language and intimacy as organizing indices for recording and analysis of observations. I used the train journeys to make extensive notes. Many of the fans would volunteer comments and query what I was going to include. My experience challenged my 'starting assumptions'. I was never frightened and saw no violence, though I was spat on by home supporters on two occasions. It all seemed quite the reverse of my assumptions, in that the crowd I travelled with appeared to be a very large extended family, and most certainly was contrary to the media portrayal of West Ham supporters. The fans themselves complained bitterly about what they saw as an out-of-date view. Lots of them told me that things had changed, that banning alcohol on trains and other such measures had had a good effect, and that it had only been a minority of their fans that had been 'rotten to the core'.

I had to accept that 'what I saw was what I got'. There was little chance that my presence had distorted in any global way the fans' behaviour and I do not think I am being dishonest here or denying the effect I might have had. There was sexist language and behaviour, I got used to being greeted with 'You all right doll?' and 'protected' by being given room at barriers etc. On one occasion the only women's lavatory for visiting supporters was out of order, so a male lavatory was commandeered by two of the older men and given over to 'the ladies', and they stood guard over it. Women supporters were there, and were there in their own right, not just accompanying men but taking a lively part in the rituals and enjoying the game. They felt that they were a good influence and a contributory factor to the changes. In conversations with them I checked on their experiences: none of them felt frightened, several of them indicated that they went to the football matches because it was a social event where they considered they could be safe in the crowd, and they enjoyed watching West Ham play football.

Chapter 10, on report writing, underlines the main points to adhere to, but I think it is important to make some specific points about writing up this particular kind of project, which has its own style. The reflexive researcher must remain self-conscious as an author; writing up is not just a technical matter because it is at the point of representation, the report, in this type of research that the researcher has most power. How you represent the group you have studied is a central concern: that I was able to enjoy the experience influenced the content and the style of what I wrote. Quantitative research writing conventionally demands the distant and the impersonal, formally written in the third person, whereas ethnographies are often embedded in and constituted by their style. Choice of language in the writing of an ethnography is vital if the quality of the observation and experience in the case is to be communicated. It was certainly difficult to make an absolute distinction between analysis and account in my West Ham study. The formal research report, which separates 'method', results and discussion, does not lend itself to commentary. There is a strong argument that ethnographies should be very much like narrative writing, with an emphasis on theme and illustration: it is essential to make clear the pattern of events and the researcher's understanding. This is not to suggest that there is no organization or systematic analysis, for the ethnographer, like other researchers, has to achieve distance and impose a coherent, analytical framework. Given the 'richness' of the material I had gathered it was tempting to split the narrative from the analysis, the narrative serving the function of giving the reader a 'feel for' the West Ham supporter culture, and the analysis accounting for the discrepancy between the reputation and my experience. However, the danger of this textual separation is that it can sometimes hide the fact that the narrative part itself is analytic selection by the researcher of material. This ties in with the ongoing debate as to whether theory-free description is possible (which is further developed in Chapter 8).

As my research had been concerned with observing male (West Ham supporters') behaviour in a new (for me) context over a period of months, in order to make sense of their reputation, I chose to use the natural history model of writing up, producing descriptions of the perspectives of a group of people and descriptions of their patterns of interaction within the particular settings. One of the claims of ethnography is that such descriptions have value in their own right, producing qualitative data which give inside and detailed information. In this study it is perhaps the absence of certain behaviours that is significant: I did not observe anything that could justify the reputation. However, this exposes one of the limitations of the ethnographic account: it cannot research history as such, it takes a 'slice of time'. Many of the fans admitted that there had been an unruly mob element in the supporters but that was over ten years ago. Clearly reputations take time to change. Rather than simply 'telling the story' as events progress over time and the picture unfolds, another approach would be to write up in terms of the developmental cycle of the actors or the setting. This is particularly useful in terms of medical interventions and illness. Current counselling psychology research, for example, which is process rather than outcome focused, lends itself to this approach, particularly when the research is looking at how and why institution-based counselling services function, or not, as the case may be.

Assessment

I was certainly led to a more empathetic understanding of the state of being a West Ham supporter, and faced with the actual behaviour, forced, in the classic Glaser and Strauss (1967) model, to find a meaningful theory to account for the behaviour I encountered. This is over and above what I already 'knew' as a counselling psychologist about male behaviour, and what I was 'told' by the media. I am in the process of writing the account up, reflecting on the collective defensive containment of violence by the use of ritual and how those rituals were negotiated, the displacement of aggression by the use of humour and the rationalization of sexism into 'gallantry'.

I was not faced with the difficulty of finding myself unsympathetic to the group that I looked at, which, of course, can be a problem for ethnography, given that it does offer the opportunity to enter and understand social and cultural worlds that other methodologies cannot reach, and therefore does highlight how the issues of motive, method and morality can be inextricably intertwined in ethnography, demanding a sharper awareness and constant vigilance from the researcher. Chapter 8, on feminist research, provides a more specific treatment of this. Any method which involves intensive contact and ongoing personal relationships carries extra ethical responsibility, in terms of both how the researcher conducts the fieldwork and how the text conveys the findings. Fielding (1981), when faced with this dilemma, saw his role in his work on the National Front as that of interpreter between the inner workings of the organization and society in general, in the hope that from his account people could understand its appeal and find constructive ways of combating it. The problem of doing ethical ethnographic research manifests around the issue of 'fitting in', given the commitment to naturalistic understanding.

One of the criticisms of ethnography's important claim to naturalness is that in the selection of meetings, time periods and people for study others are excluded, so that an entirely 'natural' setting is never really possible. Obviously this was so in the West Ham study. I did not attend all games and it is just possible that the games I attended were relatively 'low key'. However, using as informants several fans who became known to me it was possible to monitor what happened at other games. After the first two games, stories of the 'missing matches' were relayed to me without prompting. One further restriction is that as I travelled by train the hundreds of fans who travel by car are outside my post-match conversations.

Another criticism focuses on the possible influence the researcher/observer might have upon the other participants (subjects of research), which could modify the validity of the findings. The claim to naturalism is regarded as 'dishonest' by Stanley and Wise (1983), in that by claiming 'naturalism' the researchers are denying their effect on the scene. However, one of the strengths of participant observation, the method I used, was that I was able to consider my own actions as well as those around me. This was a most illuminating part of the study in terms of understanding the impact of the rituals. I was well aware that my presence as a woman led to modified behaviour but as a researcher I was largely unimportant: a salutary lesson for psychologists? However, the example I have used does have limitations for the purpose of this particular point. It was a public setting where access could be bought, so there was more equality between psychologist and football supporter.

I started as a 'stranger' but it is possible that I became too immersed in the culture and so my perception was selective. But perhaps the idea that the truth is there for the taking if we can part the veil of prejudice and preconception and observe things as they really are was challenged throughout by the situation and it was important to accept that, in ethnography, description and interpretation are a continuum structured into the history of the researcher's involvement. I 'became' a West Ham supporter by choosing the 'novice' role so that I could reduce the taken-for-granted knowings that I could have brought. I did not carry out 'covert' participant observation: if I had not have been identified during the incident about the book I would have indicated my research intention. There is strong criticism of the ethics of covert research, putting the spotlight on the relationship between means and ends. The method is time consuming. I had to spend lots of time with a relatively small group of people, but it certainly demonstrated to me that this approach 'greatly assists in understanding human actions and brings with it new ways of viewing the social world' (May 1993: 132).

Useful reading

Burgess, R. (1990). *In the Field: an Introduction to Field Research*. London: Allen and Unwin.

Hammersley, M. and Atkinson, P. (1983). *Ethnography: Principles in Practice.* London: Routledge.
May, T. (1993). *Social Research: Issues, Methods and Process.* Buckingham: Open University Press.

References

Adelman, C. (1977). *Uttering, Muttering, Collecting, Using and Reporting Talk for Social and Educational Research.* London: Grant McIntyre.
Barker, E. (1984). *The Making of a Moonie: Choice or Brainwashing?* Oxford: Blackwell.
Bruyn, S.T. (1966). *The Human Perspective in Sociology.* Englewood Cliffs, NJ: Prentice Hall.
Burgess, R. (1990). *In the Field: an Introduction to Field Research.* London: Allen and Unwin.
Fielding, N. (1981). *The National Front.* London: Routledge and Kegan Paul.
Glaser, B.G. and Strauss, A.L. (1967). *The Discovery of Grounded Theory.* Chicago: Aldine.
Glaser, B.G. and Strauss, A.L. (1968). *Time for Dying.* Chicago: Aldine.
Goffman, E. (1972). *Interaction Ritual.* Harmondsworth: Penguin.
Gold, R.L. (1958). 'Roles in sociological field observation', *Social Forces*, 36, p. 93.
Griffin, C. (1985). *Typical Girls? Young Women from School to the Job Market.* London: Routledge and Kegan Paul.
Hammersley, M. and Atkinson, P. (1983). *Ethnography: Principles in Practice.* London: Routledge.
Hunt, J.C. (1989). *Psychoanalytical Aspects of Fieldwork.* London: Sage.
Kelly, A. (1984). *Girls and Science. An International Study of Sex Differences in School Science Achievement.* Stockholm: Almqvist and Wiksell.
Lee, M.L. (1993). *Doing Research on Sensitive Topics.* London: Sage.
Marsh, P., Rosser, E. & Harré, R. (1978). *The Rules of Disorder.* London: Routledge and Kegan Paul.
May, T. (1993). *Social Research: Issues, Methods and Process.* Buckingham: Open University Press.
Morgan, D. (1972). 'Men, masculinity and the process of sociological enquiry', in H. Roberts (ed.) *Doing Feminist Research.* London: Routledge and Kegan Paul.
Reason, P. and Rowan, J. (1981). *Human Inquiry. A Sourcebook of New Paradigm Research.* Chichester: Wiley.
Reinharz, S. (1992). *Feminist Methods in Social Research.* New York: Oxford University Press.
Stanley, L. and Wise, S. (1983). *Breaking out: Feminist Consciousness and Feminist Research.* London: Routledge and Kegan Paul.
Toukmanian, S.G. and Rennie, D.L. (eds) (1992). *Psychotherapy Process Research.* London: Sage.
Wilson-Barnett, J. (ed.) (1983). *Nursing Research: Ten Studies in Patient Care.* Chichester: Wiley.
Yin, R. (1988). *Case Study Research: Design and Methods.* London: Sage.

4 | INTERVIEWING

ERICA BURMAN

Conducting interviews is a complex, labour-intensive and uncertain business, fraught with tricky issues that social scientific researchers, and particularly psychologists, are often ill-equipped to address. This is because the emphasis on detachment and the distance structured between researcher and researched within most psychological theory and research instruments is rudely challenged by the face-to-face research interview. However much this is warded off by professional and personal defences, an interview is at some level inevitably a personal and sometimes intimate, as well as public, encounter. This chapter briefly outlines the rationale for doing interviews and different theoretical models of the interviewing process. The focus here is on the researcher's role, and the analysis section will draw on examples of interviewer and interviewee relations to elaborate this further. At the outset I should make it clear that, although guidelines for good practice are presented here, as with some other qualitative research methods, the diverse and specific nature of interviews means that no blueprint of interviewing practice or analysis can be absolutely determined in advance and in abstraction from the topic and context of a particular inquiry. Rather, the aim here is to highlight some of the issues that need to be addressed when designing, conducting and analysing interview-based research. It should also be noted that this chapter, as a reflection of most of the research literature and practice, is concerned with one-to-one, face-to-face interviews. While questions about the conduct of the research and the power of the researcher discussed here also apply to group discussions (which are increasingly gaining recognition as contexts of research, from market research to action research), these may be either magnified or mitigated by distinctive group processes.

While the content of this chapter covers issues sometimes addressed under the titles of 'social research' or 'ethnography', we are dealing here with what might broadly be called 'semi-structured' approaches to interviewing. We will use the term 'thematic analysis' for the process of making sense of the interview. There is a double contrast implied in the account of interviewing practice presented here: with structured approaches, which are usually quantitative and closer to questionnaires in structuring the interviewee's responses, and with so-called unstructured approaches, which for reasons argued below we regard as at best a disingenuous and sometimes a dangerous misnomer for refusing to acknowledge prior expectations or agendas. The position taken here is that assumptions structure all research, and the least we can do is to recognize this and theorize the impact of these assumptions. Better still, we can plan and articulate our starting assumptions so as to scrutinize and promote the research goals. Accordingly, the questions raised in this chapter tie in closely with the discussion in Chapter 8 on feminist research, and some of the more critical issues about interviewing practice are taken up there.

Background

There are four main reasons for conducting interviews. First, uniting the many models of interviewing is a concern with subjective meanings (the meanings the participants accord to the topic of the interview) rather than with eliciting responses within a standard format for comparison with other individuals or groups.

Second, interviews can permit exploration of issues that may be too complex to investigate through quantitative means. That is, given the latter's aim to simplify phenomena, they can misrepresent the nature of the questions under investigation. For example, if you wanted to explore roles, relationships and ethics with a particular professional group, or even to compare perceptions of a service between service providers and recipients, it is unlikely that you would gain a sufficiently sensitive and incisive grasp of your participants' concerns by administering a questionnaire with rating scale categories. This might be not so much because the scale does not address the correct questions (although this might also be true), as because the views of the participants cannot be readily representable within that form. Hence, holding inconsistent, contradictory views is not necessarily a function of faulty reasoning, but rather may be a reflection of the real contradictions and complexities of the way the service works in practice.

Your aim in using a semi-structured interview may be to explore precisely those areas where your interviewee perceives gaps, contradictions and difficulties. Hence another advantage of using a less structured approach is that you can tailor your questions to the position and comments of your interviewee, and you are not bound by the codes of standardization and replicability to soldier on through your interview schedule irrespective of how appropriate it is for your interviewee.

Within this approach, then, you should respond to and follow up issues raised by your interviewee, including ones that you may not have anticipated. In this sense, semi-structured interviewing, as a more open and flexible research tool, can document perspectives not usually represented (or even envisaged by researchers), and hence the approach can empower disadvantaged groups by validating and publicizing their views (e.g. Mishler 1986). While in an experiment the key question is specified in advance as the hypothesis (or so the story goes), and that question is (supposedly) the only question that the experiment addresses, in an interview the focus of the interview can be (although is not necessarily) a matter of negotiation.

Third, doing interviews is a salutary lesson in research involvement and practice. Without the 'safe' distance of a one-way mirror or the position of the detached manipulator of variables, as an interviewer one is forced to confront one's own participation within the research. We can take this point further to reflect on whether this lesson is particular to interviewing, or whether questions of the social construction of research 'data' reverberate further with implications for all empirical work. At any rate, conducting interviews demands consideration of reflexivity in the research process, extending from the devising of the research question, to identifying and setting up interviews with informants, to the interview itself (your role, how you were seen by the interviewee, your reflections on the process), and including the work done to transform an interactive encounter into a piece of written research.

Fourth, necessarily associated with the process of making visible your own work in the construction of your material, is the question of power relations in research. An early account of interviewing (Bingham and Moore 1959) describes the interview as a 'conversation with a purpose'. We should stop to consider *whose purposes* the conversation is pursuing. Research sets up, and is conducted within, power relationships. We need to attend to these in terms of both the morality-politics of research practice and the academic criteria of adequate evaluation of research (though such a strict separation is of course impossible to maintain once we consider these issues). Some models of research relationships try to do more than acknowledge the structural power relationships set up by research (see the chapters on feminist research and action research), to mitigate, challenge or even reverse traditional power dynamics. The move from designating the people who form the focus of the research as 'subjects' to 'interviewees' or 'participants' or 'informants' or 'co-researchers' reflects attempts to do research 'with' rather than 'on' people. Of course, the research relationship is only one of various structural power relations that can enter into the research. We should also, therefore, consider the extent to which class, 'race', gender and age relations (for example) interact with the interviewing relationship. Again we can reflect on the extent to which these issues are specific to interviewing, or, although perhaps particularly visible here, are just as relevant to other forms of research practice. Nevertheless, we need to maintain an 'interpretive vigilence' (Figueroa and López, 1991) to ward off the ways researcher control is implicitly structured and exercised within research instruments claiming to be participative and consultative.

Models of interviewing

Broadly speaking, four approaches inform interviewing practice: ethnographic, 'new paradigm', feminist and postmodernist. While these approaches can overlap and combine, each has its own language and way of conceiving the research process and relationship. So while they have much in common with each other, it is worth identifying a few contrasts or points of tension within interviewing style and interpretation here. In all approaches, however, *reflexivity* is accorded a key role, in the sense of the researcher reflecting on her or his own experience and role within the conduct of the research.

While ethnographic work highlights informants' expertise and the dependence of the researcher on the informant for access to her or his subjective rules, meanings and cultural life, there is a clear role demarcation between researcher and researched in determining the research topic and outcome (although this is changing within contemporary anthropological work: see Nencel and Pels 1991). Further, notwithstanding its ethos of eliciting and representing descriptions, we should not lose sight of how even ethnographic work still requires prior identification and structuring of themes to be investigated. On this, James Spradley (1979: 55) provides a clear account of the differences between an ethnographic interview and an 'ordinary conversation'. There are similarities here with Jean Piaget's clinical interview process, where it is argued that 'the good practitioner lets himself [*sic*] be led, though always in control, and takes account of the whole of the mental context' (Piaget 1929: 19).

In contrast, in 'new paradigm' research (Reason and Rowan 1981), while following the ethos of valuing what people say and treating this as meaningful and informative, research is viewed as a collaborative enterprise which not only involves the full participation of the interviewees but also incurs responsibility on the part of the researcher to be accountable to, and in some cases to conduct research agendas according to the demands of, the participants (see Chapter 1). Here we see the traditional model of researcher–researched relations undergoing upheaval as the researcher strives to carry out research in a non-exploitative, non-dehumanizing way.

Discussions of feminist methodology also take as central issues of power in the conduct of research. But rather than focusing only on the interpersonal relationship set up within the research encounter, feminist approaches attend in addition to wider questions of power as they enter into the funding, popularization and uses of research (e.g. Spender 1981). Moreover, they often treat power not as something that can be removed from research, but rather as an ever-present dynamic that needs to be acknowledged as structuring the interaction in diverse ways. In this sense feminist analyses of power in terms of the social positions occupied by interviewees, and (re)produced within interviews, go beyond those offered in 'new paradigm' accounts – most noticeably, but not exclusively, in terms of gender.

Finally, there are accounts of research drawing on post-structuralist and postmodernist writings to critique traditional models of research. This might include social constructionist and narrative approaches to research (e.g. Mishler 1986; Steier 1991). Of particular relevance here is the questioning of the presumption that participants within research share the research goals. The changes to which the research is directed may well be worthy, but may be of no immediate benefit to the informant at whose expense careers are gained and whose experience is subordinated to a preconceived or more or less imposed interpretive framework (see Gubrium and Silverman 1989; Opie 1992). Critiques along these lines invite attention to the variety of interpretations that can and will be made by different parties to the research encounter, and therefore also call for a principled scrutiny of our work of interpretation as researchers. In addition, more transformative research practice would seek to identify and address this multiplicity of interpretations in terms of research goals.

Constructing and selecting interview material

It is worth remembering that work done before the actual conduct of the interview is usually amply repaid in terms of its success and ease of analysis. First, you will have arrived at a topic to research, but you should clarify the rationale for doing this. Second, you should specify who would best exemplify the perspectives or range of perspectives relevant to your research question. Third, you should generate an interview schedule. At early stages in the planning of the research this may simply be a list of headings which you can elaborate in more detail once you have sorted out who your participants are, but it is worth doing this work now so that you have a clearer focus for when you approach your participants. Fourth, now that you have decided what kinds of people you want to interview, you need to contact them. It is very important to consider the impact of the route by which you contacted your participants in terms of how this structures the ways they see you, so that, for example, if you are interested in experiences of social or health services delivery it may be difficult to dispel the image of being associated with evaluation or treatment if you initially approach them via a medical or legal agency. It may, however, be impossible to avoid such constraints, but you should at least theorize how this may limit the form and content of the accounts you elicit.

What your prospective interviewees see the study as being about will also be central to their decision about whether to participate, and, in line with codes of practice about 'informed consent', you should be as open as possible about your aims. This may include outlining the kinds of areas or questions you want to discuss with them, and this information can do much to allay participants' anxieties or reservations. You should also at this point discuss what records you want to make of the interview, as in seeking permission to audiotape, for example; it might be helpful to explain why this is useful and how you will use it. Fifth, at this point you should negotiate a research contract with your participant, which includes guarantees of anonymity, a promise to terminate the interview at any point if the interviewee feels uncomfortable, the exclusion from the transcript or other records of anything the interviewee does not wish to be seen by others and a copy of the final report if desired.

While all this may gain you your participants (and if people refuse, you should consider why this may be), you now need to plan the interview itself. First, you will need to elaborate your interview schedule. In qualitative interviews it may not be appropriate to ask your interviewees similar questions; indeed, the 'same' question may have a far from equivalent meaning depending on the interview context, the interviewee's position and the research relationship. Since what you are interested in here is divergence and variety, rather than convergence and replicability, you may be better able to address your general aims by orienting the question to the particular positions of your participants.

Some people like to prepare a detailed interview schedule, with questions addressing all the key issues they want to cover. While this can be reassuring for the researcher, it needs to be treated flexibly in the interview itself since too rigid adherence can intimidate the participant or can fail to follow the participant's train of associations and perspectives. It can therefore be more helpful to have a list of topic areas, with lists of issues you want to cover, arranged so that it is easy for you to check them out in the course of the interview. But in this case the danger is that, while responding to the particular context and moment to ask your question, you either betray too much of your own perspective in the formulation you use or, in the heat of the moment, are lost for words. This is why it is useful to pose topic headings in the form of questions so that you do not have to do so much thinking on your feet. In general you should ask open questions, not only in the sense of avoiding questions that can be answered with a simple yes or no (unless you follow this up with a 'Can you say a bit more about that?'), but also avoiding formulations that could be interpreted as prescriptions for, or prohibitions on, what can be talked about – unless you consider that the situation or topic merits you positioning yourself more clearly.

Second, while these recommendations may seem daunting, all becomes much clearer and easier when you do a practice interview, perhaps with a friend with whom you feel at ease and who can give you frank feedback on the content and process of the interview. This helps to identify and iron out problems with the interview schedule and with the recording equipment (so that you remember to switch it on, you know where to position the microphone, you know not to have the machine on autoreverse so that it records over the first side again, etc.). Not least, you will gain a lot of confidence from the experience, even if you are also made acutely aware of the demands made on you as interviewer. These include the capacities to focus in parallel on listening intently to what your interviewee says, reflecting on how this relates to your interests, preconceptions and schedule, and working out what to say and when to say it.

Example

The sample analysis below reflects the focus so far on reflexive issues. It draws on aspects of all models identified above, but is most influenced by feminist and postmodernist approaches. In looking at this thematic analysis it is important to be clear that, even when carefully selected, abstracted from its original context and juxtaposed with other examples, as are the extracts below, they do not 'speak for themselves'. Meaning inheres not only in the text but in our construction and reading of it: despite the process of selection and interpretation in the preparation of this illustrative material, the analysis is inevitably selective. We are going to illustrate features of interviewing practice through a focus on instances of metacommentary (commentary on, in this case, the research process) occurring within some extracts from interview transcripts. At the outset we need to identify the questions in relation to which the analysis is structured, present the rationale for the material used and introduce the material itself.

Analytic questions

The questions selected here concern the visibility of rules governing the structure of the interview, which here are exhibited through moments of role-shifts and changes between interviewer and participant. Through this analysis we aim to illustrate how participants hold and use their positions within the research relationship. That is, they are neither passive nor unknowing about their positioning, but rather use this to achieve specific outcomes within the interview. We would not claim that these examples are routinely found within interview transcripts, but they are certainly not unique. The fact that these examples originate from interviews in which all the interviewers knew their informants beforehand (and indeed presumably selected them as willing to talk, and to talk about the selected topic) perhaps enabled the expression of what is often either non-verbally or indirectly communicated, or commented on off-tape. In line with current reflexive work on research practice, the focus here is on making visible the researcher within the research context. Correspondingly, for purposes of exposition we are going to exaggerate the reflexive ethos to focus not on the individual interview, or interviewer, but on what these extracts can tell us about research processes (which also includes what we are doing with them here).

Construction and selection of interview material

The extracts below are drawn from three second-year undergraduate practicals where students were conducting a single semi-structured interview supervised by one of us on a topic of their choice. As is appropriate research practice, they negotiated a research contract with the participant before the interview itself, which included ensuring that the transcripts would remain anonymous and would be read only by them and the markers of the work (of which, as the supervisor, I was one). Students were encouraged to discuss the interview process with participants to promote reciprocity and feedback. Similarly, these are the conditions under which I am drawing on these interviews. I am reproducing these extracts with the students' permission and with that of their informants. The fact that I did not conduct these interviews, and moreover am presenting a necessarily selective and motivated analysis, is an issue that I flag here to take up later.

Material

It is a moot point whether the material for analysis here is the text of the interview or the interview itself. Frequently researchers take as their record, as their 'raw material' for analysis, the transcript of their interview. This is belied by the fact that a transcript is: (a) an impoverished record, a key stopping point on the road of progressive removal from encounter, to aural representation (on tape), to written representation; and (b) therefore a selective/constructive representation, as highlighted by the variety of transcription notations that embody their own assumptions, whether through spatial arrangement (Ochs 1979) or through levels of detail about what is important (discussed briefly in Stubbs 1983, and extensively in Tedlock 1984).

Furthermore, not only is the production of a transcript also part of the research process, but the interviewer brings to the transcript her experience and memory of the interview. Here too it is appropriate to articulate impressions and perceptions of emergent issues and feelings, preferably as soon after the interview as possible, and in any case before starting on the analysis. These 'field notes' can become a resource, both in informing the analysis and in reminding you of what assumptions you brought to that analysis – which may or may not be borne out. Given all this construction and selection in the process of organization and synthesis that is necessary for an analysis, we should also question what is excluded, suppressed. The material presented here for analysis is of a variety that in many accounts would be sanitized away, deemed bad research, embarrassing intrusions of the personal or even lapses of interviewer control. These are precisely what make them interesting and important to analyse as indicative of the implicit rules of research, rules which become more apparent in their infraction.

Analysis

A 'thematic analysis' is a coherent way of organizing or reading some interview material in relation to specific research questions. These readings are organized under thematic headings in ways that attempt to do justice both to the elements of the research question and to the preoccupations of the interviewees. I will start by presenting each extract separately and then move on to elaborate connections and contrasts between them in relation to the themes of power relations in research, the power of the participant and shifts in positions. The texts are longer here, for illustrative purposes, than would normally be presented within the main text of a report. The transcription and terminology (I, interviewer; R, respondent; P, participant) are as in the originals. Clearly these terms reflect different ways of positioning the person being interviewed, and precisely because of this I have chosen to retain terminology from the original transcripts. Line numbers refer to those parts of the transcripts presented here.

Presentation of text and general comments

Extract 1
An interview by a young male student with a woman friend on the topic of formative influences on occupational choice.

```
 1  I:  relax – this is nothing that will be judged
[interruption]
 2  R:  I'm not looking at the questions
 3  I:  All I want is to find out a few things concerning your family,
 4      educational, friends – aspirations, motivations etcetera
 5  R:  okay
 6  I:  and I'll give you feedback on it – later on
 7  R:  not now
 8  I:  no – you can have anything you have said which you do not want
 9      to be disclosed erased
10  R:  aha
11  I:  you can also have anonymity – you can choose your pseudonym
12      if you want to
13  R:  oh fine
14  I:  as long as it isn't (interviewer's name)
15  R:  [laughs]
16  I:  oh yes I'll be taking a few notes which have nothing to do with
17      your answers during the interview – is this okay
18  R:  you'll be taking notes – I see – okay
19  I:  no
[interruption]
20  R:  so you're going to be watching me as well
21  I:  I'll record anything that's interesting – relevant
22  R:  I'll put my hands behind my back then . . .
23  R:  . . . but that's life – as long as I learn from my mistakes – what
24      was the question again – sorry
25  I:  it's okay you've answered it
26  R:  good – stop looking at my legs [laughs]
27  I:  erase
28  R:  sorry I just wanted to say that – sorry
29  I:  Hmm – let's continue – okay – and cover your legs . . .
```

It seems that the prior friendship enables the respondent (R) to comment on the prevailing rules structuring the interview by highlighting the assumptions of control implicit within the interviewer's (I) framing of the interview: the feedback is 'not now' (1.7) but later. While it is important not to minimize the ways interviews can become opportunities for sexual harassment (see later), it is also possible to read this exchange as R asserting in a mock-threatening way her power to evaluate and censor the interview material. She comments on being scrutinized both verbally ('you'll be taking notes – I see – okay', 1.18) and visually ('so you're going to be watching me as well', 1.20). Throughout this extract there is an air of what I read as amicably sarcastic compliance with clear suggestions of how provisional this may be ('aha', 1.10) and how the resistance can enter into what is available to be recorded even before the explicit rights of later erasure can be exercised ('I'll put my hands behind my back then', 1.22). R's apparently wilful misinterpretation of I's attempts to assert his position as interviewer and hers as respondent occurs even before the critical moment of embarrassing I with 'stop looking at my legs' (1.26). Significantly, this is immediately after R's indication that she had become so absorbed in her narration that she had forgotten the interviewing context (1.23–4), and so this can be read as a correlative disengagement. It is possible to read the two times (1.8 and 1.19) I says 'no' more as dismay and suppressed repudiation of R's resistance rather than a refusal of any specific feature of it.

Extract 2
A male interviewer of a male acquaintance on his political involvement with animal rights groups. In contrast to the tense atmosphere of Extract 1, I read this extract as a more reflective and collaborative exchange in which the interview gravitates to become an interview about interviewing.

1　I:　Do you think it was a wise move for me to get into psychology?
2　R:　I thought you were supposed to be interviewing me
3　I:　what's the difference
4　R:　I don't know
5　I:　do you think the person being interviewed can get as much or
6　　　more out of the interview as the interviewer
7　R:　yes of course, they wouldn't agree to be interviewed otherwise.
8　　　People enjoy being asked questions about what they are interested
9　　　in
10　I:　But the police don't ask if you agree to be interviewed
11　R:　No, but you don't have to say anything

Extract 3
A woman interviewer of a woman friend on the topic of the importance of friendship.

1 P: . . . I know this is difficult for you (I's name) but you did ask me
2   to do this and I couldn't possibly talk about friendship without
3   talking about you
4 I: right OK then (laughs)
5 P: Right, it's very very important to me but erm it's quite difficult
6   actually because I'm talking to you actually am I talking to you,
7   the person or you an interviewer?
8 I: I think we can say you can talk about me as a person it can't be
9   objective it's subjective anyway
10 P: It's really wierd to be actually talking about you erm it's not
11   embarrassing is it? I have to do it.
12 I: a bit but you will have to be clear for people reading it where we
13   met and that
14 P: I can talk away from you if you want, right I will sort of. Yea
15   the person I'm talking about her name is . . .
16 I: do you think it [the interview] could be improved?
17 P: no I don't because I wouldn't be, if I had somebody, if the
18   interviewer was somebody who, a person I didn't know, I really
19   don't think I would convey my feelings with very many people
20   erm in actual fact I would only do this interview for you I
21   wouldn't do it for anybody else I certainly wouldn't talk about
22   friendship the topic or whatever with anybody else it would
23   have to be a close friend
24 I: how do you feel about all of this being seen by others?
25 P: How do I feel about that, I don't mind really I don't mind
26 I: There is so much material on there and I just feel I'm going to use
27   it for adverse means in a sense and I wouldn't like it er
28 P: No no I don't mind the reason I don't mind is that whatever is
29   recorded on there whatever is transcribed on to paper will be in your
30   hands that's what's important to me. No it doesn't matter actually
31   whatever you come up with it really doesn't matter. But
32   nevertheless it's in your hands you're taking care of it it's your
33   baby I'm entrusting my feelings my thoughts and feelings to you
34   which I already know I feel very comfortable with anyway this makes
35   no difference in a sense it really doesn't . . .

This interview moves from an emphasis on the meaning of friendship in
general to a focus on support, and supportive friends in particular. The
participant (P) uses the interview to tell the interviewer (I) about the importance of I's friendship to her; that is, she uses the new set of positions
within their relationship combined with the public nature of the encounter

to comment on the value of her relationship with I. The positions are explicitly marked where P asks 'you the person or you an interviewer' (3.7–8), which sets up a corresponding set of positions for her as both person and respondent. She constructs I as a research object to include her as proper material for the study by 'talk[ing] away from you' (3.15) and describing her in the third person ('the person I'm talking about her name is . . .', 3.16).

Having introduced the material, we can now use four themes by which the extracts as a whole can be viewed in relation to the analytic questions identified earlier. You might want to consider what your choice of themes might be before reading further.

Theme 1   *Using the position of respondent*
In Extract 1, R can be seen as asserting her power as respondent in a context in which I is, in this case quite explicitly, dependent on R for the completion of his work. In addition, the embarrassment ('erase', 1.27) over looking at, or being positioned as looking at, R's legs highlights the covert sexuality, in this case heterosexuality, of the research encounter. In this research encounter, the official power of definition and interpretation coincides with that of the active viewer and evaluator. These culturally masculine positions were here held by a male researcher. R demonstrates her power over the interpretation of the encounter by invoking the framework of harassment, thus enlisting a range of judicial and disciplinary practices. One reading of this exchange, then, is that by making the potential sexual exploitation of the encounter explicit, the female research participant both comments on this convergence of gender, sexual and interview power relations *and* resists being positioned as a passive subject of the research gaze by using the structures of the research (question-asking, recording) to turn the researcher himself into an object of scrutiny.

In Extract 2 it is the interviewer who sanctions the commentary about the interview process with 'do you think it was a wise move for me to get into psychology?' (2.1). The explicit discussion of interviewing roles follows from I's assertion of, and departure from, the role of interviewer by asking a question, but of a reflexive form that transgresses, transcends or reverses the current interviewing relationship.

In Extract 3 the additional positions made available by the interview appear to be used by P to enable her to thank I and express her appreciation of I as a friend. Using the rules of the interview, not only is P required to hear this (owing to the injunction upon I to listen to and respect what P says), but it is also justified within the rules of interviewing, owing to the norm of frank disclosure conventionally assumed of research participants.

Theme 2   Respondent-initiated reflexive commentaries

In these extracts, although in different ways, the respondents initiate the reflection on the research process. In Extract 1, R exploits the novice I's highhandedness in reminding her of the research contract, which he appears to inform her of, rather than negotiate. She therefore frustrates I's attempts to assume the position of authority as the one who *could* but will not judge (1.1), who defines what is relevant to record (1.21), who has defined the questions (1.3) to be answered, and who has the authority to provide feedback (1.6). In Extract 2, R challenges I's assumption that he can change the roles or rules of the interview with his 'I thought you were supposed to be interviewing me' (2.2). In Extract 3, in an interview about friendship, it is significant that P raises the reflexive issues about her friendship with I. This emphasizes how commentaries on the research process are by no means the prerogative of interviewers. Rather such cues and feedback are always present even if unarticulated, and form the infrastructure of research.

Theme 3   Public nature of the account

It is clear that the fact that these are interviews, rather than conversations, constitutes key structural conditions for the accounts generated (and the division between the 'public' and 'private' itself has a history). R's resistance in Extract 1 to the interviewer–respondent relation is exercised precisely through the public nature of their encounter. I's reaction to her request to 'stop looking at my legs' is in terms of his awareness of the tape-recording (he says 'erase', 1.27), while R reasserts her desire to record this (literally reinscribes it) with 'sorry I just wanted to say that – sorry' (1.28). R therefore enlists the broader structure of scrutiny hinted at earlier by I's prohibition that R should use his name as a pseudonym (1.14), which would place him as doubly subjected to the interview (as interviewer and respondent). (In psychoanalytic terms we might see this as a return of the repressed with a vengeance!)

Within Extract 2, I initiates the discussion over who benefits from the research ('do you think the person being interviewed can get as much or more out of the interview as the interviewer', 2.5–6). I also develops R's response in terms of people enjoying talking about what they are interested in (2.8–9) by importing a legal-political interpretation of people's 'interests' (in police interrogations) (2.10). The comparison between legal/coercive regulation and the structure of the interview is both taken up and refused by R in his reminder of participants' voluntary involvement as conditional on personal engagement or relevance, as exhibited by the strategies available for non-compliance within even the most formal structures of interrogation (2.7–11). It may be appropriate that I defers to R over the success of this strategy; the probability that he has had to exercise this is rendered more likely by the topic of the interview.

In Extract 3, the public nature of the account as well as the topic (friendship) is a prerequisite for P expressing and reasserting her trust in I. Both parties refer to a (temporally distanced but very present) audience ('you will have to be clear for people reading it', 3.13, and 'how do you feel about all of this being seen by others', 3.25).

Theme 4   Past/future relations
In all three extracts, the shifts in I–P positions are achieved by reference to, and in relation to, their relationships outside the interviews. In 1, the teasing tenor of the interview suggests that R wields her power through the prior relationship she has with him. In 2, I marks permission to digress from the previously agreed topic of the interview by asking R a question that invites judgement of I on the basis of their prior relationship. He asks R for his perception of the rules of the interview with 'what's the difference' (2.3). The past relationship is alluded to by reference to the choice to be interviewed. As interviewer 2 commented to me after reading this analysis, either his mistrust of psychology is well-placed, or else, as a prior acquaintance, the interviewer is a particularly clever policeman to trick him into thinking he has a choice. In Extract 3, by the end of the interview the research encounter is incorporated into the structure of the existing friendship as not only a test of the relationship ('it's in your hands . . . I'm entrusting my feelings my thoughts and feelings to you', 3.33–4), but as an expression of it ('I would only do this interview for you', 3.22, 'this makes no difference in a sense it really doesn't', 3.35–6), and by the end the interview itself is in the past, as 'there' on the tape (not here and now), in 'there is so much material on there' (3.27), and as a record that can be used or abused.

Reflexive analysis

In this section we locate the analysis within an account of its production, including relevant constraints, limits and possibilities wrought by our position as analysts. These are issues that might be regarded as the context of the research, and this 'context' (in the sense of what accompanies and constructs the text) can be divided into ten points.

Records – what's lost (and gained)

The tendency to confound interview with transcript discussed earlier is in some senses clarified by the fact that the analysis presented here is based on transcripts of interviews which I did not conduct or transcribe. Para-doxically, the fact that I did not conduct the interviews puts my position closer to that of other readers in both generating and justifying the analy-sis. What this brings home is the incompleteness and partiality of inter-pretation (see below), qualities intrinsic to this kind of research but made more manifest in these circumstances. I have reproduced the extracts using the notation adopted by the original interviewers/transcribers. The use of conventional punctuation and absence of explicit transcription codes in part reflected their concern about presenting to informants a formalized and inaccessible representation of the interview that might compound further the potentially alienating effect of seeing spoken language written down in all its (in terms of written codes) untidiness (Stubbs 1983). But these extracts would perhaps have gained from a more systematic coding (see the Appendix for a simplified notation suitable for most thematically based analyses).

Overinterpretation/misinterpretation

A common reaction to analyses of the kind offered above is that the material has been misinterpreted or overinterpreted, manipulated to pro-duce meanings that were not 'originally' there. It is certainly true that the process of analysis, including the shifting representational forms that the interview/text assumes, does provide new vantage points from which to interpret, and that, as Stubbs (1983) points out, close scrutiny of a tran-script can magnify tensions or aggressive elements within the text. How-ever, acknowledging this does not discredit the analysis offered; rather it supports the suggestion that this is one of multiple ways of reading the texts. Clearly if the reading is mine alone, that is, if this reading is not recognized by others, then its credibility is undermined. Similarly, the re-actions of the original interviewers and participants in the extracts are important. Depending on the model of research adopted, disagreement would invalidate the reading (within an ethnographic model) or be inter-preted within it (since from a postmodernist stance it could be argued that there may be particular investments in refusing the interpretation; Opie 1992). Here it is worth saying that the original interviewers' reactions to this analysis were very favourable, and no reservations were expressed about the readings outlined above, nor any alternatives put forward. In terms of additional points, the interviewer in Extract 1 wished to have further emphasized how much is lost in the transition from tape to tran-script. Feedback from interviewer and interviewee 2 confirmed the view of the interview process as an elaboration of mutual agendas, and indicated a view that this should be recognized and explicitly structured into inter-view procedures.

Partial interpretation

All this emphasizes the constructed and inexhaustive nature of the analysis. These features sometimes make this kind of research both frustrating and dissatisfying, since a common response is to feel acutely the partiality (in the double sense of incomplete and motivated) of interpretation. Nevertheless, this too is an instructive reflection on the research process. It is helpful here to explore the infinite regress and incoherence of the fantasy of a complete and authentic original record (Why use audiotape, why not use videotape? But what about that space behind the camera?), which parallels that of the complete interpretation. Rather, we should accept the uncertainty of unfinished analysis as an index of the arbitrary limit imposed by writing up. In principle the research process could continue almost indefinitely, both in the sense of exchanging readings and reactions between interpreter and participants, and in the analyst's shifting perceptions of their interpretations (and clearly some such mutual discussion and reflection with participants is good research practice).

Intentionality and multiple readings

There are clearly other ways of interpreting the extracts above. In fact it is often useful to present and develop alternative readings and explore the different conclusions they indicate. For my purposes I have selected one reading, but in drawing attention to its provisionality two issues should be noted. First, acknowledging the multiplicity of readings (or accounts of the account) does not mean that all readings are equal. Otherwise we are stuck in the quagmire of relativistic nihilism which disempowers us from using the research to say anything (see Bhavnani 1990; Burman 1990). There may be good reasons for privileging the reading or account of the research participants, particularly if their 'voice' is that of a disadvantaged or under-represented group (but see problems with this in Chapter 8). Second, and this is particularly relevant for the kind of meta-analysis I have presented here, it is important not to equate the *reading* with either the *intentions* of participants or their intentions *in* the interview. The analytic questions driving the analysis offered here were concerned with research process and not individual opinions, so the focus was correspondingly on implicit features of the rules or frameworks structuring research rather than on what each party said or did. In this sense other analyses of this material could be made in relation to different questions from those explored here.

Selection of material

A reflexive account could include examination of my own motives in presenting this material. Perhaps I am aiming to demonstrate something about my teaching practice through the interviewing competence of my students. Perhaps I am avoiding subjecting my own interviewing and analytic practice to critical scrutiny (but see Burman 1992a, b). A more standard criticism here would question the validity of generating this analysis from interviews conducted on different topics and by different interviewers. However, once again this approach can be defended by recalling that the analytic issues do not require absolute comparability of text (indeed such a notion is questionable, see Chapter 1), and in fact may benefit from the variety of positions adopted.

Privileged access

In more typical circumstances, the researcher has privileged knowledge both of the participants and of the experience of conducting the interviews. In this case the extra knowledge I bring to bear on this material is my acquaintance with the interviewers, the history of having supervised (and marked) their interviewing research, and therefore my access to the larger transcripts from which the above extracts were selected. Again, these differences in position from which the extracts can be read have to be acknowledged rather than erased, and can perhaps be put forward either to explain differences in or to fix interpretation (Burman 1993).

Exploitation

A legitimate question that should always be posed (both in conducting and in evaluating research) is whether the participants have been exploited, that is, whether their psychological or material conditions worsened through their involvement in the research. In this case, permission was gained from all parties to use the material, and they were consulted over the interpretations drawn. As discussed in the last three chapters of this book, issues of exploitation go beyond notions of 'informed consent' to include the use made of the research.

Effects of prior relationships

These arise in the form of the interviewers' prior knowledge of their participants from other than research contexts, and of my prior knowledge of the interviewers from a teaching context. In the first case it seems likely that this facilitated greater disclosure and reflexive commentary, as well as constituting the preconditions for some of the themes identified in the analysis. The impact of the second issue is difficult to evaluate but clearly does figure; quite how helpful or otherwise this is will depend on how persuasive you as readers find this account. We are not, however, suggesting that people should only interview their friends, but rather we want to high-light how the prior relationship (of acquaintance, or non-acquaintance, which is also a relationship) enters into the structure and content of the encounter.

Danger of fetishing particular strategies

Similarly, the analysis here should not be read as recommending particular interviewing devices in order to promote either equality or reflection on research processes. Used as techniques these can work to assert interviewer authority in indirect ways (see Walkerdine 1988: 53–63; Burman 1992a, for examples from research with children). The examples presented here arose spontaneously, and as initiated or at least taken up by the 'respond-ents'. The analysis here does not (and cannot) illustrate how interviews should be done, but rather offers suggestions about what to look for, and how to think about what happens in interviews. There are no techniques or analytic procedures that escape the dangers of exploitation. Hence it is important to structure consultation and feedback over the interpretation of transcripts with participants.

Interpretive stance/countertransference issues

Given the nine points above, it is clear that the analyst brings to his or her analysis a range of different identifications and responses. In these extracts I identify as interviewer struggling to democratize the research process and anxious about how to make sense of the material (perhaps anyone who has engaged with semi-structured interviews can identify with the sense of responsibility that the interviewer comments on in Extract 3, line 25). I also hold multiple positionings and identifications arising from structures of gender, class and so on, which inevitably enter into the particular analy-sis formulated. Where personal reactions or investments play an important part, these can be treated as a resource for, rather than 'interference' within, the analysis (for an example of this see Marks, in press).

Discussion and assessment

The analysis presented here is based on unusual material. These examples may not be everyday but they are also not unique, and are consistent with the aim of highlighting the visibility of the *researcher* rather than the re-searched. Qualitative analysis elucidates phenomena that would be missed or dismissed by other methods. Just as the exception can prove the rule, so exceptional or incidental instances can function to highlight structural dynamics that underlie research encounters.

Part of what is so arresting about this material, in particular Extract 1, is that it refers quite literally to what is absent or lost from records of research: all too often we analyse interviews as disembodied voices but interviews are interactions between embodied people. In the example discussed here, R made this visible by protesting against I's gaze. Issues of sexuality within research encounters are rarely commented upon in accounts of research, but this example illustrates aspects that must always be present, even if suppressed. Where the gender and researcher–researched positions are reversed, that is where men are interviewed by women, issues of participant resistance have been documented as being acted out in the form of sexual harassment of researchers (see also McKee and O'Brian 1983; Reynolds 1993). It seems that where traditional power relations are departed from, where men are positioned as subordinate within the researcher–researched relation, for example, this structural power relationship becomes evident through their attempts to subvert it. The disjunction or exception highlights the presence of the rule.

We should draw attention to the concept of power that has informed this analysis. Although it is concerned with instances of 'respondent' resistance or assertion, this analysis does not imply that 'respondents' have greater power than 'interviewers'. Rather, following a Foucauldian perspective, power is not conceived of as a unidimensional quality that is possessed or lacked. This analysis has illustrated how particular possibilities for assertion and resistance are produced through the structures of the research encounter. Specifically, it has been argued that: (a) once consent has been given, 'respondents' or 'participants' are not passive parties to the question–answer interviewing structure; (b) they can assume a range of strategies to resist that positioning; (c) they intervene in and comment on the research process, as well as being the research focus; and (d) they achieve both joint and separate goals through their participation in the research.

In evaluating the conduct and analysis of interviews, there are continuities between thematic and textual approaches, and similarities (although cast within rather different terminology and corresponding philosophical basis) between the account here and 'grounded theory' as elaborated by the criteria identified by Henwood and Pidgeon (1993: 24–7) of 'keeping close to the data; theory integrated at diverse levels of abstraction; reflexivity; documentation; theoretical sampling and negative case analysis, sensitivity to negotiated realities, transferability.' While most of the limits of this approach have been addressed in the reflexive analysis, it should be noted that interviewing is time-consuming, absorbing and suited to a study with a restricted number of interviews in order to keep the transcription and analysis of material manageable, and to do justice to the material generated. In terms of problems, the multiple frameworks informing semi-structured interviewing can make the approaches appear atheoretical or intuitivist. A disciplined analysis of the presuppositions guiding all stages of the research does much to ward off this criticism. The final analysis, however, lies beyond the account here in the interpretations made of this by you.

Appendix

Suggested transcription notation:

(.)	pause
(2)	two second pause (number indicates duration)
xxx	untranscribable
(xxx)	indistinct/doubtful transcription
Word underline	emphasis

Potter and Wetherell (1987: 188–9) suggest a slightly more complex notation, which in turn is a simplified version of Sacks *et al.* (1974).

Useful reading

Gubrium, J. and Silverman, D. (eds) (1989). *The Politics of Field Research.* London: Sage.

Henwood, K. and Pidgeon, N. (1993). 'Qualitative research and psychological theorizing', in M. Hammersley (ed.) *Social Researching: Philosophy, Politics and Practice.* London: Sage.

Nencel, L. and Pels, P. (eds) (1991). *Constructing Knowledge: Authority and Critique in Social Science.* London: Sage.

Steier, F. (ed.) (1991). *Research and Reflexivity.* London: Sage.

References

Bhavnani, K.K. (1990). ' "What's power got to do with it?" Empowerment and social research', in I. Parker and J. Shotter (eds) *Deconstructing Social Psychology.* London: Routledge.

Bingham, W. and Moore, B. (1959). *How to Interview.* New York: Harper International.

Burman, E. (1990). 'Differing with deconstruction: a feminist critique', in I. Parker and J. Shotter (eds) *Deconstructing Social Psychology.* London: Routledge.

Burman, E. (1992a). 'Feminism and discourse in developmental psychology: identification, subjectivity and interpretation'. *Feminism and Psychology,* 2 (1), 45–60.

Burman, E. (1992b). 'Identification and power in feminist therapy: a reflexive history of a discourse analysis'. *Women's Studies International Forum*, **15** (4), 487–98.

Burman, E. (1993). 'Beyond discursive relativism: power and subjectivity in developmental psychology', in H. Stam, L. Mos, W. Thorngate and B. Caplan (eds) *Recent Trends in Theoretical Psychology, Volume III.* New York: Springer Verlag.

Figueroa, H. and López, M.M. (1991). 'Commentary on Second Discourse Analysis Workshop/Conference'. Paper presented at the Second Discourse Analysis Workshop/Conference, Manchester, July.

Gubrium, J. and Silverman, D. (eds) (1989). *The Politics of Field Research.* London: Sage.

Henwood, K. and Pidgeon, N. (1993). 'Qualitative research and psychological theorizing', in M. Hammersley (ed.) *Social Researching: Philosophy, Politics and Practice.* London: Sage.

McKee, L. and O'Brian, M. (1983). 'Interviewing men: "taking gender seriously" ', in E. Garmarnikow, D. Morgan, J. Purvis and D. Taylorson (eds) *The Public and the Private.* London: Heinemann.

Marks, D. (forthcoming/in press) 'Gendered care dynamics and the structuring of group relations: child-professional-parent' in E. Burman, P. Alldred, C. Bewley, C. Heenan, D. Marks, J. Marshall, K. Taylor, R. Ullah and S. Warner, *Challenging Women: Psychology's Exclusions, Feminist Possibilities.* Buckingham: Open University Press.

Mishler, E. (1986). *Research Interviewing: Context and Narrative.* Cambridge, MA: Harvard University Press.

Nencel, L. and Pels, P. (eds) (1991). *Constructing Knowledge: Authority and Critique in Social Science.* London: Sage.

Ochs, E. (1979). 'Transcription as theory', in E. Ochs and B. Schieffelin (eds) *Developmental Pragmatics.* New York: Academic Press.

Opie, A. (1992). 'Qualitative research, appropriation of the "other" and empowerment', *Feminist Review*, **40**, 52–69.

Piaget, J. (1929). *The Child's Conception of the World.* London: Routledge and Kegan Paul.

Potter, J. and Wetherell, M. (1987). *Discourse and Social Psychology.* London: Sage.

Reason, P. and Rowan, J. (eds) (1981). *Human Inquiry: a Sourcebook of New Paradigm Research.* Chichester: Wiley.

Reynolds, G. (1993). ' "And Gill came tumbling after": gender, emotions and a research dilemma', in M. Kennedy, C. Lubelska and V. Walsh (eds) *Making Connections: Women's Studies, Women's Movements, Women's Lives.* London: Taylor and Francis.

Sacks, H., Schegloff, E. and Jefferson, G. (1974). 'The simplest semantics for the organisation of turn-taking in conversation', *Language*, **50**, 697–737.

Spender, D. (1981). 'The gatekeepers: a feminist critique of academic publishing', in H. Roberts (ed.) *Doing Feminist Research.* London: Routledge and Kegan Paul.

Spradley, J. (1979). *The Ethnographic Interview.* New York: Holt, Rinehart and Winston.

Steier, F. (ed.) (1991). *Research and Reflexivity.* London: Sage.

Stubbs, M. (1983). *Discourse Analysis: the Sociolinguistic Analysis of Natural Language*. Oxford: Blackwell.

Tedlock, D. (1984). *The Spoken Word and the Work of Interpretation*. Philadelphia: University of Pennsylvania Press.

Walkerdine, V. (1988). *The Mastery of Reason*. London: Routledge.

Acknowledgements

I am very grateful to the interviewers and participants whose talk and work I draw upon in this chapter, in particular for their prompt and supportive feedback on earlier drafts.

5 | PERSONAL CONSTRUCT APPROACHES

CAROL TINDALL

The balance of this chapter varies slightly from the others as I intend to look at a range of personal construct approaches. Most attention will be given to the repertory grid, as this is most commonly dealt with quantitatively and often with scant regard for its theoretical background, in a somewhat free-floating fashion. My worked example of a repertory grid with laddering is immediately followed by the associated discussion and reflexive account. I then turn to other personal construct methods.

Background

First, as George Kelly's research designs are an integral part of his personal construct psychology (PCP), some theoretical background is needed. However, this is necessarily brief and highly selective. There is some debate as to whether PCP is a theory or a complete psychology. Jahoda suggests that Kelly has both an approach and a theory. She defines an approach as

> a relatively content free point of view about how best to proceed in studying people. It is based on extra-scientific assumptions and often incorporates personal values. It contains the fundamental questions to which a psychologist seeks answers. In contrast to theories, an approach can therefore neither be verified nor falsified: you can only take it or leave it.
>
> (Jahoda 1988: 2)

Kelly's is a constructivist approach. For Kelly, objective reality is a myth. Our subjective reality is based on the meanings we have attached to previous experiences. It is the *meaning* that is influential, not the event itself. Such personal meanings are the basis of our individual theories or frameworks, through which we filter and interpret current experiences. We are constantly engaged in psychological processing, purposefully searching for meaning: operating 'as if' we were scientists, constantly applying our very personal theories to 'what's going on', shifting and restructuring our frameworks in line with new understandings; aiming to inhabit an increasingly useful personal world, one which facilitates more effective interactions with others. In this way we construe ourselves, each other and our personal reality. Kelly's focus is on the individual as the maker of meaning. It is the idiosyncratic nature of our experiencing that accounts for the difference between people. Unlike in some psychodynamic and behaviourist views, within personal construct psychology there is a dynamic element of personal agency. 'People are neither prisoners of their environment nor victims of their biographies, but active individuals struggling to make sense of their experiences and acting in accordance with the meaning they impose on those experiences' (Kelly 1955: 15).

Nevertheless, as Fransella (1990) points out, we may make ourselves prisoners by the way we construe our biography. Our idiosyncratic constructions, firmly rooted in our unique stories, simultaneously provide an anticipatory basis for future action. This anticipatory element based on our current understanding inevitably frames our reality and illuminates or alerts us to particular aspects of 'what is going on', and equally limits or blinds us to other aspects. When we predict that something will happen we are also predicting that other things will not happen. Construing (a word deliberately chosen by Kelly) is experiencing, at all levels of awareness, thoughts, feelings and actions in appropriate (personal) harmony. It is essentially a dynamic search for personal understanding, which according to Kelly is gained by recognizing similarities and differences in our experiences. 'Only when man [*sic*] attunes his ear to recurrent themes in the monotonous flow does his universe begin to make sense to him' (Kelly 1955: 53).

Our personal frameworks, or construct systems in Kelly's terms, are made up of a vast collection of similarity–difference dimensions or bipolar constructs. We each uniquely yet systematically hierarchically network our constructs. Core or superordinate constructs are those which are central to our being, those which we use to impose personal order on our lives. Each core construct subsumes a number of subordinate constructs, which in turn subsume more subordinate constructs and so on. A construct gains its meaning from both poles; similarity can only be understood in the context of difference. Constructs are highly individual and personally understood. For example, as an outsider we would recognize that two people using the construct 'friendly' are experiencing different realities if we also know that the difference pole for one is 'not so friendly' and for the other is 'hostile'. The difference pole may be a logical or idiosyncratic opposite. Thus our current construct system frames our reality, aspects of which will be clear and appropriate while others remain fuzzy. We must remember that it is our construction, the meanings are inferred by us. These meanings are not part of the event, not statements of reality.

'Constructive alternativism', the philosophical basis of personal construct psychology, acknowledges that there are different ways of seeing, that equally valid alternative constructions are always possible. We need to be aware that others are likely to construe differently from ourselves. Constructive alternativism is about exploring our construct system and selecting the most appropriate theories to apply, which must then be judged only in terms of their usefulness, not in terms of any absolute truth. They do, however, determine the range of options open to us and can be limiting. We can extend our knowledge and understanding by being continually open and prepared to update and reconstruct our theories in the light of experience: 'even the most obvious occurrences in daily life might appear utterly transformed if we were inventive enough to construe them differently' (Kelly 1986: 1).

Kelly suggested that psychologists should start their work not with theories but with involvement in the life situation of the people they have chosen to study. If our aim is to understand someone, then we must gain understanding from within that person, empathize with them, get to know their story, explore their social world through their frameworks.

Another core element of personal construct psychology is *reflexivity*. Personal construct psychology accounts for its own creation: it is a construction like any other. The richness and relevance of the personal experience of all is acknowledged and validated. Both researcher and participants are involved in interacting and construing. The aim of research is to engage in a collaborative exploration of equality and mutuality to gain an insider's view of part of the participant's reality, at the same time acknowledging that the research question is necessarily part of the researcher's construct system. Clearly the research process offers all who take part the opportunity for new understandings and self-development. The completed research is a more or less useful construction, which is, of course, open to reconstruction.

We can see, then, that Kelly's approach encourages the democratization of the process of research. The subjectivity of both the researcher and researched is embraced. People are dealt with as complex beings rather than reduced to isolated variables. Participants' constructions are valued, not seen as requiring modification and adjustment to fit more easily into another's theoretical framework.

Personal construct techniques

The repertory grid

The repertory grid is a highly flexible technique which is often used quantitatively and on occasions completely divorced from its theoretical underpinning. I will show how it can be used qualitatively. The aim of the repertory grid is to illuminate a person's current understanding of whatever it is they are concerned with. This may be done alone or with one or more co-researchers, depending on what is being explored and by whom.

The first step is to choose a topic of concern, personally relevant to the participant, which has the potential to offer insight. This may be their work situation, family, friendships, themselves, relationships, leisure activities, possible opportunities, whatever is appropriate.

Second, the participant must choose a range of elements (more than ten can become unwieldy). Elements are anything that give rise to construing: they can be people, courses, pubs, leisure activities, careers, aspects of work etc. To expose the most illuminating picture and to allow some comparison, elements need to vary on dimensions relevant to the participant and the topic. If explaining friendship, for example, it is likely that you would want to include established friends, ex-friends, potential friends and acquaintances. Traditionally, in Kellyan research, elements are roles – someone I admire, someone I dislike, someone who has influenced me etc. – or, if the focus of the research is yourself, each of your own roles – friend, partner, colleague, worker, parent etc. – or yourself over time – as a teenager, as a young adult, now, in ten years time.

You might want to look at relationships, perhaps in terms of similarity of construing and/or ability to empathize. In this case elements and constructs (see below) would be jointly negotiated, then completed individually before being jointly completed (Bannister and Bott 1973). The comparison between each individual's reality and the negotiated picture of reality can reveal connections and areas of discord.

Thomas (1979) developed these ideas and devised a similar 'exchange grid'. This involves both participants jointly deciding on the elements, then completing the grid individually using their own constructs. Constructs are then exchanged and each completes the other's grid 'as if' they were the other. Analysis of the two pairs of grids offers insight into the degree of understanding each has of the other's personal world.

To reiterate, elements need to be personally relevant to the participant, even if they appear strange to outsiders, and both appropriate to and representative of the topic explored.

The next task is to identify some of the constructs currently being used within the area of exploration. This is done by choosing any three elements and asking in what way two of the three are similar to each other and different from the third. I find it more useful to ask participants to identify a *difference* rather than a contrast or opposite, as in my experience these last two terms encourage people to search for some generally accepted contrast and therefore shift the emerging picture away from the personal.

The three elements to be compared can be chosen systematically or randomly. Each element can be allocated a number and then three numbers can be chosen. Or each element can be written on a separate card, with the cards being shuffled and the top three chosen. Used cards are returned to the pack, the pack is reshuffled and the top three are chosen, and so on. This process of choosing three elements and identifying similarity and difference continues, ideally until the person runs out of constructs. Ten to fifteen constructs often provide a useful picture.

The similarity, which may be positively or negatively stated, is written on the left and the difference on the right. In the example below it is clear which three elements a friend I will call Jo compared. The Xs indicate the two elements who were seen similarly, as egotistical, when compared with the third element O, who was identified as being group-oriented.

		Elements						
Similarity	–	–	–	–	–	–	–	Difference
Egotistical		X		X		O		Group-oriented

In this way, one of the constructs used by the participant to understand 'what's going on at work' is accessed. This procedure is repeated until the participant decides that sufficient constructs have been externalized. It is assumed that the constructs are permeable, i.e. they can and will be applied to new elements and they do indeed represent the participant's understanding of the area. It is also assumed that the language used does, to an extent, capture the personal meaning of the construct. However many constructs are generated, it must be remembered that we are only gaining access to a sample of current constructs.

The fourth task is to locate each element on each construct. Each element is allocated an X or O depending on whether the element is more like the similarity pole of the construct, marked with X, or the difference pole, marked with O.

		Elements						
Similarity	–	–	–	–	–	–	–	Difference
Egotistical	X	O	X	O	X	O	O	X	Group-oriented
Creative	X	O	X	O	O	O	O	X	Rule-bound

When the whole grid is completed in this way, patterns and associations emerge. Clearly Jo, with the exception of one element, experiences people at work who are egotistical as also creative, and group-oriented people as rule-bound. This may be a barrier to creative group-based work. We would need to see the rest of her grid and talk to her about her understanding of these two constructs to gain a clearer picture.

A slightly more subtle picture can be gleaned by using an ordinal scale to reflect person relevance, rather than a notion of absolute quantity. Each element is rated by the participant, on each construct, on a scale of 1–3, 1–5 or 1–7, whichever seems most suitable. Some elements might share the same number, other numbers might not be used at all. Jo used a scale of 1–5.

	Elements								
1									5
Similarity									Difference
Egotistical	2	4	1	4	2	5	4	2	Group-oriented
Creative	1	5	3	4	4	4	5	1	Rule-bound

It must be remembered that these numbers carry no inherent meaning but simply provide a way in which the participant can position elements in relative terms on each of the dimensions and so expose a slightly richer picture. We can now see that all those people in Jo's grid construed as group-oriented are also seen as rule-bound while only two of the four experienced as egotistical are also creative. One is rule-bound, an interesting phenomenon, worthy of more discussion with the participant. The other is given a 3, which may mean that they appear to Jo to be rule-bound in some situations and creative in others.

Analysis may be focused on elements, constructs or both. If a rating scale is used, a simple cluster analysis is possible to clarify associations.

Analysis is an integral part of the collaborative process of working up the grid to completion (i.e. it is part of, rather than succeeds, the research process). Information on how the participant understands their world emerges throughout, from the first step of identifying the particular topic to be explored, through to which elements are chosen for inclusion and which excluded, and beyond to how readily constructs are verbalized and which particular constructs are applied. As it is the *participant's* understanding that is being exposed it is for them to analyse and gain insight from viewing the completed grid. If the participant does not identify and verbalize obvious connections made explicit by completion of the grid then it is not necessarily the role of the co-researcher to voice them. Essentially it depends on the area explored and the reason for the exploration. Emergent implications may be sensitively checked out with the participant but we must be aware of the possibility of harm. The grid may highlight sensitive issues that the participant chooses not to acknowledge at this time. The understanding gained is thus framed by the participant.

A worked example

This grid was constructed by a middle manager in a recently privatized utility, who claims to be frustrated and somewhat limited by the work climate set, in his opinion, by top management's failure to act in a way that values all workers and to offer sound leadership. His frustration has been clear from numerous spontaneous discussions with him over the past two years. His aim was to clarify his view of colleagues' management styles, with the possibility of gaining new insight. Mine was actively to re-experience the process of working up a grid with a participant. Figure 5.1 shows his organizational structure.

Having outlined Kelly's theory to Alex, stressing particularly that it was his understanding of his issues, framed by him and explained in his language, that we were attempting to access, I asked him to identify a range of elements. He chose managers liked and respected, disliked and not respected, peers, middle, senior and top managers, although he stated at this point that there were no top managers he respected. All were men. His focus, then, is his experience of management styles and their implications within his work sector.

He constructed the grid very readily (see Figure 5.2). The constructs flowed in response to me repeatedly offering him a random selection of three elements. He occasionally offers further explanation of the meaning of his constructs. Ambition, for example, is construed as being prepared to knife others in the back, and if you're not prepared to take this action then you're experienced as less ambitious.

His construct choices present a picture of traditional male work culture underpinned by competition and in-house political correctness. He clearly experiences a different work climate from Jo, who, when engaged in a similar work-based exercise, revealed the following constructs: reliable–a bit erratic; clear communicator–rambling style; effective–less so; creative–more limited; socially skilled–socially clumsy; enthusiastic–too much trouble; good negotiator–directive; adventurous–doesn't take risks; facilitative–critical; weak–strong; stubborn–amenable.

Discussion

Focusing on the constructs and just choosing a few of the evident associations, we can see that those colleagues construed as supportive are also experienced as inventive, trustworthy and less likely to be politically malleable. And of course the corollary is that those experienced as non-supportive cannot be trusted, are more likely to be politically malleable and tied down by the flavour of the month – in Alex's terms the 'politically correct' current issue. He also experiences those who are less inventive to

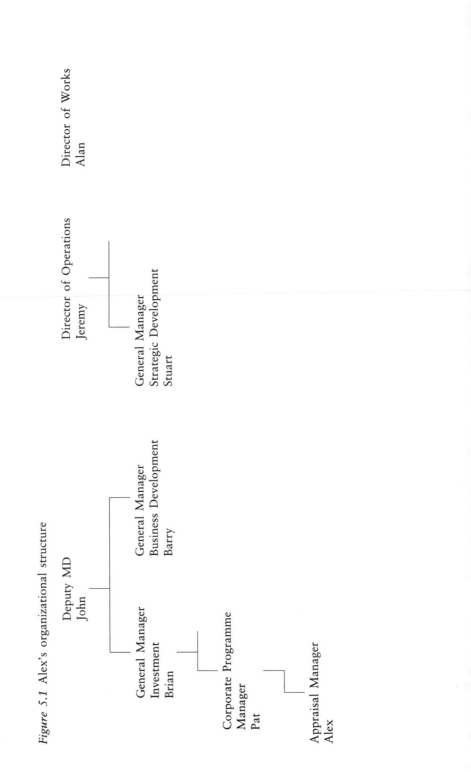

Figure 5.1 Alex's organizational structure

Figure 5.2 Alex's repertory grid

Similarity	Alex	Jeremy	Pat	Barry	Stuart	Alan	Brian	John	Difference
Non risk taking conventional	3	4	4	o4	x1	2	2	x2	Risk takers
Supportive of subordinates	x1	2	1	x1	3	o4	3	4	Non supportive
Looks after himself – totally non people oriented	4	4	5	4	4	x1	o2	x1	People oriented
Knife in the back (ambitious)	4	x4	x4	4	o4	1	3	1	Less ambitious
Non systems – bound (open)	2	2	x1	x1	o4	3	3	2	Systems bound
Non organized – day to day existence	3	3	x3	x4	o4	3	1	1	Organized long-term view
Inventive – (not tied down by flavour of the month)	2	x2	x1	1	3	3	4	o4	Tied down by flavour of the month
Takes wider view – not basic engineer	3	1	1	x1	3	3	o4	x2	Basic engineer
Not basically trustworthy	4	4	4	o4	x1	1	1	x1	Trustworthy
Perceptive – people aware	x3	x3	o5	4	4	1	1	2	Non-people aware
Not a bully	1	4	x1	3	x1	3	4	o5	Bully
Politically malleable – blows in the wind	o5	2	4	x2	1	2	x2	1	Less politically malleable

Note: x denotes similarity
o denotes difference
Alex used a scale of 1–5

be systems bound and unlikely to take risks. These people are seen as more likely to use bullying tactics to achieve their aims.

The clearest association in the grid is that those experienced as sufficiently ambitious to knife others in the back are also seen as concerned with self rather than being person-oriented. These colleagues are also described as more likely to be lacking in awareness of others. In all probability there is a core construct (possibly egocentrism–altruism or cooperative–competitive) underpinning these three slightly semantically different manifestations.

Conversational laddering, which is explained in the next section, could be used here if more depth is required, to gain access to core constructs and thus perhaps to greater understanding.

In terms of elements, he construes the senior and top managers in his sector, Brian and John, whose decisions have implications for him, in very negative terms. He characterizes them as politically malleable, lacking in long-term strategy, rarely prepared to take risks and short on inventiveness, owing to their being tied down by the 'flavour of the month'. They are also experienced as untrustworthy, prepared not only to bully but if necessary also to knife their colleagues in the back. Alan, who heads another sector, is construed very similarly.

The grid reveals that Alex sees himself as most like Pat, his immediate boss, and very similar to Jeremy, a top manager in a different sector, despite his claim at the outset that there were no top managers he respected. Brian and John are construed as most unlike him and in fact similar only to Alan, another top manager. Setting these findings in the slightly wider context, Alex maintains that he has little faith in top managers, as he claims that those who are promoted are not necessarily the most skilled and effective people, but those who play the 'politically correct' tune. Their management actions are rooted in their own uncertainty. Their need to maintain control means that their teams are not included in decision making, nor are they trusted to operate responsibly and effectively, which results in workers feeling undervalued and frustrated.

Clearly this analysis could be taken much further, the specific direction depending on the research question. However, this initial exploratory grid has captured Alex's frustration and disillusionment with the management of his organization.

There are a number of ways to extend this understanding. The grid could now be used as a basis for further grids, perhaps including his notion of an ideal manager or how he would handle the role. He might find it useful to discuss findings from such a grid with a trusted colleague who had completed a similar grid. Grids such as this form a useful focus, an initial shared understanding on which to base an interview. If Alex wanted a more illuminating picture of how he experiences his work setting, then conversational laddering based on the constructs revealed would produce a deeper understanding.

Laddering

Laddering (Hinkle 1965) is a particular style of interviewing which allows constructs to be revealed (see Chapter 4 for more details on interviewing). It may be used in addition to the grid or independently using constructs that crop up in conversations. It needs to be used wisely and cautiously (see Rowe 1988) and only when the participant is willing and keen to gain a deeper understanding. Often the grid gives rise to surface (subordinate) constructs that are not generally applicable. They have implications, but fewer than core constructs, which frame our reality as they are central to our being. Often subordinate constructs are sufficient. Laddering, however, not only allows elaborations of a more personal framework but also illuminates how constructs are personally (hierarchically) integrated, and has the advantage of being able to identify which of the revealed constructs is more important, thus offering a better understanding of how the person frames their reality.

We move up the hierarchy from subordinate constructs to those that form the core of our value system by asking where the person would prefer to be located on a particular construct and why. This is best achieved by using a conversational style, responding directly to their comments each time (rather than repeating the question why, which often feels interrogational). Occasionally laddering works neatly, when co-researchers move from initially stated superficial constructs through to more psychological core constructs fundamental to the person's understanding. Often this is not the case, and core constructs may be difficult to verbalize for a variety of reasons. Rather than climbing up the ladder of the hierarchy we can climb down to more subordinate constructs by pyramiding (Landfield 1971). This is done by asking the question 'What does it mean to be . . . ?' (organized, for example).

Alex and I used the laddering technique to try to gain a better understanding of what he means by 'political malleability'. We noted that he had put himself on the extreme position of less politically malleable. I began by asking what advantages there are to being less politically malleable.

A: Not a lot (said with a laugh) – I feel a bit more virtuous but it doesn't do a lot of good at the end of the day . . . sometimes I feel things are right . . . If I was politically malleable I'd have to go against my conscience. I'm not as politically malleable as some, but I'm not fixed –

some of our managers duck and weave to stay in power . . . that's their main aim in life.

CT: It's not yours?

A: I'm happy to be part of a team – to influence what's going on. If something is wrong I'm prepared to stand up against it, to put it right. I don't seek power for power's sake.

CT: Why don't you seek power?

A: Those who are power driven have a narrow, limited view . . . some people need power.

CT: You'd prefer to put it right?

A: Yes . . . although it doesn't necessarily win many friends – it's seen as a negative position. I'd prefer a more positive job. People have said to me 'I wouldn't have your job'.

CT: Is there anything positive about 'putting it right', about your position?

A: It helps achieve the company's aims.

CT: Which are?

A: To lower costs, to offer better value for money – which would secure more jobs and satisfy customers.

We now have a fuller view of what Alex means by politically malleable, although we have moved to a more pragmatic rather than psychological construct. It is tied up with power seeking and the consequent limitations of view. He experiences those in power as generating problems, ones that he has to 'stand up against' and 'put right' for the good of the organization and his conscience. His stated aim aligns with the company's aims, to lower costs and thus secure more jobs and to satisfy customers. In contrast, he construes the politically malleable as mainly aiming to stay in power. Although his stance does not 'necessarily win many friends' we can see that he and others construe this negativity as at least partly to do with his position. At least one of the sources of his frustration at work is now clearer.

Discussion

What we see from the analysis is a middle manager who wants more control, who wants to take part in decision making, who would prefer to work in a more supportive consultative climate. Jackson (1983) and Argyle (1989) among others claim that such an environment leads to increased health and job satisfaction.

The discussion could present some support for Alex's experiences of top managers by picking up the thread of organizational culture and looking at possible reasons for the actions of managers at different levels, particularly the lack of power sharing. Handy (1985) claims that age and middle management task experience lead top managers to dislike too much risk, to prefer a style of tight structure and control, whereas Alex's preference to work within a supportive flexible climate is typical of middle managers. This could then be developed in terms of the efficacy of work cultures, seemingly a major concern for Alex, and the creative integration of different management styles.

Alex views top management as insecure about their own management skills and there is objective insecurity in the wider organizational context, as recent privatization has brought about change and the workforce is to be halved over the next two years. A number of studies (Cobb and Kasl 1977; Dooley *et al.* 1987) suggest that the anticipation of job loss, for managers, may well be as traumatic as unemployment itself. It is also reasonable to speculate that those who feel stressed may adopt a tighter style of management. It is possible that the insecurity of the situation itself fosters a high need in Alex for participation to enhance feelings of control and professional worth. A study of managers (Roskies and Louis-Guerin 1990) in an ambiguous work context found links between perceived job insecurity and poor health, and between negative work attitudes and psychological distress.

Personal construct psychology connections and comments would need to be made, particularly the fact that we are dealing with the dynamic construing of one middle manager whose personal experiences have led to the construction of particular frameworks through which he filters and understands his current experiences. This snapshot in time is inevitably illuminating only part of the picture, and the picture itself is open to a range of alternative constructions.

Reflexive account

Personal construct psychology is reflexive. Both co-researcher and participants are, in Wilkinson's (1988) words, 'in the construing business'. The choice of topic and the interaction involved in constructing and analysing the grid would have been different with someone other than me, someone with whom Alex has a different personal history and understanding. The brief analysis, although checked out with Alex, is my construction, my way of seeing, my struggle to understand his understanding. 'The knower is part of the matrix of what is known' (DuBois 1983: 111). Essentially it is the sense that I can make, operating with my current frameworks as a woman and social psychologist with both particular interests and a previous understanding of Alex's work concerns, of the expressions of his work experiences elicited at this time by the process of constructing the grid with me.

The researcher's part in the process needs to be acknowledged. In a full reflexive account specific consideration needs to be given to how the researcher, with her particular interests, skills and understanding, influenced the process.

Other personal construct methods

Caution

Personal construct psychology methods may only give rise to superficial construing, but all, particularly laddering and the ABC method, have the potential to tap into core constructs and therefore the potential to be harmful. To a large extent the methods are participant controlled, the level of construing revealed depending on the level at which they choose to work. However, core constructs and particularly personal links between constructs of which the person was previously unaware may be externalized for the first time. Caution and sensitivity are required throughout, as such new understandings, while offering opportunities for self-development may also be threatening. Researchers need to be aware of ways of limiting participant disclosure and of supporting strategies to cope with what might emerge. Participants need to be fully informed at the outset of the possibilities.

ABC

Often we fail again and again to achieve personal change we claim to want to make. The ABC model devised by Tschudi (1977) is particularly useful for revealing possible underlying tensions (core constructs) that prevent us from making the change. Again you can do this alone or with a co-researcher asking the questions. When the change to be made has been identified, the person's present and preferred positions are stated – in this case mine.

A1 Present position

Relatively disorganized life

A2 Preferred position

More organized life

I then list the advantages of my preferred position and the disadvantages of my present position.

B1 Disadvantages of present position

Stressful
Being slightly chaotic is time consuming

B2 Advantages of preferred position

Less time and effort spent achieving tasks
Smoother life?

Untidy	Appear (and feel?) more professional
Look tense and therefore less approachable?	Appear calm and therefore more approachable?
Slightly dizzy persona	Gain some control
Occasionally feel out of control	Less stress
Achieve less?	Maybe have more time for more social life

Finally, the advantages of the present position and the disadvantages of the preferred position are listed. Often, the reason for the lack of movement becomes clearer at this stage.

C1 *Advantages of present position*	C2 *Disadvantages of preferred position*
Freer to 'go with the flow' – respond to intuition	Appear (and feel) in control and therefore strong; consequently,
Room for spontaneity	maybe, never offered support, or
Creativity and fun – self-development	approached by others to support them
Able to ask for and receive practical and emotional support when needed	Maybe more distant from friends and colleagues
More closely connected to others – more open relationships possible	Appear dull and predictable, lacking in enthusiasm?
More varied life?	Ruled by my own organization?
	More fixed – possibly less capacity for creativity
	Less open to new opportunities for self development?

Clearly, I associate being disorganized with spontaneity, creativity and the ability to act impulsively. Crucially, I also see it as allowing me to form closer relationships and offering me more opportunities for self-development, to enjoy a more interesting life. Although an organized life appeals in terms of less stress, more control and possibly more time, I also construe being organized as a potential barrier to close connections with people and self-development. As I currently value close connections with others, intuitive understanding, creativity and opportunities for self-development, it is quite clear why I do not become more organized.

Revealing such personal implications in this way can highlight why a person is 'stuck' and offer new understandings of the dilemma which then enables them to begin to make changes, to reconstruct, if that is what they choose to do.

Self-characterization

Self-characterization (see Fransella and Dalton 1990) is a method of capturing the flavour of the idiosyncratic richness of the way individuals construe themselves and their worlds. It is used a great deal in therapy, but has applications in a variety of other contexts.

The instructions given to the participant are: 'Write a character sketch of yourself, as though you were the principal character in a play. Write it from the point of view of a friend, someone who knows you intimately and sympathetically, perhaps better than anyone really could know you.'

The resultant sketch will reveal, in part, the participant's truth, her story. We are not in the business of content analysis, nor checking off constructs used. Rather, we are looking at how the person construes, how constructs are integrated and what implications they are seen to have. The overall tone and character, the non-verbals of the sketch, also offer important insight. The sketch needs, in Kelly's terms, to be 'brought in to focus.' We, as co-researchers, are attempting to empathize to gain a glimpse into the world that the writer experiences, to understand their story. Understanding is best gained via a process of negotiation between the co-researchers. Statements such as 'it seems to me that . . . Is that right?' are useful for checking understanding. It is the script writer who is the final arbiter as they alone can offer personal validity. We must remember, however, that this is our here-and-now construing, not necessarily how things were or will be. Nevertheless, useful insight can be gained.

Drawings

Participants sometimes prefer to use drawings to explore their construing. This initial freeing from language can give rise to more spontaneous expression and illuminate, perhaps more readily, the personal quality of the experience that language often fails to convey. Drawings are most often used in conjunction with other methods. They can be used in a multitude of effective ways: for example, to illustrate parts of an interview, to chart change, real or potential, to go beyond the words, to reveal more of the underlying meaning. There are clear links here with art therapy. Drawing skills are not necessary, and people can choose to represent themselves in all sorts of ways.

Cooperative analysis will include the non-verbal characteristics of the illustrations, such as size, positioning, and the use of colour. The researcher's understanding is best checked out by using propositional statements like those mentioned above, so that it is the participant's interpretation, rather than the researcher's, that is illuminated.

Assessment

I will look first at some general limitations of personal construct psychology approaches. Our aim is, to the extent that we can, to gain an understanding of our participant's way of seeing, to enter their reality. It must be acknowledged that a complete understanding, an ability to experience the world 'as if' we were them, is not possible. There are many barriers.

All the techniques rely on people's ability to introspect, to reflect on their experiences and assume that the idiosyncratic quality of such experiences can be captured and communicated via language. This is not so. Many have difficulty reflecting and the use of language is highly personal and inadequate to convey the total meaning of an event. Some experiencing is completely beyond words: listening to a piece of music or achieving a personal goal is active construing without language.

Some would claim that unconscious motives and physiology affect our experiencing but are unknown and therefore cannot be stated. Kelly had no truck with unconscious *motives*, but acknowledged that constructs are not always fully elaborated, in that one end, usually the difference, is submerged and therefore not available for conscious exploration. His concern was for the limitations this set for the individual, as people cannot be something they cannot construe. However, a knowledge of constructs lacking oppositional meaning is useful. As co-researchers our understanding is limited by our ability to relate effectively to the participants and thus to facilitate the telling of their story, by our capacity for open listening to the complete message and by our own frameworks of understanding.

There is the problem of reification, of believing that we have accessed some objective truth. All we have ever gained is our construction of a section of someone's current understanding, not their complete construct system. Reconstruction is always a possibility as the theoretical underpinning of current construing is one of change. We must remember not to generalize, that personally relevant constructs applied in a specific context are not necessarily applied in other settings.

There are further problems, which are connected to wider issues to do with qualitative research.

First is the notion that constructs oversimplify experience. Constructs are dimensions, not either/ors: people may be experienced by the construer as tense or relaxed *to some degree*. Constructs reside in our heads, they are the way we make sense of what is going on. Friendliness, for example, is a characteristic, with an idiosyncratic quality, used by me to interpret someone's behaviour – not their characteristic.

Connected to this is the debate that hinges on any distinctions between constructs and concepts. Kelly's aim was to develop a holistic approach, not one solely based on cognitions. He was clear about the distinctions. For him the world is comprised of processes (constructs), not things (concepts). He addressed this in the 1950s, actively choosing the term constructs, as unlike concepts they include an element of anticipation, based on recognition of patterns of experience and outcomes of personal actions. They are 'an interpretative act of someone' (Kelly 1955: 106), not a feature of the world. Constructs underpinned by dynamism, unlike concepts, open up possibilities and enable us to extend our understanding. The debate continues. Warren (1991) recognizes some similarity between prototypical (as opposed to classical) concepts and constructs, and claims that this 'is heartening for those who would wish to develop relations between personal construct theory and other perspectives in psychology' (p. 535). However, Warren (1991: 535) concludes that 'there is value in continuing to differentiate constructs and concepts.'

Personal construct psychology has been accused of being a cognitive approach at heart. This also has much to do with the confusion between construct and concept. Kelly distanced himself from a reductionist cognitive approach, which he regarded as a barrier to sensitive psychological enquiry, preventing study of the whole person. Experiences are rarely completely emotional, cognitive or rational. Construing is not thinking or feeling but an act of discrimination that may take place at many levels of awareness, from intuitive thought through to verbal, which then enables us to anticipate future events. We are forms of motion, an integrated whole, not separate systems of body and mind. Rational and intuitive knowing need to be acknowledged as equally valid, as integral parts of human experiencing.

There are two levels of criticism that focus on Kelly's neglect of the sociocultural context.

One concerns the lack of acknowledgement of the influence of prevailing ideologies on Kelly's understanding, and therefore on the emergent approach. It is true that Kelly paid little attention to the wider contextual influences. Although, from the vantage point of the 1990s, the values of the 1950s are clearly evident, this does not necessarily imply that they are no longer meaningful or appropriate. The format of his approach and his use of language illustrate his firm grounding in the times and his personal biography.

The second focuses on the neglect of the influence of the sociocultural context on construing. It is clear from Kelly's clinical work that he was aware of the impact of culture on people's construing. His sociality corollary and commonality corollary acknowledge that both individuals and groups influence a person's construing. Kelly's sociality corollary claims that to interact effectively we must, at least in part, successfully construe the other's construction processes, we must empathize. The commonality corollary explains similarity of behaviour, not in terms of similarity of expectation, membership of the same cultural group or having similar experiences, as due to construing experiences in the same way, using a shared framework, which will inevitably have some rooting in cultural background. 'So the individualist standpoint taken by Kelly does not preclude one from construing aspects of life from a group or cultural standpoint' (Fransella 1984: 160).

The emphasis, nevertheless, is on *individuals* as agents of their own actions, shaping themselves by attaching personal meanings to what is going on rather than shaped via social construction; that is, a personal rather than social construction (Rychlak 1990). Clearly individuals and their contexts interact. The range of contexts a person is operating in at any one time will influence their experiencing. However, it is the individual's understanding, the personal importance or otherwise of the contexts in their construing, that is the emphasis of personal construct psychology.

As the focus of personal construct psychology is the individual, we may fail to consider how our particular position in our sociocultural context frames our reality and limits our choices. However, the accounts we gain from personal construct approaches are explicitly subjective, which is indeed our aim and all that research can ever gain. Unlike positivist approaches, here it is the participant's understanding that is valued.

Useful reading

Bannister, D. and Fransella, F. (1986). *Inquiring Man: the Psychology of Personal Constructs*, 3rd edn. London: Croom Helm.

Burr, R. and Butt, T. (1992). *Invitation to Personal Construct Psychology*. London: Whurr.

Dalton, P. and Dunnet, G. (1992). *A Psychology for Living*. Chichester: Wiley.

Fransella, F. and Dalton, P. (1990). *Personal Construct Counselling in Action*. London: Sage.

Rowe, D. (1988). *The Successful Self*. London: Fontana.

References

Argyle, M. (1989). *The Social Psychology of Work*, 2nd edn. Harmondsworth: Penguin.

Bannister, D. and Bott, M. (1973). 'Evaluating the person' in P. Kline (ed.) *New Approaches in Psychological Measurement*. London: Wiley.

Cobb, S. and Kasl, S.V. (1977). *Termination: the Consequences of Job Loss*. Cincinnati: US National Institute of Occupational Safety and Health.

Dooley, D., Rook, K. and Catalano, R. (1987). 'Job and non-job stressors and their moderators'. *Journal of Occupational Psychology*, 60, 115–31.

DuBois, B. (1983). 'Passionate scholarship', in G. Bowles and R. Duelli Klein (eds) *Theories of Women's Studies*. London: Routledge and Kegan Paul.

Fransella, F. (1984). 'The relationship between Kelly's constructs and Durkheim's representations', in R. Farr and S. Moscovici (eds) *Social Representations*. Cambridge: Cambridge University Press.

Fransella, F. and Dalton, P. (1990). *Personal Construct Counselling in Action*. London: Sage.

Handy, C.B. (1985). *Understanding Organisations*, 3rd edn. Harmondsworth: Penguin.

Hinkle, D. (1965). 'The change of personal constructs from the viewpoint of a theory of construct implications'. Unpublished PhD thesis, Ohio State University.

Jackson, S.E. (1983). 'Participation in decision making as a strategy for reducing job-related strain'. *Journal of Applied Psychology*, 68, 3–19.

Jahoda, M. (1988) 'Opening address: the range of convenience of personal construct psychology – an outsider's view' in F. Fransella and L. Thomas (eds) *Experimenting with Personal Construct Psychology*. London: Routledge and Kegan Paul.

Kelly, G.A. (1955). *The Psychology of Personal Constructs, Volumes 1 and 2*. New York: Norton (reprinted by Routledge, 1991).

Kelly, G.A. (1986). *A Brief Introduction to Personal Construct Theory*. London: Centre for Personal Construct Psychology.

Landfield, A.W. (1971). *Personal Construct Systems in Psychotherapy*. New York: Rand McNally.

Roskies, E. and Louis-Guerin, C. (1990). 'Job insecurity in managers: antecedants and consequences'. *Journal of Organisational Behaviour*, 11(5), 345–61.

Rowe, D. (1988). *The Successful Self*. London: Fontana.

Rychlak, J.F. (1990). 'George Kelly and the concept of construction'. *International Journal of Personal Construct Psychology*, 3(1), 7–19.

Thomas, L.F. (1979). 'Construct, reflect and converse: the conversational reconstruction of social realities' in P. Stringer and D. Bannister (eds) *Constructs of Sociality and Individuality*. London: Academic Press.

Tschudi, F. (1977). 'Loaded and honest questions', in D. Bannister (ed.) *New Perspectives in Personal Construct Theory*. London: Academic Press.

Warren, B. (1991). 'Concepts, constructs, cognitive psychology and personal construct theory'. *Journal of Psychology*, 125(5), 525–36.

Wilkinson, S. (1988). 'The role of reflexivity in feminist psychology'. *Women's Studies International Forum*, 11(5), 493–502.

Acknowledgements

My thanks to Alex for his cooperation and to Sue Lewis for her constructive comments.

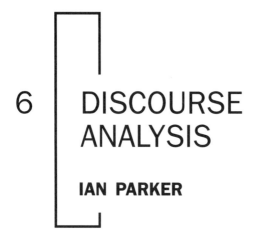

6 | DISCOURSE ANALYSIS

IAN PARKER

In this chapter we are concerned with a form of analysis that addresses the ways in which language is so structured as to produce sets of meanings, discourses, that operate independently of the intentions of speakers, or writers. Discourse analysis treats the social world as a text, or rather as a system of texts which can be systematically 'read' by a researcher to lay open the psychological processes that lie within them, processes that the discipline of psychology usually attributes to a machinery inside the individual's head. Most texts convey assumptions about the nature of individual psychology. In the example we have chosen you will see that, despite first appearances, the text is closely linked to the concerns of the discipline.

Background

The Latin roots of the word 'text' are to be found in the activity of weaving, and the tissue of material that clothed us is now the model for the tissue of meaning that holds the social world together. The recent history of discourse analysis is woven into the history of transformations inside and outside psychology, which started in the late 1960s and early 1970s. Inside psychology, the 'turn-to-language' that followed the paradigm 'crisis', events we described in Chapter 1, opened the way for what we now recognize to be a 'turn-to-discourse'. Outside psychology, a turn to language in German phenomenology and French post-structuralism gave issue to discourse theories that now enrich and dynamize studies of speech and writing in qualitative research.

The debates that prompted the turn to language were crucial for the development of qualitative research in psychology, for they permitted psychologists to break from a positivist fetish for figures to an exploration of meaning. As we pointed out in Chapter 1, the new paradigm writers gave a warrant for doing research in a way that was, they claimed, both scientific and sensitive to the sense that people construct in their everyday lives. The type of research – a form of qualitative research – that was proposed by the new paradigm writers focused on the roles and rules that govern ordinary language in the different social worlds we inhabit. Some interesting work appeared in the wake of the Harré and Secord (1972) manifesto for this 'ethogenic' approach, looking at such social worlds as school classrooms and football terraces (Marsh *et al.* 1974).

Despite Harré's (1979, 1983) ambitious theoretical reworking of Goffman's writings to produce a systematic framework for social and individual psychology, there were not many applications of that 'ethogenic' approach, and it has now all but burnt out in social psychology. Its most important legacy has been the space it provided for others wanting to do research in a non-positivistic way; the studies collected in the Reason and Rowan (1981) book, for example, are presented as part of the 'new paradigm' but range from action research to personal construct theory (approaches we believe still to be important, as our chapters in this book testify). Harré himself has moved rapidly from ethogenics through social representations to what is now the cutting edge of the new paradigm movement, discourse analysis (e.g. Davies and Harré 1990).

One important conceptual problem that the ethogenic study of social worlds foundered on was that of the *diversity* of meaning, the different contradictory ways of speaking that govern what we do (and who we can be). The figure that seemed to structure the way an ethogenic researcher looked at a social world was that of a jigsaw; here, each member carries a partial view of the whole, and the researcher gathers 'accounts' (through interviews, sometimes through the use of repertory grids) from different members to piece together what the underlying form of that world is really like. (It is no accident that the search for underlying structural forms was animating 'structuralists' in other disciplines in France and then the English-speaking world in the 1960s and 1970s.) However, the jigsaw analogy will not work, for conflicting representations of any social world enter from the language used outside (a social world is never a closed system). Meaning is continually changing (it is not static but dynamic), and language is composed of many 'languages' or discourses.

Writers heavily influenced by the sociology of scientific knowledge (looking at how science is socially constructed) and by conversation analysis (looking at the mechanisms of talk) and ethnomethodology (looking at the everyday making of sense) connected with these debates in the late 1970s. These are all approaches in sociology that privilege the 'ordinary' understanding people produce about the world over researchers' theories of what is going on. These writers made the point that rather than fetishize 'consistency', researchers into language should focus on variation, that a variety of what they called 'interpretative repertoires' constructed a sense of what was going on for members, and that language understood in this way functioned in the world rather than simply represented it (Potter and Wetherell 1987). The emphasis on variability, construction and function was already a distinguishing feature of a powerful intellectual movement – 'post-structuralism' – outside psychology (Macdonnell 1986), though the terminology was different: instead of speaking of 'interpretative repertoire', for example, post-structuralists used the term 'discourse'.

Post-structuralist writers had recognized that social relationships and our sense of ourselves is not produced by one structure but that what we do and what we are is created, 'constituted', in such a way that conflict between discourses marks all symbolic activity. For Michel Foucault (1969), discourses are 'practices that systematically form the objects of which we speak' (p. 49), and he argued that 'we are difference, that our reason is the difference of discourses, our history the difference of times, our selves the difference of masks' (p. 131). These assertions are powerful challenges to the ways we understand ourselves to be undivided, consistent individuals, and in the analytic and discussion parts of this chapter I will elaborate upon and explore these ideas.

At this point I will restrict myself to a brief example of how discourses weave together to produce a text. Three unlikely examples of phrases may serve to illustrate the operation of single discourses: if you say 'my head hurts so I must be ill', you will be employing a medical discourse; if you say 'my head hurts so I cannot really want to go to that party', you will be employing some sort of psychodynamic discourse; and if you say 'my head hurts but not in the way that yours does when you are trying it on in the way women do', you will be employing a sort of sexist discourse (whether or not, reader, you are a man). In the real world, of course, things are more complex. Take the (admittedly unreal) statement 'I've got a migraine caused by your mother-in-law's nagging which makes me relive my mother's complaints when I was a child.' Here you may find at least the three discourses, and the task of a discourse analysis is, among other things, to tease apart the discourses that are at work.

Discourse analysis in psychology is now a well-established method, and various forms of discourse analysis have illustrated how texts are not as coherent as they first seem and how they are constructed out of cultural

resources. To take some examples: Hollway (1984) argues that heterosexual couple talk is held in place by 'male sexual drive', 'have/hold', and
'permissive' discourses; Gilbert and Mulkay (1984) describe how scientists
use empiricist (resting on evidence) and contingent (relying on intuition)
repertoires to account for their choice of theory to the scientific community; and Squire (1990) shows how social psychology is organized around
detective, autobiographical and science fiction narratives.

Example

It is the Foucauldian form of discourse analysis that informs the reading
I will present in this chapter. I will take up some of the problems with the
approach, along with the reproaches of those who prefer more ethno-
methodologically inclined styles of discourse research towards the end
of the chapter. Among the advantages of Foucault's position are that we
need make no assumptions about what the writer or speaker 'meant' to
say, and that in his historical studies he has been preoccupied with the way
in which discourses, 'practices', produce types of 'psychology' (Foucault
1961, 1976). I hope to illustrate these points through the analysis of our
sample text.

Common sense psychology is reproduced through all the texts of the
mass media and different competing forms of popular culture. Rather
than taking a segment of transcribed interview material or conversation,
I have chosen a text from among the litter of contemporary consumer
packaging; my assumption is that the consumer buys the message in the
text on the package when they buy the product. In this case, the advice
that is provided as to how to use the item partakes of a wider system of
regulating practices, practices which the discipline of psychology feeds.
The instructions on a packet of children's toothpaste struck me as an
innocent and intriguing text, and my analysis flows from my first suspi-
cions about the function of this text when it was first found on a friend's
bathroom sink.

The text

The front of the white toothpaste tube bears the legend, on three separate
lines, 'MAWS', 'PUNCH & JUDY TOOTHPASTE', 'Children's Toothpaste with *Fluoride*'. This bright multi-coloured print is framed by pictures
of Punch and Judy, and there is already a multitude of meanings that
cluster around this segment of text which could be explored, ranging from
the whiteness of the tube, which signifies the whiteness of teeth, to the
happy patterns addressing the reader as child, to the connotations of
'maw' as an animal or human stomach, perhaps. As consumers, even

before reading the tube we have read the cardboard packet, and perhaps we have stood in shops and chosen the packet from among many jolly toothpastes ('Postman Pat', 'Mr Men') targeted at children and parents, and parents addressed as if they were children. These acts of reading lead us into the text at the back of the tube. This is the text I will focus on here:

Directions for use

Choose a children's brush that has a small head and add a pea-sized amount of Punch & Judy toothpaste. To teach your child to clean teeth, stand behind and place your hand under the child's chin to tilt head back and see mouth. Brush both sides of teeth as well as tops. Brush after breakfast and last thing at night. Supervise the brushing of your child's teeth until the age of eight. If your child is taking fluoride treatment, seek professional advice concerning daily intake.

Contains 0.8% Sodium Monofluorophosphate

Analysis

It will be helpful for purposes of analysis, and for pedagogical reasons in this case, to structure the reading of the text through steps to discourse analysis which have been discussed elsewhere with reference to criteria that we may use to identify discourses (Parker 1992). It should be said that these steps conceal the feelings of muddle and confusion that will overwhelm a researcher approaching a text for the first time. As the process of analysis goes on, this feeling of bewilderment will be succeeded by a conviction that the analysis is banal. What could not be seen is now seen too clearly. It is worth bearing this in mind as I trace through my reading of the toothpaste text, and when you choose a text of your own to untangle. The steps in this analysis particularize and detail the conceptual and historical work of Foucault on the construction, function and variation of discourses as they pertain to the requirements of qualitative research in psychology.

It would be possible to explore the meanings of the shape and feel of the package in more detail (and I have already referred to the ways in which the colours of the letters signify that this is a product primarily aimed at children); to do this we would take the package as a 'text', and the first step to 'reading' it would be (a) to turn the text into a written form. This production of a written text, which would then be something more akin to a transcript, allows us to bring into focus connotations that normally just twinkle on the margins of our consciousness. We can then ask questions about what it *means*, for example, that the tube is smaller than standard tubes; it is important to note here that the smaller size not only 'reflects' the smaller size of the intended user and its smaller and fewer teeth, but reproduces the child as a smaller version of the adult. It is not necessary that the tube should be smaller (tubes targeted at much older people are not smaller because they also tend to have fewer teeth), and this variation in size alerts us already to the ways in which the text functions to create particular images of the child. Alongside the point that discourse analysis can be applied to visual texts, and must then be put into words, we should also be aware that the new written text will be something different, one created by the analyst and now read, as it were, second-hand.

It is not easy, or advisable, to engage in discourse analysis on one's own; it is always better (and this advice applies to some degree to all varieties of qualitative research) to work with other people. This is particularly important in the first stages of analysis, in a second step in which you should (b) free associate to the text. In the case of a piece of text that must be turned into written form it would be helpful to note the different ways in which it could be described together with other people and also to free associate with them at that point. The chains of connotations may appear bizarre, and it is tempting to disregard them. This would be a shame, for they could be useful: what is the significance, for example, of the chain that leads from Punch to child battering, to Judy as negligent mother, to the policeman, to the crocodile with the big strong teeth? We need not presuppose that the author of the toothpaste text, the designer of the package, intended that these meanings should be available to a user of the product in order to note that the Punch and Judy narrative is one that can act as a quite specific (negative) template for the care an adult may give to their child when brushing teeth.

If we are to consider the ways in which discourses, as Foucault (1969: 49) puts it, 'systematically form the objects' that are referred to in any text, we should now, as researchers, (c) systematically itemize 'objects' that appear in this text. A useful rule to follow here is to look for nouns. Where are they, and what could they signify? If we do this, we will then be in a better position to piece together the type of world that such a text presupposes, the world it calls once again into being each time it is read. There are:

- 'directions' (procedures for application of the product, for which this text specifies the correct application);
- 'uses' (types of application, of which in this case it is implied that there is only one);
- 'choices' (actions presupposing a range of possible alternatives and the ability, comprising evaluation and agency, to select from that range);
- 'children' (the categories of being for whom certain types of 'brushes' are intended);

- 'peas' (objects of determinate size against which 'amount' can be measured);
- 'Punch & Judy' (puppet characters who exemplify bad parenting);
- 'Punch & Judy toothpaste' (specified make of toothpaste);
- 'teaching' (tutoring of others, including in the practice specified by these instructions);
- 'teeth' (with 'sides' and 'tops', identified surfaces requiring brushing);
- 'hand' (for the restraint of the child to accomplish brushing);
- 'chin' (part of the child to be grasped to restrict movement);
- 'head' (part of the child to be targeted for restraint);
- 'mouth' (part of the anatomy containing the teeth);
- 'breakfasts' (first meals after which first brushing should commence);
- 'night' (last part of the day, which should culminate in brushing of teeth);
- 'ages' (as markers of development, in which the age 'eight' figures here as a significant marker);
- 'fluoride' (substance whose ingestion is implicated in the use of the toothpaste);
- 'treatments' (regimes of health care);
- 'professionals' (categories of person charged with regulating treatment and intake);
- 'advice' (mode of communication provided by professionals, distinguished here from simple command);
- 'intake' (amount of substance deemed medically appropriate by professional);
- '0.8% Sodium Monofluorophosphate' (specified amount of active substance).

These objects are organized and reconstituted in this text through particular ways of speaking, and it will be helpful from now on in the analysis (d) to refer to these ways of speaking as objects, our objects of study, the discourses. The identification of the objects that are referred to in the text has just brought us to the edge, to the point of being able to identify the discourses that hold them together. Before we can move beyond that point to the part of the analysis where the discourses will start to take on a life of their own in our reading we should (e) systematically itemize the 'subjects' (the categories of person) who appear in this text, and (f) reconstruct, as a device to explore differential rights to speak within discourse, what each type of person may say within the framework of rules presupposed by the text. To take the fifth step, then, some of the objects I have already identified are also sentient beings, the 'subjects'. They are:

- 'children' (the categories of being for whom certain types of 'brushes' are intended);

- 'professionals' (categories of person charged with regulating treatment and intake).

In addition to these two evident categories – and leaving aside the agency attributed to 'Punch & Judy' in popular representations for the moment – there is a third category of subject, that *addressed* by the text:

- 'parent' (category of person for whom directions are intended, and the nature of this subject is constituted through the three points in the text in which the reader is addressed as the owner – through the index 'your child' – of the child for whom the product is intended).

We can now, as the sixth step, reconstruct the rights and responsibilities of this most important subject of the text and the network of relationships that are reconstituted which position this parent, the reader, in relation to the 'child' and the 'professional'. First, in relation to the child, the parent must choose for it, teach it, stand behind, restrain and brush its teeth (both sides and tops), perform this duty twice a day at specified times, and supervise the activity (which here implies the increasing self-direction of the child in the task) until a specified age (at which point, it is implied, the child can carry on without supervision). Second, in relation to the 'professional', the parent must seek advice, and follow prescriptions concerning treatment and intake. Third, in relation to the addressor (the 'subject supposed to know', to have written the text, to be speaking to the reader), the parent must follow the directions, and, as a part of the directions, seek advice, if necessary, from a 'professional'. This circuit of responsibilities positions the addressor in alliance with the 'professional' in the instruction to seek advice (but with deference, also, in the attribution of rights to the 'professional' to determine appropriate daily intake).

One of the functions of the text, as of any text, is to bring to life (again, for us now as researchers) a network of relationships, and as we move on to link this network together around the objects the text refers to we can start (g) to map the different versions of the social world which coexist in the text. As we do this we are coming closer to identifying discrete ways of speaking that are at work in this text. The instructions require the reader to behave in a rational way. They are worded in such a way as to presume that the reader is in permanent charge of a child (from every breakfast to every night). They call for agreement with the idea that the child develops in a particular way up to a particular point (age eight) and they also assume that the reader is willing to consult professionals about the health of the child.

Note that the category of the 'child' here is not gendered (it could be a boy or a girl). Not many years ago, it would have been likely to have been referred to as 'he'. This contrast in ways of specifying gender also draws attention to broader cultural assumptions that appear in texts at unlikely moments. Consider, for example, the difference between the addressee for this text, whom we have taken to be a parent (from the designator 'your child'), and the addressee who would be in charge of the child in many other cultures outside this text's frame of reference, an addressee who could well be an older sibling. We are thus arriving at some pictures of relationships at work here: rational rule-following, parental, developmental and medical.

Each of these ways of organizing the world carries with it rules for reproving those who fail to adhere to it: to break from rationality and rule-following will lead to claims that the reader is stupid or dangerous; to refuse parental responsibilities invites accusations of irresponsibility; to reject the idea that the child follows a normative developmental route and that teaching should be geared to it may lead to one being labelled as selfish and complicit in delinquency; and to challenge the call to consult medically qualified professionals is often to be viewed as deviant and anti-scientific. These possibilities are enumerated here as a step in which we (h) speculate as to how each of these patterns would deal with objections to these instructions and the cultural rules hidden within them. I have suggested how such defensive procedures might be played out after I have listed what we are increasingly taking to be the four key sets of statements, but the relationship between steps (h) and (g) in the process of analysis is messier, and it is also useful to ask how 'imaginary' authors of statements in the text would respond to those who contradicted them. This technique can help us arrive at separate discourses.

It is the discourses that 'form the objects of which they speak', and not authors who speak through the text as if the text were a kind of transparent screen upon which the writer's intentions were displayed. Our 'imaginary authors', then, are our own creations (as, indeed, are the discourses to an extent, but I will return to that issue below), and we use them to emphasize the variation, the contradictions in the text. It is helpful to focus on this contradiction and concordance between voices in the text, and to spend a little time doing this in two further steps of the analysis: (i) identifying contrasts between ways of speaking; and (j) identifying points where these ways of speaking overlap. In this case the concern with instruction, supervision and professional rights locks together alarmingly, and I shall discuss this further in our discussion (under the heading 'Repercussions of the reading'). I will also want to pursue the issue of how distinctions between the discourses could be magnified, and how 'the child' of the parent constructed here and 'the child' of the medical professional differs. We can also note at this point how the serious tone of the directions for use contrasts with the frivolity of the Punch and Judy imagery, but also how that imagery works then to confirm the position of the parent and the professional as guarantors of serious guardianship.

We can now make some comparisons with other texts (k) to assess how these ways of speaking address different audiences. It may also be possible to find expressions of the discourse in which it seems to fold around upon itself and comment on how important it is to speak that way. Although we may find it useful to look at instructions on other toothpastes, we are moving now beyond this type of text to look at how the patterns of meaning that are apparent within it also operate elsewhere. Instructions such as these are already assessed, for example, by the Campaign for Clear English, which draws attention to and praises clarity and rationality (linking these two qualities) in official documents; the ways in which parents are addressed in conservative political discourse are often explicit about the importance of the family as foundation of civilized society; the discussions of education in debates on the relationship between schooling and family values are closely tied to the claim that there are distinct identifiable stages of intellectual and moral development; and, with the increase in popularity of 'alternative' medicine, scientific and professional standards are emphasized as bulwarks against charlatanism and in the defence of correct medical terminology (and those who have the right to use it).

We have now reached the point at which we (1) choose an appropriate terminology to label the discourses. This is one way of structuring a reading of the text. I have tried to make this reading plausible, and you may disagree. In your analysis of other texts, you should also write your report in a spirit of polemic and debate. The collapsing of rationality and rule-following under the heading 'rationalist', the labelling of the terms which invoke parental duties as 'familial', the linking of themes of development and education together as 'developmental–educational' and the use of the rubric 'medical' to include the reference to professionals, daily intake and use of the chemical terminology are, in part, operations applied for convenience, tidiness in presentation, but I will have to justify these choices later, in the discussion. To summarize, so far, I can identify four discourses:

- *'rationalist'* – in which the ability to follow procedures ('directions for use') requires choices of implement and judgement of amount ('small head' and 'pea-sized amount') and is predicated on recognition of appropriate authority in health care (following 'directions' and seeking 'professional advice');
- *'familial'* – in which ownership ('your child') runs alongside supervision and continuous care (the assumption that the child is present each breakfast and 'last thing at night') and is framed by the image of bad parenting (the figure of 'Punch & Judy');
- *'developmental–educational'* – in which the teaching of the child (parental activity) precedes supervision (the child's still tutored but self-governed activity) and then reaches an identifiable stage as a developmental milestone (the 'age of eight');

- *'medical'* – in which the process of using the toothpaste is necessarily linked to hygiene (brushing after meals), professional supervision ('fluoride treatment') and the specification of ingestion and chemical composition of substances ('daily intake', '0.8% Sodium Monofluorophosphate').

Repercussions of the reading

The analysis in this type of study differs markedly from the 'results' section of an experimental report, in which the different measures are tabulated and the significance level is identified. The analysis section of the report is longer (and it shares this characteristic with many other types of qualitative research we describe in this book). The analysis is also more 'discursive' in the sense that it traces the reasoning by which discourses were located in the text (though this characteristic is exaggerated in this chapter because I am not only describing an analysis but also recapitulating a series of steps to educate a reader in technique), and in so far as the unravelling of the text into discrete discourses necessitates a discussion of associations, cross-connections and contradictions between groups of terms and their everyday uses. This is a reading of one case example. It is not necessary to read twenty different tubes of toothpaste, though it may be interesting to do so.

The analysis has applied itself to the task not only of reading the text in question but also of following 'steps', and this is certainly not the lightest and most engaging way of presenting the material. The presentation of discourse analysis marks it as a variety of qualitative research which, unless measures are taken to the contrary, tends to conceal its reflexive aspects (a characteristic it shares with observational studies and some personal construct approaches and which differentiates it sharply from action research and feminist work). We should be clear, then, that the reading I have presented here is my response to the text and that the discourses are as much our creations as they are 'objects' existing independently of us. Our encounter with these discourses as they manifest themselves in this text is not an encounter with something new to us but rather with something very familiar; for the history that bears the discourses as 'objective' phenomena is also the history that bears us as 'subjective' beings. An advantage here is that discourse analysis makes public its sources in a reading. Our subjectivity as a historically produced and contingent form of matter is, then, an important research tool for the decoding of forms of language.

My discussion of the analysis of the toothpaste text must unfortunately be restricted here to an overview of the types of points I would want to cover in a lengthier study. The discussion in discourse analytic research may extend the analysis through (m) a study of where and when these discourses developed and (n) a description of how they have operated to naturalize the things they refer to; that is, how they 'form the objects of which they speak' in such a way that it appears perverse and nonsensical to question that they are really there. These two tasks underlie questions I would want to pose concerning the role of the discourses in the life of institutions, power relations and the transmission of ideology.

In this text the discourses clearly reinforce the institutions of the family and of medicine. Foucault's way of analysing the history of discourse has been applied to the family, and the role of state and welfare practices in shaping the internal structures of the family has been closely connected with the images the medical profession has distributed over the years in prophylactic advice against bad parenting (Donzelot 1979). Punch and Judy operate in this history as a contradictory sign of familial relationships, for while they are used to illustrate the moral dangers of neglect and child abuse they also function as subversive carnivalesque emblems of revolt against the authorities. The extension of analysis into the discussion is already following here a step (o) in which the discourses' role in reproducing institutions is examined alongside a step (p) in which the discourses that subvert those institutions are explored.

Such institutions do not simply structure social life, they also constrain what can be said, who can say it and how people may act and conceive of their own agency and subjectivity. Wherever there is power there is resistance (Foucault 1975), and the analysis of institutions could be extended to look at (q) who would benefit and who would be disadvantaged by such discourses, and so also (r) who would want to support or who to discredit these ways of talking. The powers that are accorded to the parent and the medic would appear to single these figures out as subjects who are wielding power over the child. We should take care, however, not to treat this exercise of power as deliberate, or to neglect the ways in which those who exercise power are also enmeshed within it (Foucault 1975, 1976). The figure of the parent with regard to the medic is contradictory, for example.

Discourse analysis is concerned with the ways in which meaning is reproduced and transformed in texts, and when such reproduction and transformation concerns institutions and power relations we are led inevitably to a consideration of the role of ideology. At this point I can link together some of the discourses I have described in the analysis to show (s) how they also entail other discourses which enjoy power, and (t) how these reproduce or challenge dominant conceptions as to what can change and what may be possible in the future. I can only suggest here that it may be illuminating to trace connections between images of rationality in the adult, accounts of child development and conceptions of the family as the 'normal' arena for the care of the child; not only medicine, but psychology as well slips in here naturally as an institution concerned with hygiene, or mental hygiene. The descriptions of psychology as an apparatus, a 'psy-complex' which emerged alongside medicine in the last century, would be relevant here (Rose 1985, 1989). The text seems, in this light, to encapsulate an image of psychology and cognate disciplines as practices obsessed with surveillance and control. The discussion could not move much further forward without trespassing into the disciplines of sociology and history, without an account of psychology itself as an institution suffused with power and ideology.

Assessment

I will discuss some of the limitations of the approach I have adopted here, and the criticisms that may be levelled against the reading by other writers in psychology sympathetic to discourse analysis, before moving on to consider briefly some deeper problems with this type of work.

Limits

There is, as I pointed out in the introduction to this chapter, a strand of work closely tied to ethnomethodological studies in the sociology of scientific knowledge which was a conduit for entry of discourse analysis into psychology (Potter and Wetherell 1987). The concern with everyday accounting for action takes priority over the researcher's perspective, and the rhetoric that people employ is privileged over any evaluation a psychologist could give. The analytic process I have described in this chapter has been subjected to criticism from writers in this tradition, and the concerns have been to do with the tendency to reification, the ways in which the analysis presupposes what it pretends to discover, and the use of common sense knowledge in the elaboration of the categories that are eventually 'discovered' (Potter *et al.* 1990). It could be argued, perhaps, that the four discourses simply do not exist as if they were invisible girders that held language together, and that it does not do justice to the subtle strategies people engage in to make sense, to pretend that experts can detect what is *really* happening. Worse than that, there is also an element of mystification in that I have pretended to tell you what is really there *as if* you did not know in the first place; I have only re-presented to you common sense notions of rationality, the family, developmental stages and medicine.

I would agree that there is a problem with the assumption, an assumption that guides much positivist research, that the psychologist knows best, but that does not mean that there should be no critical perspective on the ways in which language is used. The discourses are not really there hidden away awaiting discovery; they are indeed produced through analysis, but they do then give a coherence to the organization of language and tap institutional structures of power and ideology in a way that a simple appeal to common sense reasoning could never do. As I noted before, I am influenced in this view by Foucault's work and the post-structuralist tradition. As a counterpart to these criticisms, however, I should also consider those that come from the other side, from writers who may argue that I have been too cautious, not too far from but too *close* to the ethnomethodological strand of work. It could be argued, for example, that a fifth discourse, 'self-regulation' is also at work in our toothpaste text, and that this discourse, like the others that were described but more so, could only be drawn out by using a prior theoretical historical framework (Foucault's). I have indeed used theory to produce this reading; perhaps, for some, not enough. Criticisms have already been directed at the ethnomethodological strand (Bowers 1988), and I could now guess how they may be adapted to apply to the analysis I have presented here.

Although I have described how notions of rationality are reproduced in this text, it could be argued that I have presented an image of the meanings in the text as fairly static, that I have slipped back into standard structuralist styles of analysis, which do not really have much to say about resistance or the desire of 'readers' and 'writers' in the process of resistance. Although the reading is supposed to focus on variation, there is too little analysis and discussion of contradiction and free play in the text. The text pretends to be a serious document, but it is bounded by fun (in the figures of Punch and Judy), and analysis needs to work more thoroughly with the idea that subjectivity is always split, anarchic. Such analysis requires, perhaps, the use of psychoanalytic ideas (Hollway 1989; Parker 1995).

Critiques

It would not be difficult to predict the objections that would be levelled against the analysis by more traditional psychologists, and a clear expression of the hostility of the experimental tradition to this type of work has already appeared (Abrams and Hogg 1990). It is not clear in what sense this text is representative of instructions on children's toothpaste tubes, and no attempt was made to compare the text with those that may appear on, for example, Postman Pat or Mr Men toothpaste. The reading I have presented is only my opinion, and I have made no attempt to validate it against other forms of analysis, or even to discover whether the procedure I used is reliable when applied to other texts. I do not even know whether parents read the instructions, let alone whether the instructions actually determine the behaviour of parents. I have drawn on accounts of the 'psycomplex' that are speculative at best, and I assumed that a reader will simply and unthinkingly accept and implement the instructions in the way I assume them to function. Such complaints could be addressed to many of the examples of qualitative research we describe in this book, and they would apply to all studies of discourse that fail to use quantitative methods. This analysis, experimental psychologists would say, is a travesty of scientific inquiry.

From the other side, however, we must note the dissatisfaction with discourse analysis of some researchers who have no such qualms about abandoning 'science'. This last set of criticisms chimes in with those who are still inspired by the radical political aspects of post-structuralist and psychoanalytic theory. One overview of problems from this position identifies thirty-two problems with discourse analysis (Parker and Burman 1993), but we have space here only to note that they include the problem of treating language (texts, discourses) as more powerful than other material constraints on action, and the fantasy that the researcher can pull out a toolbag and apply it to any and every text without reflecting on the effects of an analysis. There is more *variability* in human action and experience than that expressed in language; as researchers we *construct* our own image of the world when we reconstruct 'discourses'; and we have some responsibility for how our analysis will *function*.

We have traced the analysis of sets of statements that course through a tiny text and tracked the ways in which the discourses carry in their wake sets of assumptions about the nature of social relationships, relationships that the discipline of psychology has in the past both investigated and endorsed. Psychology which operates in these ways has traditionally relied on the rhetoric and practice of quantification and observation. In contrast we have presented an analysis that is also a critique from the standpoint of qualitative research and those who are usually subjected to the professional gaze.

Useful reading

Burman, E. and Parker, I. (eds) (1993). *Discourse Analytic Research: Repertoires and Readings of Texts in Action*. London: Routledge.

Hollway, W. (1979). *Subjectivity and Method in Psychology: Gender, Meaning and Science*. London: Sage.

Potter, J. and Wetherell, M. (1987). *Discourse and Social Psychology: Beyond Attitudes and Behaviour*. London: Sage.

Squire, C. (1990). 'Crisis what crisis? Discourses and narratives of the "social" in social psychology', in I. Parker and J. Shotter (eds) *Deconstructing Social Psychology*. London: Routledge, pp. 33–46.

References

Abrams, D. and Hogg, M.A. (1990). 'The context of discourse: let's not throw out the baby with the bathwater'. *Philosophical Psychology*, 3(2), 219–25.

Bowers, J. (1988). 'Essay review of *Discourse and Social Psychology*'. *British Journal of Social Psychology*, 27, 185–92.

Davies, B. and Harré, R. (1990). 'Positioning: the discursive production of selves'. *Journal for the Theory of Social Behaviour*, 20(1), 43–63.

Donzelot, J. (1979). *The Policing of Families*. London: Hutchinson.

Foucault, M. (1961). *Madness and Civilization: a History of Insanity in the Age of Reason*. London: Tavistock.

Foucault, M. (1969). *The Archaeology of Knowledge*. London: Tavistock.

Foucault, M. (1975). *Discipline and Punish*. London: Allen Lane.

Foucault, M. (1976). *The History of Sexuality, Volume 1, an Introduction*. Harmondsworth: Pelican.

Gilbert, N. and Mulkay, M. (1984). *Opening Pandora's Box: a Sociological Analysis of Scientists' Discourse*. Cambridge: Cambridge University Press.

Harré, R. (1979). *Social Being: a Theory for Social Psychology*. Oxford: Basil Blackwell.

Harré, R. (1983). *Personal Being: a Theory for Individual Psychology*. Oxford: Basil Blackwell.

Harré, R. and Secord, P. (1972). *The Explanation of Social Behaviour*. Oxford: Blackwell.

Hollway, W. (1984). 'Gender difference and the production of subjectivity', in J. Henriques, W. Hollway, C. Urwin, C. Venn and W. Walkerdine (eds) *Changing the Subject: Psychology, Social Regulation and Subjectivity*. London: Methuen, pp. 227–63.

Hollway, W. (1989). *Subjectivity and Method in Psychology: Gender, Meaning and Science*. London: Sage.

Macdonnell, D. (1986). *Theories of Discourse: an Introduction*. Oxford: Blackwell.

Marsh, P., Rosser, E. and Harré, R. (1974). *The Rules of Disorder*. London: Routledge and Kegan Paul.

Parker, I. (1992). *Discourse Dynamics: Critical Analysis for Social and Individual Psychology*. London: Routledge.

Parker, I. (1995). 'Discursive complexes in material culture', in J. Haworth (ed.) *Psychological Research: Innovative Methods and Strategies*. London: Routledge.

Parker, I. and Burman, E. (1993). 'Against discursive imperialism, empiricism and constructionism: thirty two problems with discourse analysis', in E. Burman and I. Parker (eds) *Discourse Analytic Research: Repertoires and Readings of Texts in Action*. London: Routledge, pp. 155–72.

Potter, J. and Wetherell, M. (1987). *Discourse and Social Psychology: Beyond Attitudes and Behaviour*. London: Sage.

Potter, J., Wetherell, M., Gill, R. and Edwards, D. (1990). 'Discourse – noun, verb or social practice'. *Philosophical Psychology*, 3(2), 205–17.

Reason, P. and Rowan, J. (eds) (1981) *Human Inquiry: a Sourcebook of New Paradigm Research*. Chichester: Wiley.

Rose, N. (1985). *The Psychological Complex*. London: Routledge and Kegan Paul.

Rose, N. (1989). *Governing the Soul*. London: Routledge.

Squire, C. (1990). 'Crisis what crisis? Discourses and narratives of the "social" in social psychology', in I. Parker and J. Shotter (eds) *Deconstructing Social Psychology*. London: Routledge, pp. 33–46.

Acknowledgements

Thanks are due to Deborah Marks for her helpful comments on an earlier draft of this chapter.

7 | ACTION RESEARCH

MAYE TAYLOR

This chapter will at first concern itself with a general view of action research as, simply, 'a way of trying out changes and seeing what happens', and put forward the view that this has particular appeal to researchers motivated by a philosophy of social change such as feminism, anti-racism or socialism. It involves abandoning the idea that there must be a strict separation between science, research and action.

Background

Action research can be seen to have evolved from the work of Kurt Lewin in the 1940s (e.g. Lewin 1946), at which time, drawing upon several traditions of the mid-century, it was lauded as an important innovation in social inquiry, and was taken up in a variety of contexts, notably industry, education and community affairs. In social psychology Lewin probably did the most to promote and popularize the idea of studying things through changing them and seeing the effect, which in essence is the argument that in order to gain insight into a process one must create a change and then observe the variable effects and new dynamics.

Lewin was a strong exponent of action research in its concern with power relations between researcher and researched and the rights of the individual, foreshadowing the new paradigm psychology of the 1980s.

Lewin's 'cycle' of planning, action and 'fact-gathering' was the forerunner of Elliott's (1980) action research spiral. This is illustrated, for example, in one project where Lewin incorporated 'guidance' by sociologists with the actions of socially disadvantaged groups in a democratic process aimed at social change in which the benefits of the research were mutual. Lewin encouraged communities to study the results of their actions and examine the origins of their own biases in an endeavour drastically to change relationships within the communities. This constituted quite a direct challenge to the prevailing practice of using 'proxy' information about 'marginal' populations, because the underlying conceptions of social pathology encouraged researchers to devalue direct accounts from respondents in favour of those mediated by professionals. Current practice increasingly accords 'equality of status' to those who are researched and with it the right to speak and have their views seen as central to the research enterprise, exemplified in Freire's (1972) concept of 'conscientization', which involves a deepening awareness of their own sociocultural identity and their capacity to transform their lives.

In psychology tensions between the need for experimental rigour and the flexibility demanded by professional standards applied in 'real-world' settings has produced acrimonious debate. According to Frankel (1986), the critics were simply lamenting the 'confusion and noise' foisted upon social science by the 'humanness of human beings'. Like the librarian who dreams of the tidiness of the bookshelves without patrons, the 'neo-positivists' fantasize a spick and span social science where researchers are all identical, unbiased, infallible, measuring instruments. Research would be so much easier if researchers did not have to interact. However, Eisner (1984) argued the need for research 'pluralism' and urged the social science world not only to accept, but also to welcome a proliferation of research paradigms and to take advantage of the new angles they provide for viewing the world. Even though, by the 1970s, action research had been 'rediscovered', there is still strong opposition to its acceptance as 'real research'. The paucity of action research projects listed in psychology departments indicates this. However, there is healthy activity in some spheres, notably practitioner research (see Sapsford and Abbott 1992). In contemporary practitioner research it is accepted that the research methodology cannot be separated from conceptual analysis; that is, even though research and action are analytically distinguishable, they are inextricably intertwined in practice. In Polanyi's (1962) terms 'knowledge is always gained through action and for action'.

Cohen and Manion (1980) argue that while it is no less scientific and rigorous than applied research, action research interprets scientific method more loosely while focusing on precise knowledge applied to a specific problem in a specific setting: its unique strength is that it is self-evaluative and collaborative, with an ultimate objective being to improve practice. This gives 'practitioners' the kind of knowledge they can apply to their own behaviour in the midst of ongoing events, in such a way that it helps them inquire more effectively with others about their common purposes.

So, in action research the research 'question' arises out of the problems of practitioners and it is an important aspect of this approach that the analysis of the situation is *in situ*. The immediate aim of the research is to understand these problems, and the researcher, who may or may not be the actual practitioner, formulates speculative and tentative general principles about the problems that have been identified. From these it is possible to generate hypotheses about what action is likely to lead to (desired) improvements. The action can then be tried out and data on its effect collected, and the data can be then used to revise the earlier hypothesis. Two useful definitions of action research are:

> the study of a social situation with a view to improving the quality of action within it. [The] total process . . . review, diagnosis, planning, implementation, monitoring effects – provides the necessary link between self-evaluation and professional development.
>
> (Elliott 1980: ii, 1)

> Essentially an on-the-spot procedure designed to deal with a concrete problem located in an immediate situation. This means that a step-by-step process is constantly monitored over varying periods of time and by a variety of techniques . . . diaries, interviews, case studies etc., so that the ensuing feedback may be translated into modifications, adjustments, directional changes, redefinitions as necessary.
>
> (Cohen and Manion 1980: 47)

One last point about ethics in action research comes into sharp focus when we consider the infamous Miligram (1974) 'experiments', which involved deceiving the subjects, and is transformed into a strong set of working principles for action research projects, as will be outlined later in this chapter.

Feminist researchers have further elaborated on the theme of action research, stressing as a matter of central importance that research should be about change. Reinharz (1992) extends the concept and talks about *action-in-research*, identifying five types of specific action in research, namely action research *per se*, participatory/collaborative research, prevalence and needs assessment, evaluation research and demystification. She argues that each has validity in its own right.

Action research   To qualify under this heading it must be research in which *action and evaluation proceed separately but simultaneously*. These would be research projects that attempt directly to change people's behaviour. While gathering data in traditional or innovative ways, they intervene and study in a continuous series of feedback loops. A good example of this would be the work of Hanmer and Saunders (1984) into forms of violence against women, where community-based, at-home interviewing with the purpose of feeding the information gained back to the community in order to develop new forms of self-help and mutual aid among women was used. The research involvement led to an attempt to form a support group for survivors of violence and to make referrals to women's crisis and safety services.

Participatory or collaborative research　The essential feature here is that the *people studied make the decisions* about the study format and data analysis. This model of research is designed to create social and individual change by altering the role relations of people involved in the project. This is very clear in feminist participatory research, where the distinction between the researcher(s) and those on whom the research is done disappears. Lather's (1988) work serves as a good example. In her project, low-income women were trained to research their own economic circumstances in order to understand and change them. This links strongly with Lewin's views on power relations, for in participatory research attempts are made to form egalitarian relations, with the researcher abandoning 'control' and adopting an approach of openness, reciprocity and shared risk. Participants thus make decisions rather than function as passive objects, they are 'co-researchers' rather than 'research subjects'. Much work with adult survivors of childhood sexual abuse is progressing along these lines, with the professional therapist acting as resource to self-help groups seeking to understand their own behaviour and change it.

Prevalence and needs assessment　Here the research seeks to *determine the absolute or relative number* of people with a particular experience or need. Conventional research in this area has relied heavily on surveys which 'distanced' results from the situation, a 'let's find out and then act if we find it' approach, often used, according to radical social workers for example, as a way of delaying interventions, in contrast to placing the emphasis on mobilizing people to set up resources and organizations to respond to the needs as they are being identified, measured and re-defined. MacKinnon's work (1979) on sexual harassment first demonstrated the power of this approach, showing how meetings called and women discovering their own experience as they spoke identified common themes which led to the size of the problem becoming evident, and the basis for necessary action being revealed without preconception or suggestion on the part of the researcher.

Evaluation research　The purpose here is *to evaluate the effectiveness of different types of action in meeting needs or solving problems.* It can be used to evaluate individual and organizational behaviour and to evaluate evaluation research itself. An important example of such work is that done on evaluating the effectiveness of different forms of individual behaviour to determine which strategies enabled women to stop a rape in progress. Bart and O'Brien's (1985) intention with this work was to generate data-based advice that could be given to schools, hospitals and courts for them to give to women.

Demystification   Central here is *the belief that the very act of obtaining knowledge creates the potential for change.* There is a paucity of research about certain groups, which accentuates and perpetuates their powerless-ness: researchers on women's employment have found little data on the employment situation of disabled or lesbian women, for example. A cru-cial point here, for action research, is that because the needs and opinions of these groups are not known their views have less influence on the conditions under which they live. The Boston Women's Health Collective's book, *Our Bodies, Ourselves* (1984) is a prime example of the empower-ing impact of action research because it enabled women to understand the working of their own bodies, become more knowledgeable about pre-vention and treatment of women's health problems and thus take more control themselves. This in turn meant that they were less frequently subjected to the power of *male* medical experts, which the research project had identified as one of the 'problems' in the first place.

Clearly, action researchers have extra responsibility in addressing the 'does the end justify the means' issue, and the response has to be unequivo-cal: the action taken has to be in the best possible interests of the people involved; ethically there can be no place for conscious exploitation. Prac-titioner action researchers must work in such a way that they safeguard the practice aspects of their professional work while maintaining a rigor-ous and reflexive research stance. Research investigating the sex life of ferns (yes, it does exist!) is quite different from that investigating the best way of carrying out first interviews with rape victims. It is also clear that action research can often involve the practitioner researcher in new sets of relations with colleagues and clients (Kemmis 1982). The ethical guidelines for research have to be stringently applied in action research, which by definition is intervening in people's lives. There has to be respect for the whole life of the person, not just as a research subject.

So far, this chapter has explored some of the definitions, principles and approaches to action research, seeing it to be essentially practical and problem solving. Perhaps the reader can see why it is the hope of admin-istrators, politicians and practitioners and the despair of many academics. Action research means intervention in a world where everything can be happening at once and it is impossible to be sure what arises from what, where there is no ethical way of controlling (or measuring) the 'interven-ing variables' because those 'intervening variables' are actually people, with their emotional responses, their conceptualizations, their needs, their defence mechanisms etc. It is all a 'scientific researcher's nightmare. There is a Marxist point being made here, that we should not just understand the world but change it. Feminists concur and currently radical social workers loudly agree. Many claim that 'objective value-free' research is a 'cop out', where the research becomes the end in itself and avoids the real issues of what you do about it, what you can do about it and what works.

Some educationalists are anxious, seeing action research as vulnerable to co-option by uncritical policy makers and managers. Teachers are already being trained to view action research in schools as a form of inquiry into the best techniques to produce *prespecified* curriculum objectives or increases in standardized test scores, which is entirely contrary to the spirit of action research. Elliott (1980) warns that it is only a matter of time before action research will be promoted as the newest strategy to help teachers improve pupil achievement in order to meet national curriculum targets. In other words, the actions action research warrants need to be subjected to a political evaluation in the terms of the context in which they intervene rather than being treated as inherently progressive or worthwhile.

Doing action research

The principle of action research is really quite simple: an existing state of affairs is seen as problematic, it is identified, named and described in an appropriate way, attempts are made to change it and these attempts are monitored, and so on. So, action research is appropriate when 'specific knowledge is required for a specific problem in a specific situation, or when a new approach is to be grafted on to an existing system' (Cohen and Manion 1980).

Planning

Action research needs to be planned in the same systematic way as any other type of research. It is useful to draw up a checklist of preliminary questions in order to develop a *description* of the situation, such as: 'What is happening already? What is the rationale for this? What am I trying to change? What are the possibilities? Who is affected? With whom will I have to negotiate?'

A general outline of the stages of action research is:

1 First you need to identify some general idea or problem and clarify just what it is that you are interested in, like ethnography and unlike conventional research, and this general idea can shift as the work progresses. It helps if you are really interested in the area. Sustaining research is often difficult, so a little bit of passion won't go amiss.

2 Spend some time describing the 'facts' of the situation at the outset.
3 Make a preliminary explanation of the 'facts' of the situation by generating hypotheses, by means of brainstorming sessions, for example.
4 Test your hypothesis, i.e. put an action into operation and see if you were right.

This is often referred to as the *action research spiral* (Elliott 1980) and looks like this:

- Select the general area. Discuss, observe, read and decide on your first action.
- Take your action (monitor the action).
- Examine the information you have collected.
- Evaluate (a) processes, (b) outcomes.
- Plan next action.
- Take next action.
- Continue.

Data collection

You need to gather data in order to be in a position of being able to monitor the action (practice) which is at the centre of the inquiry. Action research is multimethod research (several chapters in this book take a detailed look at some of those methods). The methods selected for gathering the information you need for action will depend on the nature of the information required. It is important to gather information that will tell you more as a practitioner than you already generally know. This should be in such a way that it can inform the thinking of not just you as, perhaps, 'key' researcher, but of all concerned with the intervention programmes, and so offer the opportunity to evaluate the efficacy of intervention programmes in general. This may involve a combination of the following procedures, where appropriate. It is important to stress at this point that if you are carrying out practitioner action research you *must* select data collection methods that do not distort and intrude on your practice.

1 *Collection of documents relating to the situation.* These can range from newspaper articles where appropriate, through official documents, policy satements and correspondence.
2 *Keeping a detailed diary.* It is strongly advisable to keep a research diary whatever the approach being used, but for action research it is crucial. You can record your own ideas, including anything that might not be recorded anywhere else as it seems too general. Your diary will be particularly important when writing up, particularly for the design and methodology, 'what happened when'.

3 *Observation notes*. It is helpful to keep notes of meetings, lessons etc., which could be in the form of observation schedules. Elliott suggests a 'running commentary' approach to this at first, becoming more specific using checklists of relevant phenomena derived from the earlier analyses (see the research spiral).

4 *Questionnaire surveys*. Normally these are of other people involved in the project, to gain their impressions, attitudes and experiences. At first you might find an open format helps when you are doing the initial 'exploring'. Later, when you are involved in checking or choosing between interpretations, a closed format might be more helpful.

5 *Interviews*. The more sustained interaction of interviews allows more subtle nuances of perhaps an unfamiliar perspective to be explored in detail and gradually clarified.

6 *Shadowing*. Participants in the situation may be followed by an observer over a sustained period, in the ethnographic tradition. Shadow studies can give vital information when the study extends over boundaries into different aspects of practice, as can happen in institutional life.

7 *Tape/video recording*. This allows for repeated monitoring of the data you have collected.

8 *Still photographs*. These can be very useful for subsequent participant discussion, 'freezing' a situation which is then sharply in focus.

9 *Triangulation*. This is an essential ingredient whereby you use a range of the above methods to check out information gained, interpretations and your decisions about action.

Examples

Two strands are evident: the professional ideal, which means continuing openness to the development of good practice, and the scientific ideal of the continuing growth of understanding through critique and revision. Given this essential nature of action research it is not intended here to take one completely worked example, as the chapter has already concerned itself with principles and practice. The research spiral always applies, so clearly the crucial issue for undertaking any such project is for you to identify the problem. The research can be big or small, from individual case study work to community-based projects: the choice of area will be constrained only by opportunity and context. Some illustrations should suffice.

Zamorski (1987) did a piece of action research involving a socially isolated Asian boy, *apparently* suffering from a problem of low self-esteem connected with racial tensions in his school and community. Zamorski:

- carefully observed his behaviour with other children;
- experimented with small group games with varying groups of children, examining patterns of linguistic interaction during this;
- intervened to counteract racist comments by some children;
- negotiated changes in partners for classwork and seating arrangements.

Her work 'documents' the progress of an individual 'therapy', and analyses the effect of each successive strategy in the light of a developing theory as to the origin and the structure of the problem. The research actions included using groupwork, changing the physical structure of the classroom to change the interaction patterns, actively intervening when any racist comments were made to the boy or in his hearing and giving him attention and support. Changes brought about included transforming the school and teacher's understanding of the nature of the problem: illustrating the nature of the links between attempts to *solve* the problems, i.e. the isolation of the boy, and attempts to *understand* the problem, i.e. the patterned effects of institutionalized racism.

Action research, which can start with the identification of a problem, can also start quite dramatically when the problem forces itself to our attention, as the following will show. A sexual assault centre for women found itself with a problem of referrals when a rape victim was referred on, by one of the volunteer counsellors, to a psychiatrist. The counsellor had identified that the victim needed to be seen by a specialist mental health professional, as the counsellor felt that the service the centre was able to offer was not sufficient for her needs. The woman contacted the centre some time later, highly distressed, and told this story. She had been to see the psychiatrist, who, 'in passing', in the assessment session had humorously(!) said to her, 'Well Mrs X, look on it as community service, if they had not raped you they would have raped your neighbour.' She fled. The centre counsellors, themselves already concerned about their lack of knowledge of the mental health resources and their own limitations, took the incident seriously. I would add a note here that I am quite aware of the shocking nature of this example, that the comment is extremely provocative and that this is a sensitive issue. It is quoted to underline the seriousness: *action* research concerns quality of life.

Some of the stages that might follow are:

- use the incident as a critical incident to start a discussion about the needs of such clients (the starting point for a large action research project);
- organize a day conference for all appropriate workers in the area;
- set up information networks;
- produce a directory of services in the area;
- initiate a programme of training and supervision of voluntary counsellors;

- evaluate the effects of such actions, and so on through the research spiral.

This particular action research project would obviously be a large-scale one and by its very nature is not an exemplar of the small-scale projects that you, the reader, might be envisaging. It is quoted here to underline further the emphasis on the *action* part of action research. As the action research spiral indicates, all such research starts with the need to select a general area, discuss, observe and decide on your action. At the point of taking such action the project could be 'scaled down' to manageable proportions to be carried out by one person, or several persons undertaking a collaborative study. The choice is yours, for the range of subjects and problems that could lend themselves to action research is very wide, but the topic has to lie in your own area of expertise and interest. The whole field of counselling psychology, for example, lends itself to this approach, given the increasing turn to the provision of a counselling service as a response to observed 'problems'. The centrality of the 'helping relationship' and the need for research to inform action as well as to provide evaluation of changes brought about by interventions at individual, group and organizational levels clearly places it in this research field. Organizationally a useful example would be a research action project on an in-house counselling service: is it used and does it reduce targeted behaviours?

I will further illustrate the sequence with a representative example.

Identify a problem. An attached youth worker, trained in counselling, informed by equal opportunities issues and new to a centre, might want to make changes in the light of observing the large gender imbalance in users of the centre. There are very few young women at the centre, and when they are there they seem marginalized to few activities.

The questions what, why and how need to be addressed. Reading of previous research on youth work, discussion with colleagues, users of the centre and neighbourhood contacts, and perusal of local newspapers might well elicit information pointing at a history of male domination of the centre.

Formulate a course of action. Start by setting up single-sex discussion groups with the current centre users.

The young women identify verbal sexual harassment, bullying and the exercise of territorial domination, which has 'put off' many of their friends. They say they put up with it because at least the club is better than being at home and they cannot afford many of the other places. The young men see no problem, they like things the way they are.

In the light of the fact that the young women said they had enjoyed the discussion groups, continue these as an ongoing support group one evening a week, initially for a ten-week trial period.

Monitor the increase, if any, in women's attendance and record conclusions from the group discussion about the nature of the experiences they have and what they would like to see done about them. Observe activities in the centre to see if there are informal changes in the take-up of the various resources, looking to see if the support group is giving them the confidence to challenge.

Take formal action to ensure that the young women are given equal opportunity time on, say, the pool table and other arenas of activity that are designated as 'open'.

Monitor verbal harassment and intervene. Record in detail all incidents, and set up a group with the young men to look at the issue of verbal harassment in order to get them to stop it themselves. Monitor the effect of the groups.

Perhaps take individual counselling sessions where the only other step would be exclusion. Exclude individuals who refuse to adhere to the rules.

If necessary, allocate separate time periods for use of the resources by specific groups (e.g. girls or boys) to ensure equality of access.

Continue monitoring action as the time allotted to the project allows, and to the point when you are satisfied that the changes to practice have been made and the aims of the research have been met.

Writing up of such action research is necessarily a descriptive process. The comments made in Chapter 3 are applicable here. In addition it is important to report the time sequence very carefully, highlighting the various stages and indicating the problem(s) you identified, what you did, what you saw happen, right through the whole project. It is crucial that at each of the stages where you take action you elaborate on your justification for the action. Full description is important in its own right, as previously stated in Chapter 3, but also because in action research the detail is necessary to allow for close scrutiny of the decisions taken in the light of the evidence collected, and thus to allow for ongoing evaluation.

Assessment

This chapter has already identified some of the problems and special issues that arise when doing action research. It is possible for the action researcher to take too many of their own assumptions for granted, and to become either grandiose or too cosy and thus lose the essential evaluative cutting edge of this approach. It can become 'mere cookbook style, recipe following application', according to Kincheloe (1991: 83). Furthermore, as, by definition, intervention (action) takes place as an inherent and immediate part of the research in its 'institutional' context, Sapsford and Abbott (1992: 103) point out, you can never be completely sure exactly what action produced what results. In most institutional settings many variables may be operating. In addition they cite the 'Hawthorne effect' to illustrate further the need to disentangle the research effects. However, in the example of the youth club, it would be reasonable to argue that the increase in the number of girls using the centre could be directly linked with the actions taken to change the practices that had been cited as keeping them away in the first place. Given that the girls were collaborating at every stage, their views underpin the evaluation.

Perhaps a major criticism, raised by Billig (1976), needs highlighting: action research *can* be used to subordinate and defuse debate and conflict between dominant and marginal groups rather than to empower them. However, there is a question to be raised about the concept of empowerment, in that it implies that the group being researched are powerless until empowered. To counter this is crucial. Freire's critical, democratic concept of research, which incorporates those being 'examined' in the formulation, criticism and re-formulation of the research, has to be central if we are to 'transform our idea of research from mere data gathering into a consciousness raising, transformative technique' (Freire 1972: 135).

Useful reading

Courtois, C. (1988). *Healing The Incest Wound*. New York: Norton.
Kincheloe, J. (1991). *Teachers as Researchers: Qualitative Enquiry as a Path to Empowerment*. London: Falmer Press.
Rheinharz, S. (1992). *Feminist Methods in Social Research*. New York: Oxford University Press.
Winter, R. (1989). *Learning from Experience, Principles and Practice in Action-Research*. London: Falmer Press.

References

Bart, P.B. and O'Brien, P. (1985). *Stopping Rape: Successful Survival Strategies*. New York: Pergamon.
Billig, M. (1976). *Social Psychology and Intergroup Relations*. London: Academic Press.
Boston Women's Health Collective (1984). *The New Our Bodies, Ourselves*. New York: Simon and Schuster.
Cohen, L. and Manion, L. (1980). *Research Methods in Education*. London: Croom Helm.
Eisner, E. (1984). 'Can educational research inform educational practice?' *Phi Delta Kappan*, pp. 447–52.
Elliott, J. (1980). 'Action research in schools: some guidelines'. *Classroom Action Research Network Bulletin*, no. 4. Norwich: University of East Anglia.

Frankel, B. (1986). 'Two extremes on the commitment continuum' in Fiske, D. and Scheder, R. *Metatheory in Social Science. Pluralisms and Subjectives.* Chicago: University of Chicago Press.

Freire, P. (1972). *Cultural Action for Freedom.* Harmondsworth: Penguin.

Hanmer, J. and Saunders, S. (1984). *Well Founded Fear: a Community Study of Violence to Women.* London: Hutchinson.

Kelly, A., Whyte, J. and Smail, B. (1984). *Girls into Science and Technology: Final Report.* Manchester: Manchester University.

Kemmis, S. (ed.) (1982). *The Action Research Reader.* Geelong, Victoria: Deakin University Press.

Kincheloe, J. (1991). *Teachers as Researchers: Qualitative Enquiry as a Path to Empowerment.* London: Falmer Press.

Lather, P. (1988). 'Feminist persepectives on empowering research methodologies'. *Women's Studies International Forum,* 11, 569–81.

Lewin, K. (1946). 'Action research and minority problems'. *Journal of Social Issues,* 2, p. 65.

MacKinnon, C. (1979). *Sexual Harassment of Working Women.* New Haven, Conn: Yale University Press.

Milligram, S. (1974). *Obedience to Authority.* London: Tavistock.

Polanyi, M. (1962). *Personal Knowledge.* London: Routledge.

Reinharz, S. (1992). *Feminist Methods in Social Research.* New York: Oxford University Press.

Sapsford, R. and Abbott, P. (1992). *Research Methods for Nurses and the Caring Professions.* Buckingham: Open University Press.

Zamorski, B. (1987). 'A case study of an invisible child'. *Classroom Action Research Network Bulletin,* no. 8. Norwich: University of East Anglia.

8 | FEMINIST RESEARCH

ERICA BURMAN

Discussions about feminist research are currently having a major impact on qualitative approaches to social research (Hammersley 1993), educational research (Burgess 1985) and 'sensitive' research (Renzetti and Lee 1992), as well as elaborating sustained critiques of quantitative methods (Hollway 1989; Mies 1993). The debates over what it is that makes feminist methods 'feminist' and the extent to which these can be seen as 'methods' at all are central to the interventions in the research process and product made by feminist researchers. Following current feminist thinking (e.g. Harding 1987; Abbott and Wallace 1990; Stanley 1990) the starting point for this chapter is that there is no intrinsically feminist method or methodology. Rather, how feminist a piece of research is must be evaluated in relation to its purposes or goals, what it seeks to (and does) achieve. The contribution of this chapter to this collection is therefore not to add a new instrument to the existing toolbox of qualitative methods but to highlight how feminist work develops discussions of power, subjectivity and political commitment in research. Since the debates are continuously developing and informing general discussions, the specificity of the interventions made by feminist researchers is belied by their impact. In this sense, if feminist research may appear to be simply good research then this is testimony to its efficacy, and it is in this spirit that this account is offered here.

Given this perspective, the question of whether men can (or cannot) do feminist research arises both as a reflection of the current resistance against gendering specific methodologies (which includes recognizing that qualitative work also can have its own machismo and imperialism – as the pioneer exploring uncharted territories; Morgan 1981) and as a political issue about crediting and recognizing women's (academic) work (Evans 1990; Kremer 1990). Since the role of men in feminist research is a matter of debate rather than principle (see the editors' introductory comments on this in Harding 1987, and Stanley 1990), this chapter can be read both as addressing the many women researchers in psychology and social science (only a minority of whom may be in a position to define how their research is conducted, analysed and used; see Sharpe and Jefferson 1990), and as addressing men who position themselves either as willing to learn from, or as participating in, debates in feminist research, not least for its clarity in theorizing the politics of research.

Background

In general terms there have been three kinds of feminist critiques, in relation to both research topics and processes. These range from identifying distortions or biases in research (e.g. Eichler 1988), which leads to what Harding calls a 'feminist empiricist' approach, improving or supplementing existing bodies of knowledge. The claim here is that models that ignore or devalue women's perspectives or experiences (as most do) are inadequate within their own terms, and can be corrected – as reflected in titles of courses, programmes or documents that literally add women in, as in 'women and work'. In relation to categories of feminisms in psychology, this is what Corinne Squire (1989) terms 'egalitarian feminism'.

A second strategy, associated with more 'separatist' or essentialist (seeing gender differences as fixed, essential qualities) strands of feminism (what Squire 1989 calls 'cultural feminism'), goes beyond discussing the exclusion of women's experiences from dominant knowledge paradigms to emphasize *how* these experiences are different. The consequences of a focus on difference are reflected in calls for work taking women's experience as primary in its own terms, rather than a resource with which to amend existing models. But the assumption of a unitary female experience has been challenged, in particular by black and lesbian feminists who argue that such a model excludes their experiences and therefore reproduces structures of cultural imperialism and heterosexism within feminist theory (e.g. Amos and Parmar 1984; Wilton 1993).

In addressing these problems, and reflecting debates in social theory on the inadequacy of all unitary grand theories, a third position has emerged, variously called feminist relativism (Abbott and Wallace 1990), feminist postmodernism (Harding 1987), feminist deconstructionism (Opie 1992) or feminist post-structuralism (Weedon 1987; Hollway 1989). These three different positions therefore reflect a tension between developing alternative, women-centred accounts and challenging the dominant models that have attempted to represent and research women's experiences. This tension is currently held together within revisions to Harding's (1987) widely referred to 'feminist standpoint' (see discussion of this in Stanley and Wise 1990, and Henwood 1994), which treats the assertion of difference as a strategic intervention rather than claiming a unitary or stable position for women (or feminists). All three positions can be considered 'transformative' (Harding 1987) towards the feminist project of creating an oppression-free world.

Feminist critiques of research attend to both the forms by which research is produced and the relationships in which it is produced (Graham 1983). The critique of form echoes that rehearsed elsewhere in this book, with quantitative research accused of mangling (women's) experience (whether through experiments or questionnaires) into preconceived (male-oriented) categories and presenting this as objective truth. In terms of research relations, in her influential analysis of social science interviewing and survey relations, Ann Oakley (1981) showed how the presence of the researcher is theorized only as an extension of the research instrument, and the social features of the interview are treated as manipulable variables to facilitate the research process, specifically interviewee disclosure. When the interviewing relationship becomes merely the 'rapport' that lubricates the research, this sanitizes and dehumanizes the research encounter. Instead, Oakley discusses the friendships that emerged from her more egalitarian interviews with women. While subsequent feminist accounts have warned against a romanticization of research by women with women, and corresponding suppression of structural power relations between women – of, for, example class, race or age as well as interviewer/interviewee (e.g. Finch 1984; Ribbens 1989; Phoenix 1990) – this reflects the consistent focus on the politics of research. The common basis for such feminist commentaries on research processes is to reject the traditional oppositions structuring research, between theory and method, and theory and practice. Rather, within a feminist framework, these oppositions are seen as necessarily and inevitably intertwined, united through the connections between the purposes, conduct and outcome of the research.

Feminist research, then, is a 'praxis' (Stanley 1990), a theory that connects experience and action. What makes feminist research 'feminist' is a challenge to the scientism that refuses to address the relations between knowledge (and knowledge-generating practices) and power, and a corresponding attention to reflexive issues in the form of theorizing and transforming the process of academic production, including the position and responsibilities of the researcher. In this sense Sandra Harding's (1987) distinction between method, methodology and epistemology is useful. She argues that there can be no feminist method, since a method merely specifies a technique or set of research practices which (although perhaps currently performed in anti-feminist ways) is not in principle antithetical to feminist work. Hence (warding off the equation of feminist with qualitative research as both a measure of the success of feminist critiques and in danger of reifying them) a current theme of feminist research also concerns the value of quantitative work, and the relations between method and politics (Pugh 1990; Epstein Jaratne and Stewart 1991; Kelly *et al.* 1992). Similar arguments apply to the use of particular methodologies (as perspectives or theoretically informed frameworks), which do not in themselves specify a particular method. Rather, what identifies feminist research is a commitment to a specific, feminist, epistemology; that is, a theoretical and political analysis that critiques dominant conceptions of knowledge, and poses questions about the gendered orientation of, and criteria for, knowledge. It is this assertion of the connection between being and knowing, between ontology and epistemology, that defines feminist research (Harding 1987; Stanley 1990).

Despite variations in versions, feminist methodological interventions focus on experience, in terms of whose experience is represented and validated within research; on reflexivity, as a critique of objectivity, which itself is seen as a particular (culturally masculine) kind of subjectivity (Hollway 1989); and on the conscious use of a critical, or 'strong', subjectivity (Harding 1987), as a reflexive clarity about the conditions of production of the research (Stanley 1990). These ontological or experiential concerns link up with the project to highlight oppressive power relations within social practices generally, and as also expressed within research practices. Or, in Janice Raymond's (1986) terms, feminist research is 'passionate inquiry', committed to challenging and, where appropriate (in the sense that it may not be desirable to empower further interviewees from already dominant or oppressive groups), mitigating power relations within and outside research contexts. What marks feminist notions of reflexivity and researcher accountability out from ethnographic or discourse analytic notions is that whereas the latter sometimes portray reflexivity as central to making public the routes and resources that lie behind an analysis (e.g. Potter 1988; Hammersley 1992), feminist researchers see their work as accountable not only in terms of clarity or confession but also in relation to broader emancipatory and transformative goals, and current discussions are preoccupied with what this means in practice (e.g. Wise 1987; Wilkinson 1988).

Example

It is impossible to present an examplar of feminist research, given its status as an arena of continuous debate rather than a specific technology. What is presented here is an account of a piece of feminist research, that is research informed by a feminist politics at the level of theory and practice. Consistent with the commitment to reflexivity within feminist research, my account of this account must also come in for some scrutiny. The research summarized here was conducted by Catherine Bewley as the empirical work for an MSc in Occupational Psychology, and I am grateful to her for allowing me to treat her work as the focus for this chapter, and for the reflections and discussions that doing this has prompted. The study aimed to explore the organizational functioning of three feminist organizations within one municipality: a women's centre, a service for women experiencing domestic violence, which included a safe house, and a counselling service for women who had suffered sexual assault.

I am taking this research as illustrative of some key aspects and questions posed by and within feminist research processes. In terms of its topic, it highlights a key absence within the psychological literature. Research on organizations tends to focus on industrial work contexts with a differentiated hierarchical structure that fails to engage with the ways small voluntary organizations and feminist organizations function. The theories assume a division between public and private and work and home, in both the form and relations of work, that reflects male experience and highlights the cultural masculinity of organizational theory. Feminist, like other small voluntary, organizations tend to have little formal hierarchy, few role divisions and less separation between the work task and relationships. These qualities often arise from a commitment to collective work. The failure of the literature to address these different organizational forms can be regarded as a symptom of the hetero-reality and masculinity of current theories, which define women's experiences only in relation to men (Raymond 1986).

Four issues are raised by the topic of study, work in women-only organizations. First, it challenges the dominant assumptions structuring psychological models by demonstrating them to be incomplete (feminist empiricist). Second, by taking women's experiences as central, the research works towards developing an alternative account that both highlights and interrogates the differences that emerge for their consequences for the positions of women, both in psychology and in feminist organizations. This is feminist standpoint research. Third, it extends and engages with current issues in feminist politics and theory by critiquing the notion of a universalized, global sisterhood: instead of assuming alliances between women workers and the women they work with and for, there is a focus on how relationships form and function, and what makes them more or less successful. Bewley refuses essentialist, separatist feminist frameworks as unhelpful, and draws on Raymond's (1986) work on female friendship to analyse women's working relationships in terms of histories of networks and alliances rather than as arising from some mystical or unconditional notion of sisterhood. As well as addressing feminist preoccupations, then, Bewley portrays the engagement of feminist and psychological theory as mutual rather than one-way, claiming not only that organizational theory has something to learn from the functioning of women's organizations, but also that the latter could benefit from an organizational analysis. Fourth, as will be elaborated below, the study challenges existing structures of research relations and forms of production, in terms of researcher involvement, theory generation, definitions of what makes good research and personal vulnerability and risk.

The study

The study was based on the analysis of interviews, observations and documents from each organization, and notes Bewley took after her visits. The stages or cycles of the research process moved from gaining an initial picture through these to exploring themes and writing up, and at each stage the analysis generated was discussed with the participants in the organizations – with this discussion informing the following stages of analysis and reflection. The individual interviews focused on the topics of the past, present and future of the organization, its values, atmosphere and ethos, its purpose and mode of functioning, the working environment, composition of workers, participants' experience there, who used the organization and its facilities, issues of conflict and change in the organization, and the participant's views on women's positions in society (Bewley 1993: 55). Hence the study was organized around feminist principles of consultation about the research questions, reciprocity within the process of generating the accounts and analysis, and accountability over the emerging issues. The analysis was developed by a process of feedback and revision, through asking participants whether they considered the representation offered to be accurate in content and tone, and if they shared the researcher's perception of what the main issues for the organization were (Bewley 1993: 57). This culminated in the presentation and discussion of individual confidential written reports to each organization, and included supporting them in reflecting on the implications of the analysis. For Bewley, the feminist commitment to reciprocity in research, where she both gave and gained from the study, involved working with one of the organizations for eight months after the end of the study to work through the issues it raised. Here there is a particular attention to gender issues arising from a common feminist commitment, but this study reflects the general principles of action research (see also Chapter 7).

Analysis

Bewley's account of the analysis is of a multilayered cycle of reflection and digestion from which emerged a picture of each organization. This process involved:

- reading, listening to and thinking about each piece of information many times over until I knew it inside out;
- uncovering patterns by considering the information from different perspectives;
- using large sheets of paper and coloured pens to draw spider diagrams of the points that came out of the information;
- going through the information with a list of key ideas, after an initial picture had been developed, noting down any piece of information that supported (or contradicted) that idea;
- looking for events, particular uses of language, stories, metaphors and feelings;
- considering the processes which led to the production of the piece of information (say during an interview or in a meeting);
- reflecting on my experience with the organization, whether my impression about it had changed and if so, why (Bewley 1993: 56).

While my account here focuses on research *process* rather than topic, it is relevant to summarize the structure and outcome of the analysis to convey what can emerge from the feminist orientation of this research. Using the general features identified as central defining qualities of organizations (Schein 1985, 1990), as well as relevant to feminist groups, Bewley's analysis focused on the following issues: structure (how this was perceived by the participants and researcher – what, if any, kinds of role divisions, management structure, the patterns and flow of the work day); communication and information processing (decision-making structures, regularity of meetings and who attends them, access to records, how people find out about what's going on and how democratic this is); environment (appearance, accessibility, how well resourced this was and how conducive to successful organizational and worker functioning, relations with external organizations); effectiveness (to the extent perceived by the organization, and why, whether considered in terms of personal development, success rates or mere survival); power and politics (formal versus informal forms of power, power used positively and negatively, the value accorded to expertise, confidence and time spent within the organization).

As a result of building up this picture of each organization separately, Bewley could also analyse common and diverging characteristics of each feminist organization. Given the different focus of the services and varying levels of financial security, each exhibited a different profile of strengths and weaknesses, achievements and problems (Bewley 1993: 85–7). Nevertheless, some similarities of structure were discernable, with high levels of member participation, few role divisions, high levels of trust and cooperation, and commitment to collective forms of work. The structures on which the organizations were based all relied heavily on personal networks that were used to organize the work, and that also characterized the supportive relations between the organizations. This was in part related to the sharing of a feminist perspective within an often hostile or indifferent broader context, and a clarity and commonality of aims, perspective and commitment. Despite a common preoccupation with issues of structure, communication, resources and development (in initiating and responding to change), the organizations demonstrated differences in their fluidity of organizational boundaries, differential demands made of workers and corresponding ability to cope with stress, differences in ability to take positive action over which women used and worked within the organization (particularly in relation to the involvement of black and disabled women) and different accounts of the role of political commitment within the work. Each organization was also linked to other organizations serving similar purposes in other cities, from which it gained a particular organizational history and identity (Bewley 1993: 87–9).

From a piece of research exploring the mutual engagement of feminist and psychological questions, two sets of conclusions emerged: one set about characteristics of the feminist organizations studied and another about the adequacy of the psychological theories (Bewley 1993: 125–7). In terms of the organizations, the clear feminist commitment gave each purpose and direction that was consciously expressed by those within it and reflected in what they did. The form of collective structure highlighted the uneasy balance between a feminist commitment to equality and a pragmatic engagement with external demands and processes. Hence the tensions or contradictions of feminist practice were crucially played out through organizational structures and roles. In terms of the role of personal networks, these 'are the arteries along which the blood of the organizations flow' (p. 126). They worked best when based on prior or current friendship; but, as Bewley points out, owing to their informality some members could be inadequately supported, and these were precisely those most likely to leave. Power resided in skills, control over information flow (and position in the networks), confidence and ability to support others, with a high sense of achievement gained from the feminist commitment, the work with women and the changes they were able to effect. Taking these points seriously would transform our appreciation and assessment of male models of work.

In terms of its adequacy, psychological theory appears to have little to say about organizational structures such as these, which are oriented around a feminist commitment. As well as reflecting an implicit androcentrism and hetero-reality, then, such theories fail to acknowledge the gender and sexual politics of organizational culture and are thus complicit in maintaining them (Bewley 1993: 126). Moreover, the conception of power on offer fails to address adequately its sources and nature within such organizations. In this sense, while analyses of power are vital to the study of feminist organizations, they can also inform analyses of power relations in organizational cultures generally.

The study therefore poses new questions for both feminist and psychological research, including: the role of friendship within organizational structures; strategies deployed in, and political analyses of, the process of managing engagement with outside (non or anti-feminist) structures (local authorities, police, social services) without recuperation; exploration of definitions of collectivity (since these have been little studied and vary enormously); the perception and exercise of power relations – how these are used positively and destructively, and how this relates to the position of each organization externally; and the variety of views held about these issues by members of each organization, as part of building up a more complete view of its functioning.

Reflexive analysis

Now that some of the key themes of the analysis have been outlined we can step back to focus on the production of this account. I have identified nine key issues here.

Impact on organization studied
Conducting a study like this clearly highlights how research affects what it studies. This was explicitly addressed within Bewley's research process through consultation and feedback over each stage of the project's development. The organizations themselves felt they recognized the issues posed in the analysis, as in one participant's reponse of 'It feels like someone has taken the ceiling off the room and is looking down at us' (Bewley 1993: 90). Hence the research functioned to validate participants' perceptions of how their organization functioned. Yet this comment also betrays a sense of vulnerability, which was well-founded given the hostile broader contexts in which such organizations exist. Clearly the sense of threat, scrutiny and evaluation hinted at here needed to be handled carefully and responsibly. This was especially so where critical issues were identified for one organization around staff illness and stress and inadequate communication

structures. But far from criticism being visited upon the organization from on high, and leaving them high and dry, the organization used a flare-up caused by the feedback from the study to make changes, and as a result of her report to them Bewley facilitated discussions to support the organization in working through its consequences to improve the service. While the study therefore had a significant impact on the organizations, this arose partly because the research functioned to lend clarity and credibility to issues that some participants already recognized. This highlights how researchers of organizations enter and participate in pre-existing structures and agendas, rather than function entirely outside them: the issue for the researcher is to identify the agendas and how they are being invited to be positioned in them. To deny this would still be to adopt a stance, most likely the standpoint of the management or public face of the organization (see Chapter 7, on action research). Feminist researchers, in a commitment to non-exploitative approaches, assume a greater responsibility for their interpretations and analyses, in terms of rendering them accessible and, where possible, practicable.

Necessity for researcher subjectivity

This reproduces some of the issues raised by the general discussion of feminist research. Both researcher and participants in the organizations shared an ontology, a theory of being and experience. It would not have been possible to conduct this research without being feminist, not only in the instrumental and exploitative sense of 'gaining access', but also in terms of understanding and analysing the implicit rules of the cultures of these organizations. Moreover, Bewley was not an outsider. As she makes clear in her account, she had previously worked in one of the organizations, and therefore (through the connections between them) also had some, if limited, acquaintance with the others. Like the members of the organizations, then, she was involved in the networks and friendships that structured so much of each organization's functioning. Adopting the position of detached observer would have been disingenuous in relation to the production of the material for analysis, as well as alienating to the research participants. In addition, rather than being seen as a limitation, this involvement illustrates how and why there is so little research on this topic – since some connections are required to ensure that the exposure and vulnerability that such work opens the organization to will not be abused. But a part of the topic (friendship networks) was not only a presupposition of the conduct of the research, it was also an essential resource for its analysis. Making these positions clear within the account, as Bewley does, is an example of the value of strong subjectivity in research, and reflexive clarity about the conditions of production of material, as well as a reiteration of the relation between ontology (being) and epistemology (knowing) in feminist research.

Significance of writing up
This study makes a feminist intervention in terms of both its topic and its form. Bewley uses her personal experience to inform her analysis and draws on diary material to document issues and difficulties within the research process. She discusses a key dilemma facing feminist academics seeking to make women's experiences and issues visible: how to communicate in terms that engage with and intervene in academic genres without fragmenting, objectifying or disempowering women's experiences. This includes complex questions about the nature of particular audiences and interventions, and in particular decisions about the consequences of publically criticizing a vulnerable organization (see also Poland 1990). In this context, a further measure to aid the evaluation of the research is not only being clear about the research process and the position (in terms of history and stance) of the researcher, but also drawing attention to the work of producing the written account, or what Stanley and Wise (1990: 23) describe as 'the intellectual biography of the researcher', which necessarily involves 'the complex question of power in research and writing'. This includes disrupting the pretence maintained within most research reports that they are seamless coherent texts produced within one moment by a disembodied and disinterested author. In Bewley's case, the different stages of revision of the text (discussed below) were marked by different typefaces. While in part this had a practical basis (owing to changes in word processors), this itself indicated a change in institutional location over time, and also marks for the reader key editorial breaks that were a site of struggle and resistance in the historical production of the report.

Emotion as a research resource
Personal involvement has its difficulties as well as rewards. Studying an organization and sharing its values can mean taking on some of the issues the organization works on or expresses at a deeper emotional level. The organizations that formed the basis of this study had to deal with situations of crisis and major distress. During the conduct of the study the functioning of one of the organizations was thrown into major disarray by the murder of a woman seeking refuge in the safe house. Bewley discusses how the process of analysis was punctuated by her own reactions, as she reports from the following diary entry:

> Time and time again I sit at my desk looking at the transcriber and not having the courage to put in the tape, slot in the headphones, switch it on ... My dreams are glimpses of what's going on, little puffs of vapour that rise and escape steaming out of the mind's eye ... Is all this just me? Am I picking up and crystallising the pain in the organisations? What lessons are there for doing this sort of research?
> (Bewley 1993: 95)

A clear implication of this is that in engaging in work that offers or derives from personal involvement, researchers need to reflect on the support structure they can call upon and the personal impact for them of the issues they are addressing. In particular there is a clear case here for the need for supervision as well as personal support, since a researcher should not be working in isolation. But what this also highlights is a further range of interpretive issues. For, reversing the conventional way in which this issue arises, where the involvement is less intense, what does it mean for the process and product if a researcher feels *dis*engaged from the topic or process of study? While this is the affective state usually assumed within research processes, it itself speaks of the power of the researcher and the ways in which the project of producing knowledge and truth suppresses the labour and positions of the persons producing it.

Challenge to the public–private boundary
This occurred in four ways: first, in terms of topic, it challenged culturally male models of work in that a common feature of the organizations studied was that the pattern of work did not conform to the conventionally assumed structure of work–break divisions; second, in terms of method, through the relation asserted between personal politics and academic research in bringing a political commitment into the research project and process; third, in the commitment to respect women and not alienate them by researcher expertise, as expressed either in the conduct of interviews or in the representation of women's experiences in written reports; fourth, as a feminist researching with other feminists, studying friends or political allies makes manifest the responsibilities such work incurs, as well as generating what could be quite well-founded fears of disappointing them (and fears of the personal consequences of this).

Reflexivity again
Corresponding issues of reflexivity and researcher involvement arise in relation to my selection of this study for presentation here. There is an unwritten history of this study, which is a reflection of feminist struggle within academic institutions. As already discussed, the research is an intervention at the level of topic and, in relation to the genres of occupational psychological research, method. The study resonated with my experience of working in collective and voluntary organizations (feminist and mixed), which made it of immediate interest to me, and posed in a very clear way the issues faced by women attempting to work together across and within institutions, as is also the case for women's studies within academia (Coulson and Bhavnani 1990). Moreover, the questions of organizational functioning and researcher accountability that formed the topic of the study were also centrally replayed in its academic trajectory.

The particular history of the study demonstrates how psychology puts obstacles in the way of feminist research that can efface the contributions of feminist researchers to the discipline. In particular, it illustrates the normative regulation that lies behind the overt imperative for research to be original contributions to knowledge, since, as in Bewley's case, work that has no academic precedent is deemed improper research: what is truly new and theoretically challenging is literally not recognized. There has been no prior published research applying organizational theory to feminist organizations, so there was no immediate lineage or context in which this thesis could take refuge. To create a space for a new organizational analysis of feminist organizations, the study had to mark out a territory which did not exist, being critical of existing theory, but, because of the absence of alternative published psychological research, being unable to support this criticism with specific organizational theory (although theoretical support for the research was found in feminist theory from other disciplines). The thesis was only permitted to pass after three formal submissions with substantial revisions between them. It was specifically challenged on its use of current organizational theory, reflecting the tensions many feminists experience between the need to do research within an existing, if limiting and inappropriate, theoretical framework so that their work receives recognition, and the need to find new (feminist) frameworks for research theory, process and accounts which might not exist within current psychology – precisely because they are not acceptable and are therefore silenced.

This tension – between recognition and failure, persistence and compromise – which is illustrated by the experience of this particular study, demonstrates how disciplinary gatekeeping maintains academic structures so that they continually reproduce themselves as the same, and marginalize or reject any challenge (Spender 1981) so that feminist researchers leave psychology for more friendly disciplinary territories to do their work (Sharpe and Jefferson 1990). It also raises a question about the appropriate assessment criteria for research which cannot emerge through the dominant methodologies. The institutional resistance to, and suppression of, work that disturbs dominant psychological frameworks prevents, in some sort of vicious circle, the development of the very body of published research that would provide the methodological and theoretical basis for such work (see also Kitzinger 1990).

In terms of my investments in discussing this study, the struggle to get it recognized as a legitimate piece of research mirrors my frustration with psychological theory and research, and reflects general struggles of feminists within academia, particularly in relation to the ways feminists prioritize structures of accountability that lie outside the academy. Ironically, feminist researchers are castigated as doing improper research precisely because of their engagement in doing the 'relevant' research psychologists are otherwise continually called upon to do. This also highlights a further feature of feminist research: that I, as researcher, as writer, am not detached; that I share an ontology, a politics, with that of the study I have described, and that in writing about it I am attempting not merely to describe but also to intervene. This is reflected in the way that this chapter sits uneasily within this book, as not quite either research method or research critique, but perhaps both.

What is gained by my documenting this? In immediate terms the research now has some public recognition, including recognition of the struggle and resistance that structured its production. More generally, this story extends the analysis of the power of the academy, and challenges its practice. Moreover, this struggle has had its own productivity: in the course of Bewley having to respond to and resist the possibility of the exclusion of her research through failure or through its being changed beyond recognition in order to pass, it has probably now achieved a greater hearing and impact than if it had been passed and allowed to sink into obscurity. In a particular resonance between Bewley's topic and the process she found herself enagaged in, this struggle demonstrates the value of feminist networks, as used by women in psychology to counter their isolation and silencing (since Bewley first contacted me through feminist psychology networks).

Power relations in research

Just as power was a topic of the research, so it was also a feature of the process. As the researcher, Bewley tried to set up the study in as consultative and participative a way as possible, but her anxieties over the impact of the work on the organizations and her relationships within its networks reflect the power both she and they exercised within the study. Not only were there responsibilities to address and redress inequalities within the traditional researcher–researched relations of interviews, there were also issues about not wanting to expose the women and organizations to criticisms from unsympathetic outside audiences. Hence the provision of confidential reports to each organization may have done much to ensure that all parties gained from the research, as well as raising again the political questions of audience and accountability. Parallel issues are raised by the use I have made of this research to exemplify key features of feminist research. As in Bewley's own research, the account of her work presented here is an outcome of joint discussions. There is an equivalent issue in relation to dilemmas of exposure to unsympathetic audiences raised in her research. I have not brought out some of the critical issues Bewley raises of the limitations and absences in her study. While critical evaluation is necessary, the issue of the particular audience of this chapter has been salient in my account.

Risk or compromise?

At each point in the process of revision and resubmission, Bewley was struggling with decisions about whether, as some of Bewley's friends encouraged her, to 'write it to pass' or whether doing this would so compromise the research that it would lose its value or meaning – both personally and in terms of its theoretical coherence. In negotiating a path between struggle, strategy, compromise and deradicalization, the choices were between personal integrity and (the risk of) failure. This reflects three preoccupations of feminist researchers: first, taking a principled position on the role of politics in research; second, how the write-up is as much part of the research as the study itself, thus challenging the scientist division in psychology between research and report; third, the role of other people's investments in the research. Apart from the general academic, personal and career investments that were severely exercised over this, Bewley felt some pressure from other (feminist) researchers who wanted to see her thesis passed to lend credibility to this style of work, but this would have been self-defeating had the changes been too great. The fact that the term 'compromise' carries the longest entry in the index of *Feminists and Psychological Practice* (Burman 1990) suggests that these are general questions for feminists in psychology.

Accountability

Feminist researchers claim to do different and better research because it is accountable, and accountability has been a major theme running through this chapter. However, what accountability means is not well elaborated, and in part this is because what accountability means varies according to the topic and approach in question. However, some general points can be made. Typically, the structure of accountability for research is to the funding body – this might be direct or mediated through departmental and disciplinary structures (with more indirect effects in shaping the censorship and self-censorship involved in determining what research gets funded). While it would be unrealistic to suggest that feminist researchers are not as subject to this as any others, like other politicized researchers, there are other structures they look to for recognition. In Bewley's study she made herself accountable to the participants, in terms of the conduct and outcome of the research. This was driven by their and her common feminist commitment, which brought into play accountability not only to specific organizations but also to a broader framework of feminist campaigns and networks. As noted above, these feminist networks, inside and outside academic structures, both were a source of support and incurred their own expectations and responsibilities. In other cases, especially where there is less or no political resonance between participants, the organizations and the researcher, feminist researchers position themselves as accountable to other feminists within their discipline, or within women's studies. But in order to stave off the dynamic of deradicalization to which all feminists in mainstream institutional positions are subject, these structures need to be connected to feminist campaigns and movements outside academia. In some cases this is set up in quite direct ways, through consultation with women's campaigns and services about research questions, processes and products.

Assessment

This chapter has illustrated general issues about the conduct, interpretation and reception of feminist research through the account of a specific study. The study addresses an under-researched topic, which is relevant to both psychology and feminism. It therefore extends mainstream (malestream) organizational theory to address non-hierarchical structures outside traditional management models, and challenges traditional views of research relations and reports. The study also presents questions for feminist politics; particularly on the dilemmas of maintaining a feminist culture or practice while functioning in a context which is often hostile to its aims and processes, and the consequences of implicit power structures. The study promoted change within the organizations studied through validating the experience of the women members and through contextualizing their work within the framework of other feminist organizations (that is, those sharing some similar visions). Direct consequences of the research included revision and improvement to the support and training of workers, as well as promotion of the discussion of communication structures.

In its form and function, the study exhibits features of a feminist empiricist position in extending psychological theory, and a feminist standpoint position in challenging psychology to engage with new forms of structure, including thesis forms and methods. Both features can be seen as strategic interventions. Strategies, as Elizabeth Gross points out, are not ends in themselves, and while transformative, they are, by virtue of their capacity to engage with them, inevitably collusive of the structures they seek to change. As highlighted by the discussion of strategy and compromise, feminist theory and research is no purist or separatist practice but a form of 'intellectual guerilla warfare' which 'needs to use whatever means are available, whether these are "patriarchal" or not' (Gross 1992: 64).

This status of feminist research as relational, as strategic intervention rather than as separate model, disarms some of the possible limits to this approach. The first of these is its specificity. It could be argued that the work discussed here related only to the particular organizations studied, and to a particular time and place. This criticism, however, restates what is a general issue concerning feminist researchers' claims to knowledge as local reflections relevant to particular moments, as a critique of a model of knowledge as objective, disinterested, timeless truth. The fact that there is no intrinsically feminist methodology, and that feminist research is dependent on, and arises from, a feminist ontology, means that what constitutes a feminist intervention will necessarily shift and change according to time and place. So, for example, in addition to the reappraisal of the value of quantitative methods (discussed earlier), there is a current shift from researching women's experience in order to ward off a focus on women as confirming their victim status, and a turn instead to researching men and masculinity (Scott 1985). Thus feminist research is not merely research by women with women and about women. In fact this shift also reflects a more widespread move away from asserting the commonality of women's experience to theorizing the differences between women as power relations, with implications for whether and how women identify with and build alliances with each other, and with men (e.g. Yuval-Davis 1993; Burman 1994).

The specificity problem applies to the status of feminist research in another way. The approach can look, and in many ways is, derivative of other models – in fact Bewley (1993) justified her study in terms of new paradigm and organizational culture methodologies as well as feminist research. But in order to envisage change, feminist research has to engage with existing structures to transform them: what marks feminist approaches out and unites them is an explicit political commitment. This poses a dilemma for feminist researchers: although reference to or drawing upon other models may be accurate, and may well be safer (in terms of gaining access to a favourable reception from academic structures), there is a danger of colluding with traditional research structures if they fail to document the personal political resources informing research.

Given its strategic status, feminist research is vulnerable to appropriation to conventional research approaches. The examples above highlight the ease with which a naturalistic rhetoric can creep into research reports (of gathering data like ripe corn, or uncovering pre-existing phenomena) that ignores the researcher's role in production of material. In particular, the widespread practice of employing women to conduct interviews reflects how the greater disclosure often made by women to women can extend the scope for women's exploitation (Finch 1984). Jane Ribbens (1989) has critiqued Oakley's (1981) romanticization of woman-to-woman research, and in general there is need to attend to the multiple ways power relations between women enter into research (Edwards 1990; Phoenix 1990).

The problems of continuity can also be countered by recalling that, since feminist research is more an arena for debate than a specific methodology, critique is central to the approach. Notwithstanding similarities with ethnographic and new paradigm approaches, its specific features include a sustained focus on power, on the production and use of knowledge and on problematizing who has the power to define the interpretation (the researcher, the university, the funding body, the researched, the academic community of feminist researchers, women's groups and campaigns?). For example, the earlier model of research as empowerment through the documentation of devalued perspectives is now regarded as both theoretically naive and inadequate in its presumption that research (feminist or otherwise) can uncover some already formed authentic (female) experience. Not only does this ignore how the material that forms the basis for the analysis is always an account constructed for public consumption (Ribbens 1989), it is also patronizing in presuming that the researcher has the means or that the researched necessarily accord the researcher the power to define how they benefit from the research. Moreover, as Kum-Kum Bhavnani (1990) notes, silences can be at least as empowering (and eloquent) as speech in interviews.

These debates draw attention to the ways experience is produced through research practices rather than uncovered by them. This reflects the focus of feminist discussions which have shifted away from a notion of identity as fixed, stable and unitary to one 'as process, as performance and as provisional' (Bondi 1993: 95), as a rhetorical position of identifications guiding actions rather than a statement about personal essences (Yuval-Davis 1993). The process of interpretation should not be generated from on high, but rather should be the joint production of co-researchers. Nevertheless, interpretations can be offered, but with an understanding of them as provisional and specifically directed: therefore the multiplicity of available interpretations can be fixed for particular contexts and purposes of feminist research (including by the power of the researcher in defining 'outcomes' of research). The debate on whether there can be a feminist science (cf. Harding 1986; Haraway 1991), or what constitutes feminist methodology, therefore not only touches on the question of how feminist interventions relate to existing bodies of knowledge but also centrally recapitulates discussions of how women can create ways of organizing together to challenge and transform relations of oppression.

Useful reading

Finch, J. (1984). ' "It's great to have someone to talk to": the ethics and politics of interviewing women', in C. Bell and H. Roberts (eds) *Social Researching: Politics, Problems, Practice*. London; Routledge and Kegan Paul.

Hollway, W. (1989). *Subjectivity and Method in Psychology: Gender, Meaning and Science*. London: Sage.

Kitzinger, C. (1990). 'Resisting the discipline', in E. Burman (ed.) *Feminists and Psychological Practice*. London: Sage.

Oakley, A. (1981). 'Interviewing women: a contradiction in terms?', in H. Roberts (ed.) *Doing Feminist Research*. London: Routledge and Kegan Paul.

Phoenix, A. (1990). 'Social research in the context of feminist psychology', in E. Burman (ed.) *Feminists and Psychological Practice*. London: Sage.

Ribbens, J. (1989). 'Interviewing: an unnatural situation?', *Women's Studies International Forum*, 12(6), 579–92.

Scott, S. (1985). 'Feminist research and qualitative research: a discussion of some of the issues', in B. Burgess (ed.) *Issues in Educational Research*. Lewes: Falmer Press.

Stanley, L. (ed.) (1990). *Feminist Praxis*. London: Routledge.

References

Abbott, P. and Wallace, C. (1990). 'The production of feminist knowledge'. *An Introduction to Sociology: Feminist Perspectives*. London: Routledge.

Amos, V. and Parmar, P. (1984). 'Challenging imperial feminism'. *Feminist Review*, 17(3), 3–19.

Bewley, C. (1993). 'Creating a space: for a feminist discussion of psychological theory and research into women's organisations in the voluntary sector and a case study of three such organisations'. Unpublished thesis, University of Sheffield.

Bhavnani, K.K. (1990). 'What's power got to do with it? Empowerment and social research', in I. Parker and J. Shotter (eds) *Deconstructing Social Psychology*. London: Routledge.

Bondi, L. (1993). 'Locating identity politics', in M. Keith and S. Pole (eds) *Place and the Politics of Identity*. London: Routledge.

Burman, E. (ed.) (1990). *Feminists and Psychological Practice*. London: Sage.

Burman, E. (1994). 'Identities, experience and alliances: Jewish feminism and feminist psychology'. *Feminism and Psychology*, 4(1), 155–78.

Burgess, B. (ed.) (1985). *Issues in Educational Research*. Lewes: Falmer Press.

Coulson, M. and Bhavnani, K. (1990). 'Making a difference: questioning women's studies', in E. Burman (ed.) *Feminists and Psychological Practice*. London: Sage.

Edwards, R. (1990). 'Connecting method and epistemology: a white woman interviewing black women'. *Women's Studies International Forum*, 13(5), 477–90.

Eichler, M. (1988). *Non-sexist Research Methods: a Practical Guide*. London: Allen and Unwin.

Epstein Jaratne, T. and Stewart, A. (1991). 'Quantitative and qualitative methods in the social sciences: current feminist issues and practical strategies', in M. Fonow and J. Cook (eds) *Beyond Methodology: Feminist Scholarship as Lived Research*. Bloomington and Indianapolis: Indiana University Press.

Evans, M. (1990). 'The problem of gender for women's studies'. *Women's Studies International Forum*, 13(5), 457–62.

Finch, J. (1984). '"It's great to have someone to talk to": the ethics and politics of interviewing women', in C. Bell and H. Roberts (eds) *Social Researching: Politics, Problems, Practice*. London: Routledge and Kegan Paul.

Graham, H. (1983). 'Do her answers fit his questions: women and the survey method', in E. Garmarnikow, D. Morgan, J. Purvis and D. Taylorson (eds) *The Public and the Private*. London: Heinemann.

Gross, E. (1992). 'What is feminist theory?', in H. Crowley and S. Himmelweit (eds) *Knowing Women: Feminism and Knowledge*. Cambridge: Polity Press.

Hammersley, M. (1992). 'On feminist methodology'. *Sociology*, 26, 187–206.

Hammersley, M. (ed.) (1993). *Social Research: Philosophy, Politics and Practice*. London: Sage.

Haraway, D. (1991). 'The science question in feminism and the privilege of partial perspective', in *Simians, Cyborgs and Women*. London: Verso.

Harding, S. (1986). *The Science Question in Feminism*. Milton Keynes: Open University Press.

Harding, S. (ed.) (1987). *Feminism and Methodology*. Milton Keynes: Open University Press.

Henwood, K. (1994). 'Seeing through women's eyes: qualitative methods and feminist research?' *Feminism and Psychology*, in press.

Hollway, W. (1989). *Subjectivity and Method in Psychology: Gender, Meaning and Science*. London: Sage.

Kelly, L., Regan, L. and Burton, S. (1992). 'Defending the indefensible? Quantitative methods and feminist research', in H. Hinds, A. Phoenix and J. Stacey (eds) *Working Out: New Directions for Women's Studies*. Basingstoke: Falmer Press.

Kitzinger, C. (1990). 'Resisting the discipline', in E. Burman (ed.) *Feminists and Psychological Practice*. London: Sage.

Kremer, B. (1990). 'Learning to say no: keeping feminist research for ourselves'. *Women's Studies International Forum*, 13(5), 463–7.

Mies, M. (1993). 'Towards a methodology for feminist research', in M. Hammersley (ed.) *Social Research*. London: Sage.

Morgan, D. (1981). 'Men, masculinity and the process of sociological enquiry', in H. Roberts (ed.) *Doing Feminist Research*. London: Routledge and Kegan Paul.

Oakley, A. (1981). 'Interviewing women: a contradiction in terms?' in H. Roberts (ed.) *Doing Feminist Research*. London: Routledge and Kegan Paul.

Opie, A. (1992). 'Qualitative research, appropriation of the "other" and empowerment'. *Feminist Review*, 40, 52–69.

Phoenix, A. (1990). 'Social research in the context of feminist psychology', in E. Burman (ed.) *Feminists and Psychological Practice*. London: Sage.

Poland, F. (1990). 'The history of a "failed" research topic: the case of the childminders', in L. Stanley (ed.) *Feminist Praxis*. London: Routledge.

Potter, J. (1988). 'What is reflexive about discourse analysis? The case of reading readings', in S. Woolgar (ed.) *Knowledge and Reflexivity: New Frontiers in the Sociology of Knowledge*. London: Sage.

Pugh, A. (1990). 'My statistics and feminism: a true story', in L. Stanley (ed.) *Feminist Praxis*. London: Routledge.

Raymond, J. (1986). *A Passion for Friends: towards a Philosophy of Female Affection*. London: Women's Press.

Renzetti, C. and Lee, R. (eds) (1993). *Researching Sensitive Topics*. Newbury Park: Sage.

Ribbens, J. (1989). 'Interviewing: an unnatural situation?' *Women's Studies International Forum*, **12**(6), 579–92.

Schein, E. (1985). *Organizational Culture and Leadership*. Oxford: Jossey-Bass.

Schein, E. (1990). 'Organizational culture'. *American Psychology*, **45**(2), 109–19.

Scott, S. (1985). 'Feminist research and qualitative research: a discussion of some of the issues', in B. Burgess (ed.) *Issues in Educational Research*. Lewes: Falmer Press.

Sharpe, S. and Jefferson, J. (1990). 'Moving out of psychology: two accounts', in E. Burman (ed.) *Feminists and Psychological Practice*. London: Sage.

Spender, D. (1981). 'The gatekeepers: a feminist critique of academic publishing', in H. Roberts (ed.) *Doing Feminist Research*. London: Routledge and Kegan Paul.

Squire, C. (1989). *Significant Differences: Feminism in Psychology*. London: Routledge.

Stanley, L. (ed.) (1990). *Feminist Praxis*. London: Routledge.

Stanley, L. and Wise, S. (1990). 'Method, methodology and epistemology in feminist research', in L. Stanley (ed.) *Feminist Praxis*. London: Routledge.

Weedon, C. (1987). *Feminist Practice and Post-Structuralist Theory*. Oxford: Blackwell.

Wilkinson, S. (1988). 'The role of reflexivity in feminist research'. *Women's Studies International Forum*, **11**(5), 493–502.

Wilton, T. (1993). 'Queer subjects: lesbians, heterosexual women and the academy', in M. Kennedy, C. Lubelska and V. Walsh (eds) *Making Connections: Women's Studies, Women's Movements, Women's Lives*. London: Taylor and Francis.

Wise, S. (1987). 'A framework for discussing ethical issues in feminist research', in *Writing Feminist Biography, 2: Using Life Histories*, Studies In Sexual Politics no. 19. Manchester: Department of Sociology, University of Manchester.

Yuval-Davis, N. (1993). 'Beyond difference: women and coalition politics', in M. Kennedy, C. Lubelska and V. Walsh (eds) *Making Connections: Women's Studies, Women's Movements, Women's Lives*. London: Taylor and Francis.

9 | ISSUES OF EVALUATION

CAROL TINDALL

Introduction

Qualitative research recognizes a complex and dynamic social world. It involves researchers' active engagement with participants and acknowledges that understanding is constructed and that multiple realities exist.

> This can illustrate the circular relation between method and theory, that is, how method has an effect on the production of knowledge and vice versa. Because participants gave me complex, dynamic, multiple and contradictory accounts of themselves and their experience, it was possible to develop a theory of multiple and contradictory subjectivity.
>
> (Hollway 1989: 17)

It is theory generating, inductive, aiming to gain valid knowledge and understanding by representing and illuminating the nature and quality of people's experiences. Participants are encouraged to speak for themselves. Personal accounts are valued, emergent issues within the accounts are attended to. The developing theory is thus firmly and richly grounded in personal experiences rather than a reflection of the researcher's *a priori* frameworks. In this way insight is gained to the meanings people attach to their experiencing. Newton (1989) highlights this problem in occupational stress research. He claims that the narrowly based deductive approach is largely reponsible for the current confused picture. He suggests that a qualitative approach more firmly grounded in workers' experience of stress may clarify some of the issues, and eventually result in more useful theory. The researcher's central role and direct engagement with the choice of personally relevant research topics, the process of research and the participants is made explicit. New, previously unresearched areas are often chosen for exploration. The participants are considered as joint collaborators in the production of knowledge. Researcher uncertainty and not knowing are actively engaged with. Marshall (1986) claims that such engagement is the heart of research. Knowledge is accepted as constructed, as one version of reality, a representation rather than a reproduction. It is understanding in process, which is open to multiple interpretations. There is also a focus on critical examination on a number of levels, in the form of researcher reflection on both the process and experience of doing the research and the ways in which the findings were constructed. It also incorporates an expectation of change in all involved in the research, including the researcher.

Given these characteristics of qualitative research I believe that the concept of reliability is not appropriate to this kind of work. Reliability can be defined as 'a generic term used to cover all aspects relating to the dependability of a measurement device or test. The essential notion here is *consistency*, the extent to which the measurement device or test yields the same approximate results when utilised repeatedly under similar conditions' (Reber 1985: 636).

Replication in qualitative research has more to do with reinterpreting the findings from a different standpoint or exploring the same issues in different contexts rather than expecting or desiring consistent accounts. However, some others disagree. See Silverman (1993) for a full discussion of the relevance of both validity and reliability to qualitative research.

Validity is an integral element. It has to do with the adequacy of the researcher to understand and represent people's meanings. 'Validity instead [in qualitative research] becomes largely a quality of the knower, in relation to her/his data and enhanced by different vantage points and forms of knowing – it is, then, personal, relational and contextual' (Marshall 1986: 197).

This chapter then, accepting that there is no certainty in inquiry, focuses on consideration of the creativity cycle, triangulation, reflexivity and ethics, highly connected issues of validity and good practice.

The creativity cycle

The initial process of decision making and connection between the researcher and research topic is often (traditionally) overlooked. However, from the outset qualitative researchers recognize that they are subjectively and centrally engaged with the choice of research topic and the particular questions asked.

> I try to explain how I came up with the questions I did and how they changed as I went along. It would be impossible to present these questions fully without talking about myself: the point I was at in my life and its history, the political and cultural conditions which produced it, how these shaped my interest in certain areas of contemporary social theory. These factors together produce the conditions which make possible my research questions and shaped how I addressed them.
>
> (Hollway 1989: 4)

Kelly's (1955) three-phase creativity cycle provides a useful framework for the constant process of subjective decision making and adjustment throughout the research. The first phase is *circumspection*: a phase of unbounded wild speculation and free association, complete openness to a host of possibilities. It involves the use of a wide focus lens to gather all thoughts, issues and materials of potential relevance. The issues we are open to in this highly creative phase are inevitably bounded by personal experience and frameworks (we all have our insights and blind spots) and by the literature search.

An effective way to open up the area and extend the research issues beyond our own frameworks is to convene a group of volunteers relevant to the research, to consider the topic in open discussion. Notice boards are useful to alert and engage potential volunteers. This technique often results in interesting and lively debate that highlights a number of issues relevant to those people involved, which might otherwise have been neglected and which now can be incorporated into the research. Thus the research is grounded from the outset in the personal experiences of those participants involved. At the end of this stage a range of relevant issues from a variety of sources will have emerged.

The second phase is *pre-emption*. The range of emergent issues from phase one are thoroughly explored and evaluated by the researcher, often with volunteer and/or colleague involvement, with the aim of focusing on those issues considered crucial. This process of progressive focusing, checking out the pertinence and appropriateness of issues, continues throughout.

The final stage is what Kelly calls *control*. The work is brought into sharper focus. The research questions are chosen by either hypothesizing or proposing issues or questions that can be explored. The whole process is one of clarification, of ensuring that the material gathered is grounded in participants' experiences, not merely in theoretical background. In fact the issue(s) we finally choose to address may well target a gap or omission in previous research, as much feminist work does.

Research is not a neat linear progression of understanding; rather at any one time ongoing work is likely to involve a number of issues, which may well be at different stages in the cycle. The theory that is developed from the material gained then guides, to an extent, the subsequent collection of material, which in turn refines the ideas and develops the theory. Griffin's (1986) work with working class young women and their transition from school to the labour market illustrates how this interplay between work in the field and the developing theoretical framework operates in practice. Initially Griffin failed to recognize that leisure was an important issue in the lives of these young women. 'Once I realised just how crucial a role leisure played I was able to change the research design to accommodate a continuing focus on the young women's leisure during the second phase of the project' (Griffin 1986: 179). This movement from field to theory and back to field is also apparent in Hollway's work. 'Throughout the process of data collection and analysis, I was evolving the theoretical framework which fed back to inform both my analysis of data and the way in which I generated discussion with participants' (Hollway 1989: 4).

More valid theory can be developed by the use of multiple cycles. It is necessary to be sensitive to personal accounts, to attend to *emergent* issues and to *re*search the material in order to develop adequate and grounded theory. To deepen understanding and ground the developing theory more firmly we need to check out our interpretations with participants and treat their comments and understandings as an additional source of information and insight. Participants' understandings can be incorporated with our own to suggest new areas to explore and to inform the next stage of material gathering and theorizing and so on. Reason and Rowan (1981: 247) claim that 'The validity of research is much enhanced by systematic use of feedback loops and by going around the research cycle several times.'

Triangulation

Triangulation is essentially the use of different vantage points and takes a variety of forms, which I discuss and illustrate below. Triangulation allows illumination from multiple standpoints, reflecting a commitment to thoroughness, flexibility and differences of experience. Traditionally there has often been reliance on one method of data collection and analysis. We need to recognize that all researchers, perspectives and methods are value laden, biased, limited as well as illuminated by their frameworks, particular focus and blind spots. Triangulation makes use of combinations of methods, investigators, perspectives etc., thus facilitating richer and potentially more valid interpretations. Exploration from a variety of sources using an appropriate combination of methods increases our confidence that it is not some peculiarity of source or method that has produced the findings. As you would expect, the particular combination(s) is driven by the issues of concern and the questions being asked.

Data triangulation

This involves collecting accounts from different participants involved in the chosen setting, from different stages in the activity of the setting and if appropriate from different sites of the setting. Insights that rely on only one source of data are clearly limited. Accounts from people differently positioned within the context are unlikely to fit neatly together. They do, however, highlight how experiencing and thus understanding are context bound. Triangulation allows for considerable extension and depth of description.

Griffin's (1985) research, exploring the experiences of young working class women as they transferred from school to the labour market, is a good illustration of the use of data triangulation. She gained accounts from a *range of different* participants: school heads, careers officers, form and careers teachers as well as the young women and 'some boys'. These participants were drawn from a *variety of schools*: single sex (girls), co-educational, Catholic, Church of England and non-denominational, ranging in size from 500 to 1,500 students. The young women who were the central focus of the study included middle class and working class students, Asian, Afro-Caribbean and white women from the final four years of school. These young women were observed and interviewed *across sites*: at school, at leisure and in their workplace. Kitzinger (1987) also highlights the importance of a variety of sources in her study *The Social Construction of Lesbianism*. The lack of diversity she identifies within her interviewees is owing *in part* to her use of the snowball technique of contacting participants, beginning with her friends, which inevitably led to her interviewing women who were very much like her. 'I deeply regret the resultant loss to my understanding and description of the full richness of lesbians' experience, identities and ideologies' (Kitzinger 1987: 255).

It is often useful to compare data gained from different stages of the fieldwork, to research material, to check if any issues have been neglected or over emphasized to extend understanding.

Investigator triangulation

This is the use of more than one researcher, preferably from different disciplines or perspectives, or adopting different roles, thus reflecting the commitment to multiple viewpoints and providing potential to enrich the resultant theory. However, an amalgamation of (necessarily) limited views of reality might be problematic and will reflect researchers' preferred models of understanding. Multidisciplinary research teams may have difficulty understanding each other's interpretations. It may be that gaps in understanding are widened rather than reduced. Such information, wisely used, can be productive. Reason and Rowan (1981: 247) go so far as to claim that 'valid research cannot be conducted alone'. Yet conventions of academic research militate against this, as the emphasis is on competition, originality and individual achievement. We need to develop a group culture that is supportive yet facilitates challenge and an ongoing forum for debate. Collaborators need to be 'friends willing to act as enemies' (Torbert 1976), people who will contradict and challenge in a constructive manner. Challenges need to be attended to and evaluated, as they can extend understanding and illuminate issues. The main problem to be avoided here is consensus collusion or groupthink, which means all collaborators going along with the group norm, not questioning the adequacy of the theory and failing to explore alternatives. This limits possibilities and undermines the main purpose of working collaboratively.

We must recognize that much research is conducted alone. If this is the case, as it is for many of us, then it is advisable to invite friends and colleagues to talk through, comment on and challenge our work at various stages of the research. This ongoing provision of opportunities for extending frameworks and illuminating blind spots facilitates understanding and reflects a commitment to thoroughness. Oakley highlights the advantages as well as the limitations of research carried out by one person:

> In an important sense a piece of research planned executed and analysed by one person derives both its strength and weakness from this source. The strength comes from the coherence and consistency that a single perspective makes possible. The weakness hinges on the fact that the research is only as 'good' as the integrity and judgement of the person who carries it out.
>
> (Oakley 1985: 36)

Method triangulation

This entails the use of different methods to collect information. All methods have their limitations, their own validity threats and distortions. A danger of using only one method is that the findings may merely be an artefact of the method. If, however, an appropriate cluster of methods is used, each allowing different information through, then we can have some confidence that the material is more than a product of the method. We must remember that we are not gaining the impossible, a complete picture:

we may in the final analysis be made more aware of gaps in our understanding.

Some researchers combine qualitative and quantitative methods. For example, Griffin (1985), in her work mentioned above, used systematic observation and informal interviews. Brannen and Moss (1991), in their *Managing Mothers* study, began by using a totally quantitative approach but over time also developed a qualitative approach, a combination of long and short interviews. These were in part highly structured with coded and statistically analysed responses and in part open-ended and qualitatively analysed. In their words: 'In general the data analysed qualitatively proved useful in the identification of conceptual issues; the qualitative analysis fleshed out the coded responses, elaborating the meanings already encapsulated in the codes or adding new meanings' (Brannen and Moss 1991: 19).

Some long-term studies are more ambitious and creative in the range of methods used. Melamed (1983) explored women's reactions to ageing and found over time and with increased understanding of her research topic that at different stages of the research different methods were most useful. She began by exploring her own increasing self-awareness, then she talked to women but, she believed, failed to get through to how they really felt. So she then disclosed her own feelings before interviewing; this brought up new material and she realized that she had created a focus or consciousness-raising group. This raised the influence of cultural context on ageing, so she went on to include a cross-cultural perspective. 'I talked to academics, actresses, farm wives, prostitutes, jet setters, house cleaners, lesbians, nuns and others. I talked to over 200 women in seven countries' (cited in Reinharz 1992: 209). Finally, she included various experts who had studied ageing and the reactions of men. The eventual outcome was a feminist agenda for action. Such openness, flexibility and pursuit of deep understanding is impressive, but unfortunately prohibitively time consuming for most of us, most of the time. We can, though, still commit to thoroughness and rigour by initially choosing an appropriate combination of methods, one that suits the issue(s) to be explored and the questions asked. Beyond that, we need throughout the course of our work and emerging theory to be aware of and open to the possibilities that alternative methods offer, to check continually the appropriateness and ability of our methods to increase our understanding and facilitate rich interpretations.

Theoretical triangulation

Theoretical triangulation embraces multi-theories and breaks through the parameters and limitations that inevitably frame an explanation which relies on one theory. It recognises complexity and diversity and that multiple realities exist. There are clear links here with investigator triangulation and working in a multidisciplinary team. There is, however, a dearth of reported multi-theory studies. One, cited in Reinharz, is Valli's (1986) investigation of women's work and education, which is informed by and rooted in sociological, economic and psychological literature as well as feminist theory. Margaret Wetherell (1986), looking at how we might reconceptualize our understanding of gender, argues for the use of insights and critical awareness gained in other disciplines, in this case feminist literary criticism, to throw new light on and enrich debates in social psychology. 'This debate clarifies the tools and emphasis that a new social psychological approach might adopt and suggests that we can begin to learn from the upheavals and questionings in other disciplines' (Wetherell 1986: 93).

Levels of triangulation

It is desirable to include different levels of analyses to gain a fuller *contextualized* picture, one which allows connections to be made between individual and societal explanations. A recent study I was involved in, looking at stress in factory workers (Lewis *et al.* 1991), used both quantitative questionnaires and semi-structured interviewing around worker-identified critical incidents. These men, despite working in an objectively secure workplace (there had been no redundancies at the site), identified perceived job insecurity as one of their main stressors. Clearly, we cannot explain this finding in terms of what is going on in a factory. It is too simple to claim that no compulsory redundancies equals no problems. We need to look beyond the site at other levels of analysis to contextualize the information. At the organizational level, redundancy had been used at other sites to reduce the workforce and, within the wider societal context, unemployment is certainly an important factor. It seems, then, that elements in the wider contexts strongly influence the workers' construction of job insecurity.

Reflexivity

Reflexivity is perhaps *the* most distinctive feature of qualitative research. It is an attempt to make explicit the process by which the material and analysis are produced. It is a concept integral to personal construct psychology (see Chapter 5) and feminist research (see Chapter 8), in which both the researcher and researched are seen as collaborators in the construction of knowledge. Both can be explained using the same framework. According to Wilkinson (1988: 493), 'at its simplest, however, it may be considered to be disciplined self reflection'. The research topic, design and process, together with the personal experience of doing the research, are reflected on and critically evaluated throughout. Wilkinson develops the concept and identifies personal, functional and disciplinary reflexivity. The first two, which are most relevant to this chapter, she regards as inextricably connected.

Personal reflexivity is about acknowledging who you are, your individuality as a researcher and how your personal interests and values influence the process of research from initial idea to outcome. It reveals, rather than conceals, the level of personal involvement and engagement. Callaway (1981: 470) talks about the use of 'ourselves as our own sources', and Marshall (1986: 197) acknowledges her level of engagement from the start: 'I have always chosen as research topics issues which have personal significance and which I need to explore in my own life.' Examples of the researcher's interest in and connection to the research topic being made explicit can be seen in Oakley's (1985) *Sociology of Housework* Marshall's (1984) *Women Managers: Travellers in a Male World,* Kitzinger's (1987, 1993) extensive work on feminism and lesbianism and Hollway's (1989) work on the meanings of gender in adult heterosexual relations.

This centralizes, rather than marginalizes or denies, the influence of the researcher's life experience on the research and the construction of knowledge. In turn, the experience of exploring personally relevant topics, and being actively engaged with participants, feeds back into life experiences, often triggering personal change. Marshall (1984: 190) charts how she became a feminist through the process of research involved in *Women Managers.* 'The research both prompted and was facilitated by my development as a feminist.'

There are problems with this level of engagement. We need to develop a reflexive quality, be critically subjective, able to empathize with participants, yet be aware of our own experiencing in order to achieve a resonance between subjectivity and objectivity. Critical examination on a number of levels is required. If we fail to be critically aware and to know ourselves then we are in danger of undermining the validity of our work. Our findings, rather than being firmly grounded in people's accounts, may merely be a reflection of our own unconscious issues, disturbed by the research.

Reason and Rowan (1981: 246) claim that 'high quality awareness can only be maintained if co-researchers engage in some systematic method of personal and interpersonal development.' Researchers have their own preferred techniques for working through personal issues to raise and maintain self awareness. Heron (1973) and Reason and Rowan (1981) prefer co-counselling. Marshall also engaged in co-counselling and assertion training. She also discussed her ongoing work in a staff/student research group:

'without the support and challenge of these various arenas, I would not have achieved what I did through the research' (Marshall 1986: 203). Hollway (1989: 2) involved herself in a variety of activities to increase her 'understanding of self and others; writing a journal, recording my dreams, being a member of women's consciousness raising groups, teaching group dynamics through experiential methods and above all, talking endlessly to friends – about them and about me.'

Clearly there are numerous ways to heighten awareness, to gain a balance between engagement with participants' material and our own understandings. I would recommend discussing work in progress with trusted others who will be both supportive and challenging, even with the most minimal piece of work. It is a useful way of extending understandings and gaining clarity.

Functional reflexivity is defined by Wilkinson (1988: 495) as entailing 'continuous, critical examination of the practice/process of research to reveal its assumptions, values and biases.' The focus here is how who we are directs and shapes the course of the research. We need to monitor our role and influences as researchers throughout to chart the personal rationale behind decisions and to acknowledge the impact that our values have on decision making, the research process and eventual outcome. Chapter titles like 'Myself and my method: from separation to relation' (Hollway 1989) and 'Introducing my topic and myself' (Marshall 1984) reflect how the personal qualities of the researcher are intertwined with the process and thus the product of research. Indeed Hollway (1989: 9) claims 'that it was impossible to separate "me" from "theoretical ideas" from "field notes".'

Reflexivity, then, is about acknowledging the central position of the researcher in the construction of knowledge, that 'the knower is part of the matrix of what is known' (DuBois 1983: 111), that all findings are constructions, personal views of reality, open to change and reconstruction. We need to make explicit how our understandings were formed. This is best done by keeping a detailed journal or reflective diary which explores who you are, why you chose the particular topic, your initial purpose(s) and intention(s), procedural notes, what you did when and in what context (field notes and diagrams), decisions made with rationales, how you felt, confusions, anxieties, interpretations, what led to clarification: in fact anything that you believe has affected the research. The journal may then be used to structure a reflexive account or be included alongside the research report and transcripts. The purpose of providing a reflexive account is so that, in Marshall's (1986: 195) words, 'readers can then judge the content in the context of the perspectives and assumptions by which it was shaped.' It also allows readers to reanalyse the material, to develop alternative interpretations and explanations.

Validity in qualitative research is focused on personal and interpersonal qualities, rather than method. It is 'knowledge in process, which is tied up with a particular knower' (Reason and Rowan 1981: 250). This focus is clear in Marshall's (1986) reflective checklist, which I include here as I and many others have found it extremely useful and reassuring while struggling to understand (it is reproduced with permission of the author and the Open University Press).

How the research was conducted
Were the researcher(s) aware of their own perspective and its influence?
Were they aware of their own process?
How did they handle themselves?
Did they challenge themselves and accept challenges from others?
Were they open in their encounters?
Did they tolerate and work on the chaos and confusion? (If there is no confusion, I become suspicious that deeper levels of meaning were neglected.)
Have the researcher(s) grown personally through the research?

Relationship to the data
Is the level of theorizing appropriate to the study and its data?
Is the theorizing of appropriate complexity to portray the phenomena studied?
Are alternative interpretations explored?
Is the process of sense-making sufficiently supported?

Contextual validity
How do the conclusions relate to other work in the area?
Are the researcher(s) aware of relevant contexts for the phenomena studied?
Is the research account recognizable – particularly by people within the area studied?
Is the material useful?
'Good' research addresses most of these issues – it does not do so 'perfectly' (whatever that means); rather, the researcher(s) develop their capabilities for knowing.

Ethics

We need to be aware of the ethical implications for participants and researchers throughout the process of research, from planning through to outcome and sometimes beyond. Participants need to be protected from harm; their psychological well-being, health, values and dignity need to be preserved at all times. Feminist accounts and action research go further, aiming for outcomes that will bring positive benefits.

We must remember that we as researchers will not always be sufficiently well informed to identify fully the implications for participants. This is most likely to be the case if our participants are from a different ethnic group, different cultural group, different social group or of a different age or gender from ourselves. In this event we need to talk through the research with a range of people from the appropriate group(s) in order to gain information and advice. It is likely too that occasionally people we hope to include will not wish to be included. Kitzinger (1987) critically considers the range of reasons why certain groups of lesbians refused to be involved with her research for *The Social Construction of Lesbianism* and the impact that the relatively narrow base of participants had on the resultant theory.

Ethical guidelines have been produced by various professional bodies, including the British Psychological Society (1993), Ethical Principles for Conducting Research with Human Participants and the British Sociological Association (1982). In addition, many organizations and departments often have their own ethics committee, whose members may be consulted for advice and guidance on dilemmas and whose approval will need to be gained before the study can begin. It is worth noting, however, that Sue Wise (1987: 56) claims that such guidelines 'have little bearing on actual research practice . . . Their main usefulness lies in acting as sensitising devices, alerting researchers to areas of operation which require careful thought.' Below I consider four closely intertwined ethical issues: informed consent, protection of participants, confidentiality and anonymity, and accountability.

Informed consent

Good research is only possible if there is mutual respect and confidence between researcher and participants. This is gained initially by open and honest interaction. All elements of the research need to be fully disclosed, including your position and involvement as researcher in the issue, the purpose of the research, what is involved, how it is to be conducted, the number of participants, the time it is likely to take and, importantly, what is to happen to the material collected. Only when prospective participants are fully informed in advance are they in a position to give informed consent. Positivists claim that such information contaminates the subsequent material gained, but it is inevitable that people will construct their own understanding of what is going on.

It should be clear at the outset that initial consent is just that, and that participants have the right to withdraw at any time, even retrospectively. This rarely happens in my experience, but if it does the material gained from that person must be destroyed.

Prospective participants may be informed in a variety of ways: by letter, an informal chat or group discussion, with the researcher. It is important for a researcher to be available to prospective participants, to provide them with the opportunity to query and comment on any aspect of the research. A group discussion also allows them access to others' interests, anxieties and expectations and may enable them to air their own more freely. It is good practice to remain available and easily contacted by participants right the way through the research to outcome, so that they are fully involved and provided with the opportunity to withdraw consent if they so choose, or more usually to have ongoing queries and comments responded to. This is also part of the democratizing process dealt with below.

Initially people will have been fully informed of the intended uses of the research material. If this changes, or at a later stage the work is published, then participants need to be contacted for their permission and, if it is granted, informed of when and where the research will be published.

Protecting participants

The aim here is to equalize the power relationship, to democratize the process to the extent that we can and to ensure that there is no exploitation. This begins from the very first point of contact and has much to do with researcher qualities and values, their interpersonal skills and the degree to which they choose to become actively engaged with participants. Oakley (1985) chose to become very involved with her interviewees, in a variety of ways, in an attempt to democratize her relationship with them. However, Wise maintains that as Oakley fails to address adequately the power imbalance between herself and her participants, that 'in encouraging reciprocity and intimacy within the research relationship, Oakley may indeed be fostering the patronisation and exploitation that she seeks to avoid' (Wise 1987: 66).

It is important as qualitative researchers to disclose sufficiently to locate ourselves firmly within both the research issue and the participants' world. Interpersonal connections need to be made, participants need to understand our position as a researcher. However, disclosure often invites reciprocation, it is therefore crucial that participants know at the outset that they are in charge of their own degree of disclosure. They do not have to answer all questions or comment or continue talking about an issue that becomes uncomfortable for them. Participants need to know that at any time they can ask for the research to be halted for a while, or for the tape recorder to be switched off. Sometimes, if the participant becomes distressed, and it seems appropriate, the researcher needs to take the responsibility for switching the tape off, or taking time out. The problem in my experience is not encouraging people to talk, but rather getting them to stop. It is important that as researchers we have strategies to limit disclosure and that we are able, if required, to deal effectively with whatever arises. We must recognize that taking part in research may be disturbing, it may trigger some level of disruption. Often a listening ear, a friend, is all that is required. Occasionally issues will arise after we have left, so participants should be able to contact us if they want to talk things through. Giving them the means to contact us also gives them some control, and to a minor extent reduces the power differential. Sometimes, during the course of the research, participants ask for advice; if this happens, and it is serious, it is wise to recommend appropriate professional advice, with names, addresses and telephone numbers if possible.

Another way of reducing researcher power is to make clear to people that the material they give is owned by them. Once an interview tape (say) is transcribed, then participants should receive a copy for information and reference with a covering letter reminding them of their ownership rights and inviting them to delete any part of the transcript they choose to. Any deletions need to be made to all copies, including those on disks.

It must be acknowledged that the power imbalance between researcher and researched remains, despite the use of democratizing practices and the efforts of the researcher to disown and shrug off the role of expert. It is the researcher who is firmly positioned by participants as knowledgeable, who sets the process in motion, who decides on the initial research issue, which frameworks to use, which prospective participants to contact and what happens to the final product. In the final analysis it is the researcher's version of reality that is given public visibility. It is not possible to achieve complete mutuality and equality.

Confidentiality and anonymity

Confidentiality and anonymity are issues that are closely interwoven with protection. There is always the potential for harm when we are dealing with personal information, particularly if the information is made public. The Data Protection Act requires that 'information obtained about a participant during an investigation is confidential unless otherwise agreed *in advance*.' If the information is published, anonymity should be guaranteed.

There is often confusion between confidentiality and anonymity. Claims of confidentiality are made when this is clearly not the case, as the material has been made public. *The Penguin Dictionary of Psychology* (1985) provides the following definitions:

anonymity – any condition in which one's identity is unknown to others.
confidentiality – having the characteristic of being kept secret, an intimacy of knowledge, *shared by a few who do not divulge it to others* (italics added).

This is a particular problem in qualitative research as we are dealing with personal experiences. The personal detail required for understanding makes participants easily identifiable to people who already know them. What we should be claiming, in the main, is anonymity. But how can we ensure anonymity? Wise (1987: 52) claims to have developed for herself an 'acceptable risk' of disclosure. She states that 'my main responsibility was to ensure that they would not be recognisable to their next door neighbours.' To this end she included 'misinformation' or lies; for instance, she sometimes changed the number, ages and sex of the children. She also omitted 'publicly known' information. Her justification was that anyone who was still able to identify participants must already be 'in their confidence'.

It is crucial that we as researchers are in a position to assure our participants of anonymity.

Accountability

Accountability is not an all or nothing issue but a matter of degree or nuances. Who researchers are accountable to has to do with the purpose of the research. Marshall (1986: 208), when considering who the research is for and what functions it serves, identifies three main audiences:

> research is *for them* in that it contributes to understanding within the research community; it is *for me* as I use it to explore topics of personal interest and develop my competence as a knower; and it is *for us*, as taking part in research impacts participants' lives.

Although Marshall favours concentrating on 'me and us' rather than 'them', researchers are required to publish. They are, in part at least, privileging themselves and their profession. Research must conform to house or organizational style to get by the all-powerful gatekeepers and achieve publication. This is often a problem for qualitative researchers: Catherine Bewley's experience of having to rewrite her MSc numerous times before it was accepted by the institution is an illustration of how gatekeepers control the representation of information (see Chapter 8 for more detail). Qualitative researchers aim to make visible people's experiences, and thus see themselves as accountable to their participants. Feminists and action researchers particularly aim to empower participants and to bring about social change. Clearly both researcher and researched will develop through the course of the research. The question is *who* is to change, who decides on the direction of change and who is authorized as recognizing whether change has taken place. The problem with such consciousness raising is that the movement is often one-way, towards the researcher's understanding. However, in action research, where change occurs within a group, the role of researcher as agent of change is less central and the group itself more powerful. Maria Mies (1983) borrows the term 'conscientization' from Freire, to capture this very different, more egalitarian, quality of change that directly incorporates the notion of change in the researcher too.

One way to publicize accounts of experiences and, importantly, to allow the greatest number of people access to research findings is to use the media. This, however, can be problematic as issues are often trivialized and findings distorted. Perhaps the most effective way is the one adopted by Oakley (among others), who in the 1970s made her academic work on housework and motherhood accessible to the women involved in her studies by writing books specifically for them, in advance of her academic publications (Oakley 1974, 1979, 1980, 1985).

Accountability should be an integral, but is an often overlooked, ethical issue of research. As researchers we must not underestimate our ability to disrupt people's lives, albeit with their permission, and be clear to whom we consider ourselves accountable. We need to know just why we are doing our research.

Conclusion

In conclusion, our aims as qualitative researchers are to access and represent adequately the research phenomena, to ensure that we act responsibly and engage in effective practices in our search for useful and illuminating ways to construct reality. Within the criteria usually applied to research, taking the above issues seriously opens our research to numerous and potentially vast validity threats, but within the revised definition of validity presented here we argue that qualitative research can be just as, or even more, valid.

This chapter has dealt with some ways to increase validity, to increase the confidence we have in our knowledge, and includes illustrations of what I believe to be good practice. Many specific issues are taken up and developed within individual chapters. However, we must bear in mind that *completely valid* research, which captures and represents an unchallengeable 'truthful' view of reality, is not possible. We must recognize that *all* research is constructed, that no knowledge is certain, whatever the claims, but is rather a particular understanding in process, and that different understandings, different ways of knowing, exist.

Validity in qualitative research is 'tied up with a particular knower' (Reason and Rowan 1981: 250). The inclusion of field notes and transcripts together with the reflexive account that reveals the researcher's story allows the reader to identify the level of understanding at which the researcher worked, their tendencies, preferred models, biases, preoccupations and blind spots. This then enables others to reinterpret the findings to 'read' the analysis differently.

The problems remain and must be acknowledged. Following Marshall, agreeing with Reinharz (1980), we believe 'that many "methodological problems" are not resolvable, but are dilemmas which must be experienced and endured' (Marshall 1986: 194).

Useful reading

Wilkinson, S. (1986). *Feminist Social Psychology*. Milton Keynes: Open University Press.
Reinharz, S. (1992). *Feminist Methods in Social Research*. Oxford: Oxford University Press.
Stanley, L. (1990). *Feminist Praxis*. London: Routledge.

References

Brannen, J. and Moss, P. (1991). *Managing Mothers: Dual Earner Households after Maternity Leave*. London: Unwin Hyman.
British Psychological Society (1993). 'Revised ethical principles for conducting research with human participants'. *The Psychologist*, 6, 33–5.
British Sociological Association (1982). *Statement of Ethical Principles*. London: British Sociological Association.
Callaway, H. (1981). 'Women's perspectives: research as revision', in P. Reason and J. Rowan (eds) *Human Inquiry: a Sourcebook of New Paradigm Research*. Chichester: Wiley.
DuBois, B. (1983). 'Passionate scholarship: notes on values knowing and method in feminist social science', in G. Bowles and R. Duelli-Klein (eds) *Theories of Women's Studies*. London: Routledge and Kegan Paul.
Griffin, C. (1985). 'Young women and the transition from school to un/employment: a cultural analysis', in R. G. Burgess (ed.) *Field Methods in the Study of Education*. Barcombe: Falmer.
Griffin, C. (1986). 'Qualitative methods and female experience: young women from school to the job market', in S. Wilkinson (ed.) *Feminist Social Psychology: Developing Theory and Practice*. Milton Keynes: Open University Press.
Hollway, W. (1989). *Subjectivity and Method in Psychology*. London: Sage.
Heron, J. (1973) *Re-evaluation Counselling: A Theoretical Review*. Human Potential Research Project. University of Surrey, England.
Kelly, G.A. (1955). *The Psychology of Personal Constructs, Volume 1*. New York: Norton (reprinted by Routledge, 1991).
Kitzinger, C. (1987). *The Social Construction of Lesbianism*. London: Sage.
Kitzinger, C. and Perkins, R. (1993). Changing Our Minds: Lesbianism, Feminism and Psychology. London: Only Women Press.
Lewis, S., Sutton, G. and Tindall, C. (1992). 'Stress in factory workers: a dual purpose study'. Paper presented to the International Stress Management Association, Paris.

Marshall, J. (1984). *Women Managers: Travellers in a Male World*. Chichester: Wiley.

Marshall, J. (1986). 'Exploring the experiences of women managers: towards rigour in qualitative methods', in S. Wilkinson (ed.) *Feminist Social Psychology: Developing Theory and Practice*. Milton Keynes: Open University Press.

Melamed, E. (1983). *Mirror Mirror: the Terror of Not Being Young*. New York: Simon and Schuster.

Mies, M. (1983). 'Towards a methodology for feminist research', in G. Bowles and R. Duelli-Klein (eds) *Theories of Women's Studies*. London: Routledge and Kegan Paul.

Newton, T.J. (1989). 'Occupational stress and coping with stress: a critique'. *Human Relations*, **42** (5), 441–61.

Oakley, A. (1974). *Housewife*. London: Allan Lane.

Oakley, A. (1979). *Becoming a Mother*. Oxford: Martin Robertson.

Oakley, A. (1980). *Women Confined: towards a Sociology of Childbirth*. Oxford: Martin Robertson.

Oakley, A. (1985). *The Sociology of Housework*. Oxford: Blackwell (first published by Martin Robertson, 1974).

Reason, P. and Rowan, J. (eds) (1981). *Human Inquiry: a Sourcebook of New Paradigm Research*. Chichester: Wiley.

Reber, A.S. (1985). *The Penguin Dictionary of Psychology*. Harmondsworth: Penguin.

Reinharz, S. (1980). 'Experiential analysis: a contribution to feminist research methodology', In G. Bowles and R. Duelli-Klein (eds) *Theories of Women's Studies*. London: Routledge and Kegan Paul.

Reinharz, S. (1992). *Feminist Methods in Social Research*. Oxford: Oxford University Press.

Silverman, D. (1993). *Interpreting Qualitative Data: Methods for Analysing Talk, Text and Interaction*. London: Sage.

Torbert, W. (1976). *Creating a Community of Inquiry: Conflict, Collaboration, Transformation*. New York: Wiley.

Wetherell, M. (1986). 'Linguistic repertoires and literary criticism: new directions for a social psychology of gender', in S. Wilkinson (ed.) *Feminist Social Psychology: Developing Theory and Practice*. Milton Keynes: Open University Press.

Wilkinson, S. (ed.) (1986). *Feminist Social Psychology: Developing Theory and Practice*. Milton Keynes: Open University Press.

Wilkinson, S. (1988). 'The role of reflexivity in feminist psychology'. *Women's Studies International Forum*, **11**(5), 493–502.

Wise, S. (1987). 'A framework for discussing ethical issues in feminist research', in *Writing Feminist Biography, 2: Using Life Histories*, Studies in Sexual Politics no. 19. Manchester: Department of Sociology, University of Manchester.

Acknowledgements

My thanks to Sue Lewis for her constructive comments.

10 | REPORT WRITING

PETER BANISTER

This chapter covers a number of related areas, which to some extent are intertwined; all the issues touched upon here are important, and qualitative research needs to bear them all in mind when it comes to writing up. The chapter starts by looking at ways in which one should present findings, and emphasizes that qualitative methods should place due emphasis on reflexivity. Consideration of ethical issues is vital in any psychological research, and should especially permeate qualitative methods, which have partly developed as a result of the growing disquiet with more conventional methods in psychology (as has been touched upon in Chapter 1). Personal and cultural values are also an important area to consider, and the chapter concludes by making some points about the role of psychology in producing social change.

Introduction

The first point to remember is that there are no completely 'right' or 'wrong' ways to write a report up; what you are endeavouring to do is to produce something which accurately reflects what you have done, and communicates your findings in such a way as to enable the reader to follow what you have done and why this has led you to your conclusions. Some of the points covered below are common to *all* report writing, while some of them are more specific to the writing up of qualitative research. There is thus the aim of sharing your understandings, which have developed as a result of carrying out the study with others. The precise way in which this can be best done will obviously be partly dependent on the actual methods which you have used; what this chapter does is to provide a number of suggestions that will be of use when it comes to writing a report up. The general model of producing a report suitable for publication as a journal article is overall a reasonable aim here, but do remember that the different methods may suggest different appropriate ways of writing up the report (and that different journals may have different preferred required formats); in addition, whom the intended audience is will be worth considering.

General considerations

It is important to note that not all these considerations are of equal importance, and they are not listed in any particular order.

Although it sounds a very trivial point, the language utilized is very important (as has been pointed out in Chapter 6, on discourse analysis). Thus, do be sure that you realize that you are not engaged in writing up an 'experimental report'. It is important to ensure that you are using appropriate discourses: avoid using words such as 'experiment', 'experimenter', 'subject', etc.; instead, talk about the 'researcher', 'co-researchers' (or 'participants'), etc.

Although it might be initially difficult to do it (as this goes against traditionally accepted methods of writing up scientific reports, which you may be more familiar with), it is generally desirable in writing up qualitative reports to use the first person (e.g. 'I'), rather than reporting the research in the more traditional stylized impersonal fashion. This is not essential, but it may help to emphasize the somewhat different philosophy underlying qualitative research, as it helps to acknowledge the position of the researcher as owning the research. However, it must be remarked that conventions do vary here as to the acceptability of such a position. Do remember that there is of course a danger in doing this; namely, forgetting that you as an individual will have information that only you are privy to, and assuming similar knowledge in the reader (as has been pointed out in the chapter on feminist research). Thus, if you are writing in the first person, be careful to ensure that you do not lapse into unsubstantiated assertion, that you make it very clear as to who you are, that your assumptions and position are clearly stated, and that any pre-existing relationships with participants are clarified.

Often, it is useful to write with a mixture of the active (e.g. next I joined the fans at an away match) and the passive (e.g. football programmes were next examined) voices. In particular, do use the active voice if you want to stress that the agent of the activity is important.

There is a need to be aware of sexism in the use of language, and steps should be taken to avoid it; thus, for example, the word 'he' should never be used to refer to people in general. Use instead 'he or she', or (and preferably) try to write in such a way that it is not necessary to make general statements in the third person singular. By using the third person plural (e.g. 'they'), all such problems are avoided, but it must be noted that this may create the further problem of producing the fiction of a genderless subject. Both the American Psychological Association and the British Psychological Society insist that this convention be followed in any of their publications. This book does not totally follow this format, to emphasize the very point of problems of gender invisibility.

Be careful to make sure that your use of verb tenses is systematic. In general, the accepted method in quantitative research is to use the past tense in the introduction and methods sections (e.g. football matches were attended), and the present tense when it comes to looking at the results and subsequently discussing them (e.g. the findings may indicate that . . .). In qualitative research, however, this convention may be less appropriate.

Always keep in mind that the main point of a write-up (at which many published journal articles are lamentably poor, serving to obfuscate, rather than to illuminate) is to communicate clearly your findings to others, to share your understandings of your results, to tell others what has possibly been learnt from your particular piece of research. The style to adopt and the detail necessary will of course vary depending on to whom the report is to be presented; what are offered here are general comments, which it is hoped will be of use in the production of any reports. Always bear in mind, however, who it is that the report is aimed at. What is necessary for a journal publication is likely to be different from what is needed for a report on the progress of your studies for a research council, for instance.

A key point to aim for is replicability (but not necessarily in the quantitative sense). Ideally, the model here should be to present sufficient detail about what you actually did to enable the reader to pick up your report, and to repeat your study from the information provided. Even if the readers do not wish to replicate your study, they should be provided with sufficient material to allow them clearly to understand precisely what it was that you did; this means that they should be able clearly to visualize the setting, the participants, etc. from what has been written. As is pointed out in Chapter 1, replication may not mean the production of identical results.

Although this is related particularly to the previous point, clarity is something that should permeate your report. Another stylistic aim is conciseness: we recommend parsimony rather than verboseness.

As has already been stressed above, reflexivity is a very important aspect of writing up reports (both qualitative and quantitative), and must be included. This part is so important that it is considered in further detail in a separate section later in this chapter.

It is often useful to make a plan for your report, before you begin to write it up. This needs to be flexible, but it will help you to produce a better structured eventual report. The area of interest that you are researching into needs to be kept to the forefront, possibly written down on a card to keep in front of you throughout the process; this will aid relevance and focus. Bem (1991) makes the interesting point that there are often two possible reports which can be written: the report you thought you were going to write when you started to do your research, and the report that will make the best possible sense of your findings. The scientific method suggests that one follows an inexorable process, which starts from a literature review and proceeds forward in a linear fashion, step-by-step, while real-life research practicalities (as has already been suggested above) may be somewhat different to this. Bem rightly concludes that usually it is the second report which one should be writing, and this is the one which you will need to be devising your plan for.

The bibliographic reference list always takes much longer to produce than originally thought. One strategy which might be useful here is to write down the full details of each reference that you are likely to be subsequently using as you come across them on an individual file card, and to put these on one side in a box. When it comes to doing the bibliography, all you will need to do is to take the cards out of the box and shuffle them into alphabetical order.

It is important to leave yourself enough time to write up your report, and invariably it takes longer than is envisaged. It is important to give yourself some leeway, as reports can usually be improved by reviewing them (see the next point below), and extra time is inevitably needed for such a process.

Related to the above, important activities that also take up a lot of time are the proofreading and spell-checking of your report.

Reviewing your report is often helpful. There are a number of ways in which a review can be carried out. The simplest is to write a draft report, and then to put it on one side for a few days, turning to something else in the meantime; return to it, and re-read it. The extra few days will allow you to become more detached from it, and the extra distance from the report will allow it to be looked at more as if you were an outsider. An alternative, which although it may be more difficult is generally preferable, is to show the report to a colleague or friend who is unfamiliar with your research, to see if they can follow the write-up. The view from a different perspective is often most useful: as well as checking for clarity, replicability, etc., an alternative slant on what you have done can get you to look at your findings in a different light, and can help to point out things which you have missed, even to the extent of offering alternative explanations. If relevant, tutors or supervisors can be used here, but do remember that they may (like you) be too closely involved in the research; consequently, they may not be able to distance themselves sufficiently from the work to be able to evaluate it critically.

The structure of a report

As has been stressed above, there is no set way of producing a report of qualitative research, providing that the general points mentioned above are carefully considered; there are a variety of ways that are equally appropriate. What follows here is a general outline of a conventional and typical write-up, very much following standard journal practice. Some of what follows may thus repeat what is covered in many standard undergraduate psychology courses. Such courses normally spend a lot of time trying to encourage the clear structuring of reports (often to a standardized format), but despite this, this is an area where many researchers still have a lot of trouble; it is felt that any repetition here is worthwhile, as it is likely to lead to improved report writing.

A general guideline to bear in mind is that the shape of a report is ideally like that of an hourglass, starting off in the introduction with very general considerations, and going on gradually to focus in on the specific area of interest. The methods and the results narrowly attend to the research itself, while the discussion gradually widens out again to encompass broader issues. Thus you might start off, for instance, by reference to examining the impact of television on people's lives, before going on to look more specifically at the influence of *Star Trek* on people's social relationships by interviewing people at a Star Trek Convention, finishing by speculating on the possible global impact of science fiction on the social world. As Bem (1991: 456–7) says, 'if your study is carefully executed and conservatively interpreted, you deserve to indulge yourself a bit at the two broad ends of the hourglass. Being dull only appears to be a prerequisite for publishing in the professional journals.'

It is suggested that the report is easier to follow if it is subsectioned; what is presented below is the minimum that would be normally used. Do remember that in a lengthy report it is often useful to subsection further within the broad sections, both to enable the reader to appreciate better the structure of your report and to help you, as the writer, to produce a more carefully thought out and developed argument. If this is done, do signal clearly to the reader what particular format you are utilizing, and why.

Title

The title should clearly and succinctly indicate the area of study, and should be sufficient to inform the reader precisely what the study is about. Thus avoid general titles such as 'Insights into persons' lives', instead being more specific, such as 'Interviewing black people about their experiences of racism in England'. Remember that a number of databases and journals such as *Current Contents* only provide article titles, either free-standing, or along with abstracts; thus someone searching (for instance) a CD-ROM database (such as *PsycLit*) would only discover the relevance of your article for their research if your title clearly indicated the precise nature of your study. The title, as well as being as informative and as specific as possible, should also endeavour to be as concise as is practicable. As a broad rule of thumb, it should never go beyond a maximum of twelve words. Snappy or punning titles may attract the reader's attention, but should generally be avoided, as they usually end up being more concealing than revealing; for instance, who knows what 'Would you rather take orders from Kirk or Spock?' (Sternberg 1993) might be about? Sometimes, however, an interesting title fronts a boring article; remember that appearances can be deceptive.

Contents

Although this is not generally necessary in journal articles, in other contexts it is often useful to provide a brief contents index, to enable the reader to consult the relevant parts of your report quickly. In this context, it is important to paginate, to aid reference.

Abstract

Practice concerning abstracts varies, some journals preferring a 'conclusion' or a 'summary' at the end of an article, but the usual (and probably most useful, for reasons which are spelt out below) practice is to provide an 'abstract' at the beginning of the report. This should provide a succinct summary of what the research was designed to investigate, what precisely was done, what was found and how the results were interpreted. As with the title, remember that databases (for instance, *Psychological Abstracts*) often rely on only this section, so ensure that appropriate keywords are included in what is written here. Given that qualitative methods are fairly distinctive, and that the methodology adopted may be of importance to other researchers, it might be useful to the reader to give some indication here as to the type of analysis that was used (e.g. naturalistic observation, feminist interview, discourse analysis, etc.). Thus, by the end of this section, the reader has a very clear general picture of your study, which will be a useful overview to keep in mind when reading the rest of the report, and will allow the developing arguments and logic to be more easily followed. It is difficult to specify a word limit here, as reports will vary enormously in terms of their size and breadth of coverage, but 150 words might be a suitable upper target to aim for.

Introduction

It is often very useful to subsection this part of the report, especially if the section is a long one. If this is done, then start with a brief outline of the structure of your introduction; this will aid both the reader and the writer to follow better the developing thesis of this portion of your write-up.

Remembering the hourglass suggestion earlier, start off with a general introduction to the area. Commence at the macro level (e.g. 'social behaviour', 'gender expectations'), before gradually concentrating on the precise area of interest (e.g. 'queuing behaviour', 'mothers' gender expectations of their children'). Briefly review relevant and up-to-date literature in the area (often, the first thing readers do on starting to look at an article that interests them is to turn to the references, which will give a good idea of the scope and context of the work), before going on to more detailed discussion of studies which are of direct relevance to your research. Sources are important, and must be clearly cited, setting the background and context for your particular study. Do realize that often you may come across absences and gaps in published research, which your study will attempt to remedy. This literature review should end with at least a clear statement of what the study is going to investigate, possibly indicating any expectations about what the findings are likely to be (hypotheses may be appropriate here, depending on the nature of the investigation, and what has been revealed in the previous literature that has been reviewed). When reviewing the literature, it is essential to concentrate on only those studies which are of direct relevance to your research. Often, you will have read far more than you are likely to need, and there is consequently a temptation to put in as many as possible, to demonstrate how wide your reading has been. Do try to avoid this temptation.

Most importantly, in a study that relies on qualitative methodology, this section should also include a brief justification for the precise methods adopted in the research, indicating clearly why they were chosen. What should be argued here is why it is considered that qualitative methodology in general and the chosen method in particular may be the most appropriate to utilize in answering the particular research question under investigation. Alternatives should be briefly considered, and the reasons for their rejection should be made clear to the reader. It is critical to include this, and it might raise issues that need to be returned to in later parts of the report. For instance, it might be necessary to indicate why action research was chosen, rather than a field experiment.

The reader should, by the end of this section, have a very clear idea of what you are intending to do, why you are doing it, how you are doing it and why you have chosen this particular way to investigate it. To some extent, the introduction is almost like an exercise in 'selling': it needs to convince the reader that this will be an interesting and worthwhile study, and that it is going to use the most suitable research methods possible.

Method

As has been stressed above, this section should provide sufficient detail to allow the reader the opportunity to replicate the study on the basis of the material presented here. All too often, 'methods' take too much for granted, or simply leave out vital information. Some justification for the method chosen may occur here, particularly detailing why the *specific* variety of method which is to be used has been chosen. The precise structure of this section will obviously differ depending on the particular methodological approach being used, but in general needs to include the following points.

Give a general outline of the design of the study, making it clear to the reader what the general methodology is (for instance, 'this is a participant observation study, where the people being observed were not aware of the researcher's identity', or 'this is a feminist interview').

Give an outline of any pilot studies that were carried out. As has been argued above, such studies are often vital, to attempt to iron out potential pitfalls. Practice interviews, for instance, may indicate that important questions have been left out, or may need to be rephrased; moreover, such interviews may provide valuable experience in interviewing for the interviewer. Trial observations will indicate what is possible and what is impossible to observe in a given social situation. Clear indications should be given as to what procedural and other changes were instigated as a result of experience gained from this stage of the research. Often, pilot studies are the appropriate place to carry out any necessary reliability checks; if these have been done, then the results could be usefully outlined here. Precise details of pilot work (e.g. preliminary interview question schedules) can be provided in the appendices.

Give details as to whom it was the study was carried out with, and how precisely the people concerned were selected (indicating, if appropriate, any prior links between the researcher and the participants; in an interview, for example, how was access gained to this particular interviewee?). As much detail as possible of the participants (demographic and other) should be included here, of course bearing in mind principles of anonymity (see the section on ethics below for a further discussion on this point). If it was felt necessary to carry out any selection or control procedures, then the reasoning behind such preliminaries needs to be clearly spelt out, with reference to the appropriate literature. If (for instance) discourse analysis is being carried out, the reasons for the choice of the precise texts used need to be clearly stated. Examples of what other texts were considered and what criteria were used to reject them as being unsuitable need to be provided.

Some indication is needed as to who the researcher is, including your demographic and other social characteristics (these might affect the answers given in terms of personal constructs, for instance).

A clear description should be given of the location of the study. If it is outside, then do not forget practical variables such as the weather. If it is inside, then variables such as extraneous noise, lighting and interruptions will need to be remarked upon. In many studies (including observations and interviews), sketch plans are often helpful, to allow the reader to visualize better the precise setting.

Stipulate clearly when the study took place, including both the date and the time. You may also want to include some chronology of the development of your interpretations.

Precise details of the procedure followed must be given, from (if appropriate) the initial approach made to the participant to any 'debriefing' or feedback that was carried out. The way in which a study is introduced to the co-researcher, for instance, may influence what is subsequently found; an example of this might be the initial calling of oneself a 'psychologist', which may well conjure up images such as that of the 'psychoanalyst' in many members of the general public. If this does occur, then the others in subsequent interactions might become more concerned with ensuring that they present themselves as being mentally healthy, rather than indicating what they really think about the matter under discussion. This has occurred to the author of this chapter. When I was carrying out work on vibration-induced white fingers (see Banister and Smith 1972), forestry workers initially refused to take part in the study until they were reassured that psychologists were interested in other things than Freudian theory and their sex lives. To avoid problems of this nature, it is often much better to describe oneself as a 'researcher', perhaps from a specific institution, interested in a particular research area, i.e. you should take into account co-researchers' perceptions of the nature of the investigation.

An outline needs to be provided as to what precisely was recorded, and how. If, for instance, a tape recorder or a video recorder was used, this must be clearly specified. Again, pilot work is likely to have taken place in the development of suitable recording instruments, and changes as a result of such procedures need to be mentioned here. If (for instance) interview transcripts were subsequently produced, these need to be put in the appendices, preferably with each line separately numbered, to aid subsequent easy reference to them. How and when these transcripts were produced needs to be clearly stated, along with a clear key as to what form of notation is being used (to indicate pauses, inflections, paralinguistic aspects, etc.). An example of this is in Jefferson (1987).

If any permission was needed for the study to be carried out, this should be included here. If a contract was made between the researcher and the participant, this also should be referred to here, including commitments made and adhered to.

Ethical issues (as stressed in detail below) need to be very carefully considered in any study, and must be included here. Even if it is felt that the method involves no ethical concerns (which is probably impossible), this nonetheless needs to be painstakingly thought through and clearly stated.

Analysis

Once again, the exact format to be followed here will very much depend on the precise methodology used, so the following is intended more in the way of general points to bear in mind when writing up this part of the report. Sometimes, it may be more appropriate to combine the results and discussion sections together. If you are doing a thematic analysis of interview material, for instance, it would be best to do this as one section, and then to go on to discuss wider issues.

Overall, what should be aimed for is a clear and unambiguous statement as to what was found, in such a form as to enable the reader to understand it from the material presented in this section. Remember that some readers will only look at some sections of the report, and it is much more 'user friendly' to try to ensure that each section can be clearly understood if read alone. It is often useful to start by initially reminding the reader what precisely the study was looking at, to go on to give an overall general picture of the results, and finally to examine them in detail. Again, some of the more specific aspects (e.g. detailed observational notes) might be better placed in the appendices.

If any attempt has been made to validate the data (e.g. through triangulation, through repetition over time or with different people, etc.; see Chapter 9 on evaluation in this context), then this should be included in this section. Make it clear to the reader which points seem to be well established from your work, and which are more speculative.

As has been mentioned above, often unsolicited and unexpected comments from the participants prove as interesting as whatever it is that the research is concentrating on. It is thus often worth considering including briefly such remarks in this section, as they not only help to give some idea of the 'flavour' of the research, but also may provide explanations of the results gained as well as useful pointers for future research. If this is done, however, do remember your commitments to the co-researcher and ethical issues that may be involved here.

Discussion

As has been mentioned in the previous section, on occasions it may be more appropriate to combine the analysis and the discussion sections together, and this should be kept in mind when preparing your report. In many ways, the discussion is the most important part of your whole write-up. Again, it should start with a brief reminder to the reader as to what the focus of interest of the whole project is, and then should go on to present an overall summary of the findings. These should then be discussed in detail with reference to the purposes of the study (as argued in the introduction) and relevant literature. Do remember that there may be a whole variety of reasons why your findings differ from those of others, all of which will need to be carefully considered. These include differences in methodology (does discourse analysis tap material at a less conscious level, for instance?), differences in sampling (who co-researchers are may well lead to different results), differences owing to your impact on the situation (your demographic characteristics, your skill in utilizing qualitative methods, your expectations), environmental differences (extraneous noise, interruptions), as well as differences related to time and space. (Studies carried out in another culture and/or at another time may not be universally generalizable from. For instance, with respect to the example given in Chapter 2, the social rules governing queuing behaviour may be different in Jerusalem and Manchester (or New York, or Sydney, etc.) and may be different between 1977 and 1993.)

What this section should provide is an interpretation of the findings, exploring their meaning, building on the literature cited in the introduction. Are they in line with expectations, what generalizations can one make from them, what unexpected results are there and how might they be interpreted? Bem (1991) makes the somewhat heretical suggestion that if your results are startlingly new, and lead to a new theory, it might be worth going back and rewriting the whole report so that it begins with the new theory; this seems to be sound advice.

What is extremely important here is the provision of a reflexive analysis, which may even be in a separately headed subsection. Reflexivity is vital in qualitative analysis, and is considered to be so important in such research that it is emphasized by being given a separate heading later in this chapter. There is a need here to include a section that stands back from your study, and looks at it, analysing how appropriate the methods were in retrospect, what it felt like to be the researcher doing the study, what it might have felt like to be a participant (including any reports from the participants themselves), what flaws in the design came to light in the experience of completing the study, how it might be improved if it were to be replicated in the future, what other ways it could have been done and what further research needs to be done. The emphasis here should thus be on constructive criticality (see also Chapter 9 in this context).

References

Detailed references must be given of all cited literature, systematically using the standard full procedure, as in journal articles (or as used in this book). If some material has been gathered from a secondary source, this should be made plain to the reader; if you are quoting from such material, then do remember that secondary sources can be misleading. Idiosyncratic interpretations can be given of the work of others (sometimes to fit an argument), and at times inaccuracies will creep in (like the debate over whether Watson's Little Albert study initially involved a white rabbit or a white rat).

Appendices

These have been referred to above, and are often useful to help the reader to understand precisely what it was you discovered in your research, and how you set about doing it. It also allows sufficient space to put material which is too bulky or detailed for the report itself. The provision of appendices will often allow the reader to follow better the arguments put forward, and may even permit reinterpretation of the material. Appendices should be clearly labelled and sensibly ordered; they can include raw material, transcripts, details of pilot studies, etc.

Reflexivity

This has already been mentioned above under the 'discussion' heading, but is sufficiently important in qualitative research to warrant a separate section here, to give it due emphasis. As is argued in Chapter 1, qualitative methods attempt to remedy many of the perceived shortcomings of more conventional ways of carrying out research; the roles of ethics, values and the potential impact of findings all need to be carefully considered, and all are given separate headings in this chapter. Another key feature is that of reflexivity, the realization of the relative nature of social reality, that there are multiple realities, the questioning of whatever it is that one does, the refusal to be satisfied with outcomes, the seeking of alternatives and other possibilities. Points that are mentioned here inevitably overlap with other parts of this chapter, but there is no harm in reiterating them, as part of the aim of this book is to get the reader to think about their own research practice and to become more aware of possible problems and pitfalls. Qualitative methods may avoid many of the problems faced by other methods of doing research, but none the less aspects of such research still need to be carefully considered; in particular, such methods may involve other features which are potentially exploitative.

Reflexivity should involve both thinking about oneself and thinking about one's research; Wilkinson (1988) defines these two aspects as 'personal' and 'functional' reflexivity respectively, but points out that the two are so closely intertwined as to be inseparable in practice. Thus there is a need to realize that inevitably you as a researcher will have biases, interests, predilections, values, experiences and characteristics that will affect your research and your interpretations of it. The examples given in chapters of this book, for instance, are likely to reflect whoever it is who has written the particular chapter; the topics chosen are likely to be influenced by the person choosing them – readers can ascertain some of my interests from this chapter. The authors have got together to discuss their contributions collectively, to attempt to minimize such potential difficulties, but they are inevitable in research.

Discussion with participants and colleagues will help to gain a broader picture, but reflexive writers must be aware of their limitations. Thus you should always be questioning in a disciplined manner what it is that you have done, asking yourself whether your choice of methods was appropriate, what alternatives could have been utilized, what your impact on the setting, situation, participants, results, etc. is likely to be, what alternative interpretations might be put forward (as Chapter 2 suggests, for instance, when considering interpretations of observations). Sometimes, keeping a diary as your research progresses is very useful here (as is noted in Chapter 9). Thus, as well as thinking carefully about your own particular study (and yourself), you also need to think about more macro issues, which include research methodology and questioning psychology itself (what Wilkinson 1988 calls 'disciplinary reflexivity'). Power relationships are likely to be particularly important, and must always be given due consideration. As has been emphasized above, this whole process needs to be done in a constructively critical fashion.

Ethics

Quite rightly, and as has, we hope, been duly emphasized above, psychologists have become increasingly worried about ethical issues concerned with research; indeed, part of the impetus behind the recent turn towards more qualitative methods has been the growing realization of the ethical problems involved in a lot of traditional research. In this context, the argument between Zimbardo (1973) and Savin (1973) concerning the famous Stanford mock prison work is particularly interesting as an illustration of debates on the ethics of experimentation (see also McDermott 1993, for a more recent commentary by Zimbardo on this controversy). It is felt by many that qualitative methods have the potential to avoid a number of the usual ethical pitfalls of more conventional psychological methods.

There are now published ethical guidelines for conducting research, and the reader is urged to consult those of the American Psychological Association (1992) and the British Psychological Society (1993); the full text of these guidelines should be essential reading for any researcher. All psychologists who are engaged in research are expected to abide by the principles espoused in these documents.

Ethical concerns must be part of the fundamental design of any research project, and ideally any proposed research (including even undergraduate, A level and GCSE practical work) should be talked through with an ethics committee and/or colleagues, to ensure that the research does not, as a minimum, contravene the published ethical principles. The proposal should also be talked through with members of the population with whom the research is going to be carried out. The broader perspective so gained will help to reduce the possibility that the proposal is too one-sided, and may assist it to take on board such issues as (for example) living in a multicultural society. It will be argued below, however, that many think that the current guidelines do not go far enough, and need to be further discussed and developed; in this context, it is worth pointing out that the guidelines themselves are subject to constant review and modification. Those mentioned above are very recent, and were last revised in 1990, indicating that they are still very much under discussion. There is thus continuing healthy debate concerned with the further development of these principles. Guidelines do not tell us much directly concerning what to do if one observes somebody committing a criminal act, or doing something which is harmful to another. The withholding of possible benefits from some participants (for instance, in some control or comparison group) is also an area of concern which is often not considered.

The guidelines are rightly very clear on a number of points; these will be outlined first in general terms, and then their impact on qualitative research will be considered. An overall principle is that of the welfare and protection of participants in research. It must be emphasized that studies should, among other things, be concerned with establishing mutual respect and confidence; we should respect participants as individuals, we must treat them as having fundamental rights, dignity and worth. Moreover, we should be appreciative and grateful for their helping us. Participants should leave the research situation with their self-esteem intact, feeling glad to have made a valued contribution to a worthwhile piece of research and happy to take part in further studies in the future.

The following paragraphs take as their general framework the British Psychological Society (1993) guidelines.

A vital point the guidelines rightly emphasize is the necessity of avoiding anything that has any possibility of harming the individual taking part in the study; the definition of 'harm' here also includes discomfort and embarrassment. Any potential threats to psychological well-being, mental or physical health, values, attitudes, self-worth or dignity must be fully thought through. Thus, all possible psychological consequences for the participants need to be carefully considered and discussed with colleagues, including *inter alia* the study from the standpoint of the participant.

There is a paramount underlying precept of informed consent; participants in a study should be very clear as to what the research entails, and should have agreed to take part. Why we are carrying out our particular research should be made clear to them, along with full details as to what is proposed. Any aspect that might conceivably affect willingness to take part in the study needs to be brought to the attention of the other. Often, it is useful to draw up a full written contract with the other, explaining the procedures, what you intend to do with the results and how confidential or anonymous they are going to be, giving the other the right to terminate the study at any point, to withdraw or modify their contribution (for instance, it is desirable common practice for co-researchers in interviews to be given a full copy of the interview transcript, with the invitation to modify or delete anything written there), to refuse to answer any question, etc. The guidelines recognize that some potential participants may not be able to give consent; research studies involving children or those with various impairments are obvious examples here. In such cases, those *in loco parentis* or similar positions must give their consent. People should never feel pressurized into taking part. (This is often difficult to ensure, especially in situations involving explicit power relationships between participants, such as in prisons or in universities. It may even be that such power relationships in some settings are impossible to avoid.)

If for some reason withholding of information, misinformation, misleading or even deception is deemed to be essential to ensure that a more accurate picture is gained, this should only be execptionally done, and only after detailed discussions with colleagues and disinterested independent advisers has produced no suggested feasible alternatives (and it is agreed that it is necessary for the research to be carried out). Moreover, it is vital for consultation to occur with people from the same background as the proposed participants in the research, to explore their possible reactions to such a procedure. If this does take place, it is essential that participants are fully debriefed, the reasons for the misinformation being fully spelt out, and again guaranteed the right to withdraw their contribution to the research. This session should also include a discussion with participants concerning their experience of the research, in particular checking for misconceptions and any negative effects.

As a general principle, report write-ups should guarantee confidentiality or anonymity, unless explicit identification of participants is discussed and agreed in advance. Publication of results should ideally be of such a form as to guarantee anonymity for individual participants, and should not have the potential of causing harm to persons who might identify themselves from such a report.

Qualitative methods have both particular advantages and disadvantages when it comes to ethical considerations, and the points raised above will now be systematically, though briefly, commented on.

Researchers utilizing qualitative methods are usually aware of possible harmful consequences, and indeed prefer to use methods that treat and respect the other in the research situation as an equal; thus, full and open discussion is usually encouraged, which it is hoped will minimize any problems in this area. By their nature, qualitative methods tend to be less intrusive, but there is still the need to guard against potential harm to the psychological well-being (e.g. self-esteem) of participants. The method is generally far less reactive (i.e. the actual act of carrying out research has less of an effect on what is found) than more quantitative methods, which again is an advantage.

Similarly, this very openness generally means that research often fulfils the desirable general principle of 'informed consent', avoiding problems of deception which beset a lot of psychological work. The very use of terms such as 'participants' (or 'co-researchers', depending on the precise methodology adopted) rather than 'subjects' emphasizes the realization of the imbalanced power relationships inherent in much research, and attempts to address and remedy such problems.

On the other hand, deliberate attempts are made in some circumstances to study people in real-life contexts when they are unaware that they are being used as part of a study; examples here include some kinds of both participant and non-participant observation. Here, the principle of 'informed consent' is usually impossible to maintain. The British Psychological Society guidelines explicitly point out that in such circumstances we must respect the privacy and psychological well-being of the people being studied, and unless we have obtained informed consent, we should really only observe in situations where observation by strangers is normally expected. Thus we should restrict ourselves to settings such as public social situations, but even then we need to be aware that variables such as local cultural values need to be taken into account.

Qualitative methods also have specific problems when it comes to the writing of research reports; the general aim of confidentiality and anonymity is much harder to guarantee, especially in using people from a limited population. A guarantee of anonymity is no assurance that a participant will not be recognized; interviews within my institution with staff, for instance, mean that who the participants are is obvious to colleagues. This means that special care needs to be taken in writing up such research, which needs to be done sensitively and with the realization that at least it is likely that participants will be able to recognize themselves.

It should be realized that one's responsibility as a researcher does not end at the end of the research; as is mentioned in Chapter 2, observation has been called an 'act of betrayal' by some, as it is making public something which previously is private, often to the benefit of the researcher and to the detriment of the observed.

This leads on to an important ethical debate, which is related to the whole issue of the relationship between psychology and social change (which is briefly considered below); namely, in whose interests is the researcher being carried out? One of Savin's (1973) criticisms of the Stanford Prison Experiment is that it was not carried out primarily to attempt to make people aware of prison conditions, and in the hope of leading to improvements in prisons, but was carried out because the researchers thought the resulting publications would aid their careers. One position that could be adopted here (which goes beyond the standard ethical guidelines) is that one should not carry out research purely for the benefit of the researcher; ideally, there should be possible benefits to the participant, possibly in general terms (e.g. contributing to the debate on the necessity for an improvement in prison conditions for prisoners), if not in specific terms. Sometimes these benefits may be incidental to the participant, but nonetheless valuable; for instance, there may be value in talking to somebody else about one's experiences since being diagnosed as suffering from a serious illness may prove to be beneficial to the co-researcher.

The role of values

Again, this is intertwined with many of the points above, but it is worthy of its own heading to signify its importance, even if it is only briefly mentioned here. As has been stressed under the heading 'Reflexivity' above, qualitative methods are trying to increase awareness of many of the influences on research and their findings, which are conventionally either ignored, left unsaid or taken for granted.

'Values' have already been touched upon above; in this context, one is admitting that a researcher and research cannot be value-free, and that the general 'objectivist' notion that science can be value-free is impossible, given that we are all rooted in a social world that is socially constructed. Psychology (at least in the West) has general values (even if these are often left implicit) of communicating broadening knowledge and understanding about people, with a commitment to both freedom of inquiry and freedom of expression.

Inevitably, researchers themselves will have their own notions as to what the 'right', the 'correct', way of doing things is, and this needs to be clearly recognized in carrying out and writing up research. One also needs to admit one's values, and to stipulate them clearly. This is not to say that such revelations will minimize their impact, but it is a step in the right direction at least to admit their existence. The American Psychological Association (1992) ethical guidelines stress that it is important for 'psychologists . . . to be aware of their own belief systems, values, needs and limitations and the effect of these on their work' (p. 1599).

In this context, an important point to remember is that one's choice of research methods will inevitably influence the outcome of the research; different research techniques generate different kinds of material, ask different questions and produce different answers. As a very minimum, one should at least acknowledge that this occurs.

Psychology and social change

Inevitably, the question needs to be asked as to what use research is; here, we could get tied up in interminable arguments about 'pure' versus 'applied' research. This distinction, however, is rather an artificial one, as all research will have some implications (even if one is not aware of it at the time). In terms of our own values, we would prefer to see research as having outcomes that directly relate to the 'real world', but this is not to decry other forms of research. The insights gained by some qualitative studies, for instance, may be sufficiently interesting to persuade psychologists who prefer more traditional ways of doing research to re-examine their principles (which, in itself, would be a laudatory outcome). Overall, though, I would concur with Shepherd (1993: 42) that 'most people working at the sharp end however would of course take a different line again. What matters to them, indeed what should matter to all of us, is not philosophical arguments about the superiority of one research methodology over another, rather the utility of research results.' The implications and implementation of findings are of importance, and need to be carefully addressed in writing up research; as has been stressed above, research inevitably involves both values and moral dilemmas.

Another question which needs to be touched upon here (and which is mentioned above in the section on 'ethics') is the thorny one of who pays for the research, and what the real motivation is for doing it. At the very least, this needs to be made overt in any write-up, and there is a need to try to establish at least the limits of the independence of the researcher from whoever is paying for the research. Who the gatekeepers (who may also include journal editors and the reviewers of articles) are is important, and this needs to be acknowledged.

It must also be realized that there are ethical issues involved in the utilization of research results. Such results can be (and have been) misused in other settings and cultures, and can be used to further other political and social ends. It is thus important to attempt to state clearly limits of what it is that one has found, and to try to anticipate and forestall possible misinterpretations. Responsibility does not end with publication, and we need to be always aware of who is using our results, and for what ends.

When it comes to assessing this utility of qualitative research results, however, it might be worth bearing in mind that there are very different criteria which can be used here. Reason and Rowan (1981) raise questions as to what appropriate validity criteria might be for looking at research, emphasizing that we need to go beyond asking 'Is it right?', to ask 'Is it useful?' and 'Is it illuminating?' Sapsford (1984) picks this up, suggesting that we can assess research by the three criteria of agreement (do participants agree with the accounts of life which we, as researchers, provide them with?), consensus (is there general agreement?) and plausibility (does the research make sense of all the evidence?). Thus an appropriate criterion when considering qualitative research is to adopt that of examining the illumination provided by the research, rather than just asking about the validity of the results; what qualitative methods may be about is attempting to enhance understanding of the social world by helping to reveal the multifaceted nature of social reality. The change is one for psychology, as well as one for our conceptualization of that world; moreover, it may be a change for the researcher. We hope that this book has helped this reflexive process.

Useful reading

Judd, C.M., Smith, E.R. and Kidder, L.H. (1991). *Research Methods in Social Relations*, 6th edn. Fort Worth, TX: Holt, Rinehart and Winston.

Miles, M.B. and Huberman, A.M. (1984). *Qualitative Data Analysis*. London: Sage.
Robson, C. (1993) *Real World Research*. Oxford: Blackwell.

References

American Psychological Association (1992). 'Ethical principles of psychologists and code of conduct'. *American Psychologist*, 47, 1597–611.

Banister, P. and Smith, F.V. (1972). 'Vibration-induced white fingers and manipulative dexterity'. *British Journal of Industrial Medicine*, 29, 264–7.

Bem, D.J. (1991). 'Writing the research report' in C.M. Judd, E.R. Smith and L.H. Kidder (eds) *Research Methods in Social Relations*, 6th edn. Fort Worth, TX: Holt, Rinehart and Winston.

British Psychological Society (1993). 'Ethical principles for conducting research with human participants'. *The Psychologist*, 6, 33–5.

Current Contents, Social and Behavioral Sciences. Philadelphia: Institute for Scientific Information.

Jefferson, G. (1987). 'Appendix: transcription notation', in J. Potter and M. Wetherell (ed.) *Discourse and Social Psychology*. London: Sage, pp. 188–9.

McDermott, M. (1993). 'On cruelty, ethics and experimentation: a profile of Philip G. Zimbardo'. *The Psychologist*, 6, 456–9.

Psychological Abstracts. Washington, DC: American Psychological Association.

PsycLit. Washington, DC: American Psychological Association.

Reason, P. and Rowan, J. (eds) (1981). *Human Inquiry: a Sourcebook of New Paradigm Research*. Chichester: Wiley.

Sapsford, R. (1984). 'Paper 10 – a note on the nature of social psychology' in R. Stevens (ed.) *D307 Metablock*. Milton Keynes: Open University.

Savin, H.B. (1973). 'Professors and psychological researchers: conflicting values in conflicting roles'. *Cognition*, 2, 147–9.

Shepherd, S. (1993). 'Review of "Suicides in Prison" by Liebling, A.'. *Inside Psychology*, 1(2), 42.

Sternberg, R.J. (1993). 'Would you rather take orders from Kirk or Spock?' *Journal of Learning Disabilities*, 26, 516–19.

Wilkinson, S. (1988). 'The role of reflexivity in feminist psychology'. *Women's Studies International Forum*, 11, 493–502.

Zimbardo, P.G. (1973). 'On the ethics of intervention in human psychological research with special reference to the "Stanford Prison Experiment"'. *Cognition*, 2, 243–55.

INDEX